Applied Behaviour Analysis and Autism

of related interest

Parents' Education as Autism Therapists
Applied Behaviour Analysis in Context
Edited by Mickey Keenan, Ken P. Kerr and Karola Dillenburger
Foreword by Bobby Newman
ISBN 1 85302 778 2

Raising a Child with Autism
A Guide to Applied Behavior Analysis for Parents
Shira Richman
ISBN 1 85302 910 6

Asperger's Syndrome
A Guide for Parents and Professionals
Tony Attwood
Foreword by Lorna Wing
ISBN 1 85302 577 1

Parenting a Child with Asperger Syndrome
200 Tips and Strategies
Brenda Boyd
ISBN 1 84310 137 8

Asperger Syndrome, the Universe and Everything
Kenneth Hall
Forewords by Ken P. Kerr and Gill Rowley
ISBN 1 85302 930 0

Achieving Best Behavior for Children
with Developmental Disabilities
A Step-By-Step Workbook for Parents and Carers
Pamela Lewis
ISBN 1 84310 809 7

People with Autism Behaving Badly
Helping People with ASD Move On from Behavioral
and Emotional Challenges
John Clements
ISBN 1 84310 765 1

Applied Behaviour Analysis and Autism

Building a Future Together

*Edited by Mickey Keenan, Mary Henderson,
Ken P. Kerr and Karola Dillenburger*

Foreword by Gina Green

Jessica Kingsley Publishers
London and Philadelphia

Diagnostic Criteria for Autistic Disorder in Figure 3.1 reprinted with permission from the Diagnostic and Statistical Manual of Mental Disorders, copyright © 2000 American Psychiatric Association. 'Resources for Parents' on pp.255–286 reprinted with permission from Eric V. Larsson, copyright © Eric V. Larsson.

First published in 2006
by Jessica Kingsley Publishers
116 Pentonville Road
London N1 9JB, UK
and
400 Market Street, Suite 400
Philadelphia, PA 19106, USA

www.jkp.com

Library of Congress Cataloging in Publication Data
Applied behaviour analysis and autism : building a future together /
edited by Mickey Keenan ... [et al.] ; foreword by Gina Green.
p. cm.
Includes bibliographical references and index.
ISBN-13: 978-1-84310-310-3 (pbk. : alk. paper)
ISBN-10: 1-84310-310-9 (pbk. : alk. paper)
1. Autism. 2. Autism in children.   I. Keenan, Michael.
[DNLM: 1. Autistic Disorder—therapy—Child. 2. Behavior Therapy
—methods—Child.   WM 203.5 2006]
RC553.A88A77 2006
618.92'85882—dc22

2005024312

British Library Cataloguing in Publication Data
A CIP catalogue record for this book is available from the British Library

ISBN-13: 978 1 84310 310 3
ISBN-10: 1 84310 310 9

Printed and bound in Great Britain by
Athenaeum Press, Gateshead, Tyne and Wear

Contents

Foreword

Imagine the following hypothetical scenario: you have a beloved young child whose health just does not seem to be normal. You observe that she has persistent fevers, is lethargic and tired much of the time, and has aching joints and bones. You express concerns about your child's health to your family physician, who tells you that it's just a phase that she will grow out of, or not to worry because girls tend to be less active than boys. So you wait a while, and you watch your child closely, and the symptoms don't go away; in fact, they seem to worsen. Still the physician does not think your concerns are sufficient to warrant the trouble and expense of a bunch of tests, so he recommends giving the child aspirin for the fever and aches, and a vitamin to boost her energy level. But your child does not get better, and your anxiety mounts. You begin to compare notes with parents of other children near the same age as your daughter, and do some reading on childhood illnesses. From the information you obtain, it seems that the symptoms you have observed in your child could signal any of several conditions, including childhood cancer, so you decide to take her to a professional who specializes in diagnosing cancer in young children. To your dismay, you learn that there are not very many of those professionals around, so you have to wait a long time for an appointment. Finally the evaluation is done, and your daughter is given a diagnosis that stuns and chills you: acute lymphocytic leukaemia (ALL).

Now, imagine further that the diagnostician – who has not actually treated any children with ALL – tells you that although the cause of ALL is unknown and there is little hope that your child's health will be restored, there are many different treatments or therapies that can help those with ALL. She refers you to your country's national association for ALL for further information, and suggests that you and your spouse join a support group for parents of children with ALL. With a mixture of fear and hope, you immediately contact the national association, which provides you with some descriptions of ALL that you find quite confusing and frightening, and a long list of treatments or therapies for ALL that other parents and some professionals

7

have reported to be beneficial. The names of the treatments are Greek to you; you're still trying to figure out what ALL is and what you should do for your child, and feeling an increasing sense of urgency because your precious little girl is not getting any better.

You seek more information about the treatments on the list from the national association and various websites dedicated to ALL. For virtually every treatment you find glowing testimonials from people who swear that the treatment is a miracle cure for ALL or, if not a cure, is wonderfully beneficial for their children or themselves or their patients. You notice that many of those people are eager to have you buy their books, diet manuals, DVDs, drugs, 'natural' remedies or electronic devices, to attend their 'workshops', or to purchase services from them, often for a hefty fee. For some of the treatments, you see references to 'research' that is said to show that the treatments are effective. Proponents of some treatments for ALL assert that scientific research is not necessary to determine if a treatment works – opinions, stories and 'clinical judgement' are said to be sufficient – and some maintain that science is not only unnecessary, it's bad. As you wade deeper into this morass of information, you also find criticisms of many of the treatments, even an occasional mention of research showing that a treatment did not work or that it had harmful effects. Being new to this ALL business, and not being a researcher or trained in research methods yourself, you find it difficult to evaluate any of those often-conflicting statements.

So how do you decide which of the many treatment 'options' is best for your child? The national ALL association and a number of other sources strongly encourage you to manage your child's treatment yourself by picking and choosing, mixing and matching from the list of treatments you were given originally – now grown longer by the addition of other treatments and therapies that you read about on the web, or saw reported on television or in a magazine article, or heard about from other parents of children with ALL. The notion that you should treat your child yourself seems a bit odd to you, since you are not trained in medicine or a related field and knew nothing about ALL until your child received that diagnosis. But by now you have seen a number of reports from parents who say that they have successfully treated their child's ALL using a variety of treatments, and their stories are very compelling. So you try the 'mixed' approach for a while, or perhaps you try one of the treatments that particularly appealed to you. You so want the treatment to help your child that you put your heart and soul, all your hopes, and considerable material resources into it.

After a while, however, you stand back and look at the situation objectively and realize that your little girl really isn't getting better. You remember reading on some website or hearing at some conference that there was one specialized treatment for ALL that seemed to have more research behind it than the others, including several studies in which children who received an intensive form of that treatment did much better than similar children who received more generic treatments or a combination of treatments. In fact, some children who received the specialized treatment actually had their health restored, though others did less well. The researchers had professionals who were not involved in the treatment use objective measures to evaluate the effects of the treatment on the various symptoms of ALL, and showed that the specialized treatment alleviated several symptoms to a considerable degree in many children. Some researchers followed the children who participated in the study for years, and found that those who responded well to the specialized treatment remained healthy. You ask the physician and the diagnostician who saw your daughter about that specialized treatment. To your surprise, the physician knows nothing about it. The diagnostician tells you that the studies on the specialized treatment were flawed (neglecting to mention that she has never done any treatment research herself, and has not actually read all of the research on the specialized treatment), and that she knows many people who believe that the specialized treatment is 'narrow', 'old', 'unnatural' and too 'intrusive' for a young child. She again strongly recommends a mixture of treatments that does not include the specialized treatment you enquired about. Puzzled, you return to the website of the national ALL organization where you find a description of the specialized treatment – written, you later discover, by someone who is not trained in that speciality – that is sketchy and quite disparaging. You notice again that many of the other treatments are given glowing endorsements, though no supporting research is mentioned. In fact, you have now learned on your own that studies have found several of those treatments ineffective or harmful, but that research isn't mentioned either. Among them are the treatments recommended for your child by the professionals who have evaluated her. Your confusion and anxiety deepen.

Nevertheless, you are determined to learn more about the specialized treatment, so you consult a number of other professionals who work in ALL. Several of them admit candidly that they know little about the specialized treatment or the research behind it. Some criticize it vehemently and with great conviction, without informing you that they are not trained in that speciality and have not actually seen that treatment delivered by individuals who do have that training. Those professionals urge you to pursue a treatment that they have developed, or one to which many in their discipline ascribe. When you ask each of these professionals for published research on the treatment they're recommending, one hands you a paper that she wrote and published in a journal of which she is the editor. Another gives you a self-published manual, and still another shows you a summary of consumer satisfaction surveys completed by parents of children with ALL who received his treatment. Some provide you with a few articles published in peer-reviewed professional journals. The articles include lots of statistics, which seem impressive at first glance. On closer inspection, however, you find it difficult to figure out exactly how many children got better with treatment, and how much they improved. In the articles from which you can glean that kind of information, you see that only a small proportion of the children actually improved over the course of treatment, and in most cases the improvements were small. You also notice that most of those studies did not compare the treatment the professional is recommending with any other treatment. Some did, but used just one test to measure a subset of the symptoms of ALL, and the researchers administered that test themselves rather than having independent evaluators do it. No studies compared the recommended treatment, by itself or in combination with other treatments, with the specialized treatment. Several of the studies were short-term: the children who received the recommended treatment were followed for only a few months. It seems to you that the research on the treatments that are being recommended by many professionals who work in ALL does not stack up all that well in comparison to the research on the specialized treatment, but many people are very enthusiastic about those other treatments nonetheless. And many of the professionals you speak with claim (without proving it) to know a great deal about the specialized treatment, which they disparage or dismiss.

Eventually your explorations lead you to a website that provides a lot of information about the specialized treatment, written by professionals who are trained in that speciality and have used and studied the treatment for years. You are surprised to learn that the specialized treatment is not just a treatment for ALL, but is one of many successful applications of a particular scientific discipline. Like other disciplines, specialized academic training and practical experience are required to practise this one competently – a fact that none of the professionals with whom you've spoken so far have mentioned. You learn that even more specific training is necessary to use the discipline's methods effectively to treat ALL, but you have become aware that many people who do not have that training nonetheless claim that they do, and happily take money from parents to provide what they say is the specialized treatment. You also learn that the specialized, intensive treatment you've read about actually consists of many techniques developed by many members of this discipline, and that each of those techniques has been studied in scores of studies published in scientific journals over the past several decades. You read descriptions of this discipline's approach to the treatment of ALL and even read some of the published studies. Although the articles contain unfamiliar technical terms, you find that you can usually figure out how the specialized treatment affected the children with ALL who participated in each study, because many articles include graphs that show the degree to which each individual child exhibited one or more of the symptoms of ALL before treatment started, and how much the symptoms changed over the course of treatment. You read more, and communicate directly with professionals in this speciality as well as some parents whose children with ALL have had the specialized treatment. You see data from multiple sources indicating that many children who got the specialized treatment recovered from ALL or had most of the symptoms ameliorated to a considerable extent, but the researchers and parents are candid about the facts that the treatment is not cheap or easy to do, and that some children do not respond that dramatically. Still, you determine to pursue this treatment for your child because it seems to offer more substantial hope than the others you have learned about.

Unfortunately, you then experience another series of unpleasant surprises. Your private health insurance refuses to pay for the specialized treatment, deeming it 'experimental' even after you supply them with copies of the supporting research articles, based on a review of those articles by a professional from an entirely different discipline who was hired by the insurance company. The government agencies that are required by law to help care for children with ALL do not offer the specialized treatment because their employees are not trained in the relevant discipline. You ask them nicely to pay for a properly trained person to provide the treatment to your child, as provided by law, but your request is turned down because the agency opposes the treatment on 'philosophical' grounds or considers it too expensive, or because the law does not require them to use proven methods or to provide maximally effective treatment for children with ALL. Never mind that both the private insurer and the government agencies willingly use and pay for many treatments for ALL that have never been tested properly, and others that have been proved ineffective or harmful. Not to be deterred, you hire an attorney to help you get the specialized treatment for your child. To your astonishment, the insurers and public agencies that complained about the cost of the specialized treatment now tell you that they will see you in court, and proceed to pay many times the cost of the specialized treatment to attorneys and 'experts' to fight your effort to secure treatment with demonstrated effectiveness for your child. By this time you have also confronted the unfortunate reality that there are not very many professionals with proper training in the speciality and experience in treating young children with ALL, so you drain your savings or remortgage your home in order to bring the specialists to your home periodically, or you move your family across the country or even across the globe to be near a centre that provides the specialized treatment. Finally your little girl begins receiving the treatment. There is no miraculous, overnight 'cure', but for the first time you see her health improve, and over time you see more improvements occurring, often in small increments but steadily moving in the right direction.

Now change hypothetical hats and imagine that you are a member of the relatively small scientific discipline that has developed the specialized treatment for ALL. You have treated children with ALL for some time and have seen for yourself how they have improved. But as a scientist you know not to rely on your own observations and impressions to determine if a treatment works, so you have painstakingly had the effects of the treatment measured by independent observers and evaluators, and have had the resulting data analysed by experts on research methods. You have repeatedly submitted your work to critical peer review and published your studies in respected journals. Others in your discipline have done the same, and some of them have compared the specialized treatment with other treatments for ALL. You've looked carefully at all the research on the speciality treatment, and at what research you could find on other treatments for ALL, as have a number of other professionals, several multidisciplinary task forces, and the Surgeon General of the United States. Of course, there are some variations in details of the treatment, research methods and results, but all of those reviewers conclude that, taken together, the studies show quite clearly that the specialized treatment can result in large and lasting improvements for many children with ALL, and a better quality of life for their families. They also conclude that, so far, the relatively small body of scientific research on other treatments for ALL does not show that they produce comparable effects.

Yet almost every day you hear from parents like the one described in the previous scenario about the tremendous obstacles they encounter when they seek the specialized treatment. On scores of ALL websites, in reports in the popular press, and even in professional journals and textbooks, you read grossly inaccurate descriptions of your discipline, its approach to treating ALL, and the supporting research. Task forces and committees are formed at the highest levels to promulgate ALL treatment and research guidelines, presumably based on research evidence. But most of those groups either completely exclude knowledgeable members of your discipline, or include them only in marginal roles; not one of them is chaired by a member of your discipline. Given those facts, it is not surprising that their reports and recommendations often misrepresent your discipline, paint an incomplete or skewed picture of the research on your discipline's approach to treating ALL, and endorse other treatments for which there is little or no supporting evidence from sound studies. Those reports are nonetheless treated as gospel by government agencies that fund services for children with ALL. When you and other members of your discipline question those reports and the processes by which they were produced, and lay out the documented facts about your discipline and its treatment for ALL, you are labelled 'arrogant', 'non-inclusive', 'close-minded', 'self-serving' and worse.

Okay, now set aside the hypotheticals and enter reality. Substitute 'autism' for ALL and applied behaviour analysis (ABA) for 'specialized treatment' in the scenarios just described, and you have a reasonably good picture of the situation facing many parents who seek ABA treatment for their children with autism, as well as many behaviour analysts working in autism. Their collective experiences provide the framework for much of this book. Like ALL, the original cause of autism is unknown at this time, and to my knowledge there is no universal cure that eradicates ALL or autism in 100 per cent of cases. But there are scientifically validated treatments that can eradicate the symptoms of both conditions in many children, and substantially improve the lives of many others. Of course, if scenarios like those just presented actually happened with respect to ALL, in all likelihood there would be a public outcry, exposés in the media, ethics investigations, and malpractice lawsuits galore. In autism, those scenarios occur routinely, but consequences like those just described rarely follow. Many countries make effective, science-based treatment available for most children with ALL, even if their parents cannot afford to pay for it out of pocket. In some countries, it is the case that more children with autism can get ABA now than just a decade ago, thanks largely to Catherine Maurice's 1993 book *Let Me Hear Your Voice* (New York: Ballantine), which brought the research on early intensive ABA for autism out of professional journals into the everyday lives of families dealing with autism and started a grassroots movement to make ABA more widely available. But for many families in many countries, including the US, obtaining effective, science-based treatment for children with autism still entails a costly and stressful struggle.

The analogy between ALL and autism is far from perfect. There is probably more known scientifically about ALL than autism; unlike autism, there are reliable, objective medical tests for diagnosing ALL; and the treatment of ALL is mainly the purview of one discipline (medicine), whereas many professions are involved in autism intervention (various specialities in medicine, special education, speech-language pathology, occupational therapy, physical therapy, music therapy, recreational therapy, various specialities in psychology, behaviour analysis, and others). Although the everyday practice of medicine is not uniformly scientific, the treatment of ALL is underpinned by principles and methods derived from natural sciences like biology, physiology and chemistry as well as scientific laboratory and applied research in medicine. Certainly there are those who promote treatments for ALL that are not grounded in sound science, but in general when parents have a child diagnosed with ALL, they can be reasonably confident that the treatment recommendations they receive are grounded in sound scientific research. Many autism treatments, on the other hand, are drawn from research using social science methods, clinicians' impressions, and various and sundry practices that are frankly pseudo- and antiscientific. (Behaviour analysis is an exception, because it is a natural science approach to behaviour.) Perhaps it is this difference between a mostly 'hard science' and a mostly 'soft science' treatment context that accounts for the fact that greater advances have been made in understanding and treating many childhood disorders like ALL than in understanding and treating autism. Or perhaps it is the longstanding pervasiveness of pseudoscience and antiscience in the autism culture that has retarded the acquisition of reliable knowledge about autism.

For the past few years I have been privileged to observe the efforts of the Northern Ireland organization Parents' Education as Autism Therapists and their principal mentor, behaviour analyst Mickey Keenan. Those efforts – supported by Karola Dillenburger, several of the authors of this text, and other parents and professionals in Northern Ireland and elsewhere – have been, in my opinion, nothing short of heroic. My hope is that the analogies offered in this foreword will help readers understand the frustration, despair and outrage expressed by some of the contributors to this book. I also hope readers will appreciate the tremendous joys and accomplishments described in this text, often against incredible odds. At the same time, I would encourage readers to exercise healthy scepticism about *all* interventions for autism, including those described here, and to demand objective evidence from methodologically sound studies to back up every claim.

I know that the editors and authors will be very happy if this book convinces even a few readers to take an objective look at ABA and what it can do for children with autism and their families. If it ultimately helps more children with autism get truly effective treatment, I think I can safely say that all of us will be ecstatic.

Gina Green, PhD, BCBA
San Diego, CA

Preface

This book follows on from a book we wrote in 2000 together with parents of children with autism (Keenan, Kerr and Dillenburger 2000). The first book was designed to inform those who care for these children, or those who are charged with their education, about the application and effectiveness of the science of behaviour analysis. We hoped that professionals, agencies and the education system would embrace this science and welcome it into the valley of tears. This did not happen. Instead, misinformation and prejudice were rife and even those who wanted to help were not enabled to learn about behaviour analysis.

What should you do when nobody listens? Walk away? Or do whatever it takes to get things changed? Love for their children made sure that parents did not give up. They wanted applied behaviour analysis (ABA) because they had seen the evidence with their own eyes, in the progress made by their children. But the system did not help. It left them to fend for themselves. Mickey Keenan had been the only one who cared enough to go public. His initiative had led to the establishment of the charity Parents' Education as Autism Therapists (PEAT) in Northern Ireland. Together with his PhD students he persisted and behaviour analysis was introduced to parents in the north and south of Ireland.

To our surprise, we found that when Mickey was on a lecture tour of New Zealand in 2003, people there were faced with the same problems. We asked them to join us and this was when the idea for the current book became reality.

The book in your hands is about the rights of children to benefit from scientifically validated educational practices; it is about the rights of parents to be fully informed about these practices; it is about how the intransigence of powerful people has created a deplorable position where parents of children with autism are forced to turn to the courts to receive the support they need to educate their children; and, finally, it is about how these parents, empowered with basic scientific skills, have become more adept in bringing the best out in their children than are the vast majority of professionals employed to look after the children.

The science of behaviour analysis is sketched out and the struggle of bringing this science to the community is documented. Parents then join hands with an international group of professionals to describe how together they designed and ran their own home programmes, how they set up their own self-help groups, pre-schools, schools and after-school facilities, how working with older children can be approached, and how they fought through the courts the very system that was supposed to help. Siblings describe what this has meant for them. Basic applications of the science of behaviour to other areas are outlined briefly and parents tell us what they think of ABA. Finally, resources have been made available to help those who are asked to show the evidence for ABA. Feel free to copy the references at the end of this book and slap them on a table at some meeting or other. Don't forget to demand an equivalent list evidencing the effectiveness of non-ABA interventions used with your child.

We hope you find this book useful and informative in the fight for our children's right to the most effective help available. We want to leave the last word to Colin, who was the first child in Northern Ireland to benefit from ABA in 1995 and who today attends the same grammar school as his brother and sisters.

> Dear Mickey,
>
> I didn't realize what all those games and work we did was really for at the time but now I realize it has helped me overcome the parts of autism that were holding me back. When I was little I couldn't speak properly and I didn't listen well to people. I used to be a bit of a whirlwind and never sat still (except for dinner). The activities we did helped me overcome this. I remember the looking game which helped me look at people. This is called good eye contact. Now I really like conversations and my interests include reading newspapers, playing video games, watching action movies, swimming and walking with Dad and my youngest sister. My favourite subjects at secondary school are technology, art, history and home economics. I feel very comfortable about having autism (sometimes I make a joke about Asperger's syndrome and call it hamburger syndrome). The good thing about autism is that, when I want to, I can concentrate really hard and I find learning quite easy. If it weren't for ABA I don't know if I would be at secondary school with my brother and sisters. Applied behaviour analysis has helped me so much. (Letter from Colin, Saturday 27 September 2003)

Karola Dillenburger and Mickey Keenan

CHAPTER 1

Empowering Parents with Science[1]

Mickey Keenan

New perspectives

At the heart of any science lies an unquenchable thirst for new ways to understand the world in which we live. Evidence of progress is found usually in developments at a conceptual level along with innovations in technology. The picture in Figure 1.1 captures something of the essence of being a scientist, an inquisitive spirit that is the main driving force of science. Called 'The Celestial Sphere', this play on a 19th-century image shows a man peeking out of his everyday world and experiencing a whole new other world. Metaphorically speaking, the transition made by the 'scientist' in this picture represents the changed perspective he has now on his everyday world. No longer will things be the same. But what is he to do with his new perspective? Will he be able to communicate this perspective to others who have not peeked in the way that he has peeked? Will he meet resistance to the idea that there is another way to look at the world? If he does, what should he do? Should he water down his science so that others might be more accepting of it? These kinds of questions provide the focus for this chapter. My overall aim is to acquaint you briefly with a science called behaviour analysis. Of particular concern are the kinds of

---

1   Parts of this chapter were presented at an invited address to the British Psychological Society annual conference, 2003, for the Award for Promoting Equality of Opportunity. A shortened version appeared as 'Autism in N. Ireland: the tragedy and the shame' in *The Psychologist* (2004) Vol. *17*, No. 2, 72–75.

Figure 1.1: The Celestial Sphere

issues that arise when the findings of this science are brought to the attention of the community concerned with the treatment of autism.

In the opening chapter to his book *Science and Human Behavior* B.F. Skinner (1953) talked about the possibility of a science of human behaviour. The context for his discussion was in reference to the irresponsibility with which science and the products of science have been used.

> Man's power appears to have increased out of all proportion to his wisdom. He has never been in a better position to build a healthy, happy, and productive world; yet things have perhaps never seemed so black. Two exhausting world wars in a single half century have given no assurance of a lasting peace. Dreams of progress toward a higher civilisation have been shattered by the spectacle of the murder of millions of innocent people. (p.4)

Later he indicates the challenges faced by a science of behaviour, not least the possibility that we may have to accept changes in the way in which we look at ourselves and the world. What he was referring to here was the scientific study of voluntary behaviour, something that has far-reaching implications about how we understand why we do the things we do.

> Science is…an attempt to discover order, to show that certain events stand in lawful relations to other events. No practical technology can be based on science until such relations have been discovered.
>
> If we are to use the methods of science in the field of human affairs, we must assume that behaviour is lawful and determined. We must expect to discover that what a man does is the result of specifiable conditions and that once these conditions have been discovered, we can anticipate and to some extent determine his actions. (p.6)

Cooper, Heron and Heward (1987) discuss one of the first studies to report on the application of the findings of the science of behaviour analysis. In 1949 a scientist called P.R. Fuller worked with an 18-year-old boy with profound learning difficulties who lay in a 'vegetative' state:

> He lay on his back, unable to roll over. Fuller filled a syringe with a warm sugar-milk solution and injected it into the boy's mouth every time he moved his right arm (that arm was chosen because he moved it infrequently). Within four sessions the boy was moving his arm to vertical position at a rate of 3 times per minute.

[In Fuller's own words:]

> The attending physicians…thought it was impossible for him to learn anything – according to them, he had not learned anything in the 18 years of his life – yet in four experimental sessions…an addition was made to his behavior, which, at this level, could be termed appreciable. Those who participated in or observed the experiment are of the opinion that if time permitted, other responses could be conditioned and discriminations learned. (p.12)

Quite a breakthrough! But notice something important here. It was the practical demonstration of changes in behaviour that are persuasive. The steps taken to produce these changes in behaviour are called the 'technology' of the science of behaviour analysis. Also important here is the fact that prior to this demonstration the attending physicians had a world view that left them impotent with respect to being able to produce similar changes in behaviour. Here is our first link back to the image of the celestial sphere – that is, they had been unable to look through their celestial sphere to see that it was possible to teach this person.

Here are some other examples of world views that in retrospect were shown to have inherent blind spots.

> In the American South before the Civil War, a physician named Samuel Cartwright argued that many slaves were suffering from two forms of mental illness: 'drapetomania', whose primary symptom was the un-

controllable urge to escape from slavery, and 'dysathesia aethiopica', whose symptoms were destroying property on the plantation, being disobedient, or refusing to work. (Tavris 1999)

In this example we see that the establishment had a view of their world that justified their treatment of black people. Slave owners thought that mental disorder made slaves seek freedom, and that it had nothing to do with the conditions of slavery. A point here is that the way in which people conceptualize a problem is related to how they deal with the problem in a practical manner. In this instance medicalizing the behaviour of slaves itself poses another problem. While, for today's readers, it may appear rather daft, the serious undertones are that the medicalization of problem behaviours still goes on today (e.g. Friman 2002; Kirk, Kutchins and Rowe 1997). As in Fuller's case, the attending physicians were impotent when it came to providing solutions that are clear to us today.

This next example concerns a child with learning difficulties. The view that we should care for people with learning difficulties has a long tradition. However, before we held this view, people with learning difficulties were regarded as godless, without soul, and possessed by the devil or demon (Cogan 1995). We now see things differently. Or at least I thought so until I read the following in the *Skeptical Inquirer*.

> On Friday, August 22nd, 2003, 8-year-old Terrance Cottrell, who suffers from autism, was wrapped in sheets and held down by church members during prayer service at the Faith Temple Church of the Apostolic Faith in Milwaukee, Wisconsin. He was held to exorcise the evil spirits they blamed for his condition. According to the *New York Times* '[h]is shirt was drenched in sweat when the church members who were holding him down, saying they wanted to rid him of demons, finally noticed that he was dead. He had urinated on himself, and his small, brown face had a bluish cast.' According to the medical examiner, there was extensive bruising on the back of the little boy's neck and it appeared that he died of mechanical asphyxiation from pressure placed on his chest. (Christopher 2003, p.11)

Undoubtedly this is a tragic accident. However, the reason for recounting this story is that it did not happen in the middle ages; it happened recently. This time, instead of medicalizing the problem behaviour, a different kind of inner explanation was invented, a demon instead of a mental illness. What it shows is that people still are using pre-scientific explanations for behaviour in one of the wealthiest countries in the world. So what is the alternative, or at least, in what ways can the science of behaviour analysis help us to see differently?

Like all natural sciences behaviour analysis uses special techniques for systematic observation; indeed it is the word 'systematic' that helps to differentiate the layperson from the scientist. From these observations general laws of nature can be identified, if there are any. Are there any? Sure! And what is so special about finding these laws is that we can use them to do things differently than we would without this knowledge.

Does talk about laws of nature mean that there are laws of nature operating all of the time but that the layperson is blind to them?

> The answer to this is a mixture of 'Yes' and 'No!' This is because there is a difference between being intuitively aware of certain laws and being able to talk about them in a scientific sense. For example, an important basis for the lay person's skills in social interaction is his/her ability to predict the behaviour of those with whom he/she is interacting; something a scientist would be interested in doing. The fact that someone's behaviour can be predicted suggests that a law of nature is operating. From the point of view of behaviour analysis, the behaviour of the person in question can be said to indicate the operation of a basic principle of behaviour. A principle in this sense is a statement which describes the lawful relation between the occurrence of a behaviour and the circumstances in which it reliably occurs.
>
> By making this statement, the scientist brings our understanding from the intuitive level to a level that can now form the basis for a different type of communication. Metaphorically speaking, the scientist might be conceived of as a friend who accompanies the lay person and provides him/her with a vocabulary and language for talking about their existing ability to accurately predict the behaviours of another person. To help convince their friend that a principle of behaviour does exist, the scientist…might say something like this:
>
> 'Look, it was you who predicted what Fred was going to do. Somehow or other, you assessed the ingredients that made up the situation he was in. You then used this information, together with information gathered from previous interactions with him, to predict his behaviour. Now, although we can't put back the clock to look at his behaviour again, what we could do is to set up another similar situation with him or with someone else and see what happens. This time you tell me in advance how you expect him to behave. If we do this, and if his behaviour is in accordance with your expectations, then we can begin to formulate a principle of behaviour. Once we have constructed this principle, it is this that is then referred to if someone else requires an explanation for Fred's behaviour. In other words, describing which principle is in operation is what behaviour analysts do when they are asked to provide an explanation for someone's behaviour.' (Keenan 1997, pp.328–9)

Figure 1.2 portrays a scientific observation of behaviour. The filmstrip represents the average life span of a person that extends across over 2000 million seconds. This 'streaming' of a person's life across time is called the 'behavioural stream'. It is an important consideration when we try to make sense of instances of behaviour, a point we will return to shortly. Now, depending on the level of magnification of the microscope, the segments of the strip in this diagram can represent different time spans. Different levels of magnification might include observations of behaviour across one minute, or one hour, or one day, or one week, etc. At another level, we analyse behaviour according to dynamical systems (Dillenburger 2005; Glenn 2004; Moynahan 2001; Novak 1996). In any case, scientists collect data on behaviour. Once collected, these data give an overall picture of what the behaviour is like and how it is likely to appear in the future if nothing is done to try to influence it. A point to remember in all of this is that when we talk of behaviour here, we are referring to changes in the whole person. It is the whole person (with an inner world of thoughts and feelings), after all, who extends across time.

Let's turn our attention now to an example of how the perspective painted above affects the way in which one conceptualizes something familiar to us all, education. Education is essentially a system for arranging specific experiences for a student. The nature of the experiences depends on the goals of the curriculum. The curriculum in turn depends on the current behaviour of the

Figure 1.2: The behavioural stream

student. The success of the student with this curriculum, however, depends on how it is delivered.

This last point is the nub of the education issue (Howard *et al.* 2005). How does one ensure that a student is successful? How do you bring out the best in someone? An important starting point is to examine whether the delivery of the curriculum incorporates fundamental principles of behaviour. That is to say, is the curriculum designed with the knowledge of how laws of nature affect behaviour?

Usually the goal of a curriculum is to increase the likelihood that a person behaves in a certain way in a given situation. In everyday terms this means bringing a person to a point where they have the confidence and skills to live in a world that places a wide range of demands on them. We can take as an example a parent teaching a child to be sociable. Whenever the child is behaving in a way considered inappropriate, the parent follows this behaviour with a consequence normally referred to as a reprimand. On the other hand, if the child does something that finds favour with the parent, then a different consequence is arranged; normally we call this praise. A parent might not know this, but operating within these two scenarios are extremely powerful laws of behaviour. On each occasion a consequence is delivered, the effect of which is to influence the future probability of the preceding behaviour. Because a scientist would have techniques for observing this behaviour very carefully, and for collecting data, s/he would be able to draw graphs showing how and when the behaviour changed during these exchanges between parent and child. The basic principle formulated by the scientist would look something like this:

> When a behaviour is followed by specific consequences the likelihood that this behaviour will occur again depends on the effect of these consequences.

Basic principles of behaviour like this (and remember, we are talking about facts, not theories) have been studied extensively across a variety of situations and with many different types of organisms. Martin and Pear (2001) said the following:

> Applications are occurring with an ever-increasing frequency in such areas as education, social work, nursing, clinical psychology, psychiatry, community psychology, medicine, rehabilitation, business, industry, and sports. (p.14)

What differentiates parents from the behavioural scientist, then, is the knowledge of principles of behaviour and how these are translated to the design of educational programmes. With enhanced knowledge and awareness comes increased versatility to adapt educational programmes to match individual needs.

> Applied Behavior Analysis is the science in which procedures derived from the principles of behavior are systematically applied to improve socially significant behavior to a meaningful degree and to demonstrate experimentally that the procedures employed were responsible for the improvement in behavior. (Cooper *et al.* 1987, p.14)

Earlier I mentioned that a scientific perspective on the behavioural stream has implications for understanding instances of behaviour more generally. Research from both the laboratory and in applied settings indicates that, when there is no reference made to the operation of principles of behaviour, serious errors of judgement can be made in the explanation of behaviour. These errors are similar to the errors described at the start of this chapter. To illustrate this point further consider the following. In our day-to-day affairs it is possible to identify patterns of behaviour. We all engage in repetitive behaviours generally referred to as routines. These routines can extend across different time frames (such as the sequence of steps involved in a specific skill, like getting dressed, or maintaining personal hygiene), routines that occur across the day in work settings, routines that extend across the week as in going to work each morning, coming home, making the dinner, relaxing in the evening, going to bed, getting up again the next day, and socializing at the weekend. All of our patterns can be measured and in many respects they are the fingerprints of our individuality. In addition, these patterns can be accounted for by principles of behaviour.

Once a pattern has been identified any instance of behaviour only makes sense in terms of its relevance within the whole pattern. In other words, any instance of behaviour is only a segment of a larger pattern. This means that it would be mistaken to explain this instance without reference to the principles of behaviour that account for the whole pattern. Unfortunately, though, many people not familiar with the principles of behaviour make this very mistake. Because of their initial mistake in not recognizing the role of principles of behaviour in producing a more general pattern, they end up looking in the wrong place for the explanation for a particular instance of behaviour; as happened in the examples at the start of this chapter, where people searched for internal explanations for behaviour.

There is an additional problem. People who use internal or mentalistic 'explanations' have no reason to look elsewhere for an explanation for their observations. They have their explanation and that is that! Persons inside this particular celestial sphere might not even be aware that they have an explanatory system for understanding the world. In usual circumstances there may be no need to look for, let alone challenge, premature conclusions about why certain behaviours occur. But what happens when a crisis arises and there is a need to change behaviour? In the case of autism, the limitations of someone's explanatory system, or their skills deficit with respect to behavioural technology, is exposed by their inability to facilitate meaningful and long-lasting changes in behaviour. Parents or professionals need to know what they can and cannot do. More to the point, they need to know what the child can and cannot do. What are his/her limitations for learning? You can't answer this question if you don't investigate. You also can't answer it if you don't know how to maximize the child's chances of success using the existing body of knowledge uncovered by a science of behaviour. You certainly can't answer it if the curriculum doesn't build upon the child's successes and stretch him/her in the way that any good curriculum would stretch any learner.

Bringing ABA to the community for the treatment of autism

In this section we will take a closer look at how a science of behaviour impinges on the world of autism. The patterns of behaviour of children with autism are different from the typical or the norm. These children engage in some behaviours more often than other children and they engage in other behaviours less often. For example, a child may engage in sorting and stimming behaviours significantly more often than other kids, and in social behaviours significantly less often. The label 'autism' is useful in so far as it provides a category for classifying characteristic patterns of behaviour that if left unchecked will result in major problems later in life. For those not familiar with autism here is some background information:

> 'Autism' is a descriptive label for a developmental disability often manifest before age 3, affecting verbal and nonverbal communication and social interaction. Other characteristics may include persistence in repetitive activities and stereotyped movements, resistance to environmental change or change in daily routines, and unusual responses to sensory experiences. (NAS 2005)

> Autism is a spectrum disorder (ASD) – The symptoms and characteristics of autism can present themselves in a wide variety of combinations,

> from mild to severe. Two children can have the same diagnosis but act very differently from one another and have very different skills. (NAS 2005)

In the United Kingdom (UK) the National Autistic Society (NAS 2005) has calculated prevalence rates of about 91 per 10,000. Elsewhere figures are similar. A recent article in *The Scotsman* noted that 'Campaigners believe that Scotland is facing a crisis, with the number of cases of autism rising from one in every 2500 of the population to one in 166 over the past ten years – an increase of 1600 per cent' (Thompson 2003). In the United States over 1.7 million individuals live with autism, making it more prevalent than Down's syndrome, childhood diabetes and childhood cancer combined (Autismspeaks 2005).

Although it had long been my vision to bring ABA into the community, if it had not been for a wonderful mum, Lynne McKerr, who worked diligently with me to bring out the best in her little boy, I may not be actively involved in the area of autism today. When Lynne first came to me I found it hard to come to terms with her predicament. I was well aware that there were hundreds of journal articles detailing the success of applied behaviour analysis for children with ASD (Cambridge Center for Behavioral Studies 2005; Green 2003; see also the 'Resources for Parents' section compiled by Eric Larsson at the end of this book). What I couldn't understand was why this mum was coming to me, an academic in a university setting, and not to a professional in the community? I was aghast to learn from her that there was nobody to whom she could turn. There was nobody who had sufficient knowledge of ABA to help her teach her son how to learn. So it fell to me, a behaviour analyst with no prior practical experience of working with autism, to help her. Details of our work together are contained in Keenan, Kerr and Dillenburger (2000). Here is a brief summary of that story.

After extensive assessment by a number of professionals (see Table 1.1) Colin was diagnosed by the consultant psychiatrist as having Asperger's syndrome and attention deficit/hyperactivity disorder.

Unfortunately none of the professionals who had worked with Lynne gave her any practical advice on how to educate Colin. Without appropriate education he was destined for an institution for the rest of his life. I knew that if I could teach Lynne the principles of behaviour analysis that are integral to the design of educational programmes that she would eventually be able to design her own programmes, that she would become a skilled teacher for her own son. Basically I had to design an intensive course in ABA for Lynne. Over

Table 1.1 Assessment by professionals

Age	Assessment
2 years	Speech and language therapist: 'Colin has a severely disordered communication development. Both comprehension and expression were severely affected. Self-distracting behaviour and echolalia were present.'
3 years 9 months	Teachers/educational psychologist: 'Colin has a very pronounced lack of social awareness. He pays scant regard or ignores group and class activities. He often wanders about the classroom oblivious to the main class activity. While peers in close proximity are reacting off each other [Colin] remains egocentrically preoccupied with the toy cars, having no urge to engage socially.'
3 years 10 months	Educational psychologist using the Childhood Autism Rating Scale (CARS): 'The results specifically indicated a language delay, social aloofness, some degree of obsessiveness, poor adaptation to change, high level of activity and low level of attention control.'

the course of a year she came to our house each week with Colin. Karola Dillenburger and I devised programmes tailored to his skill levels on each occasion. Colin and Lynne made great progress together as evidenced by a report on his special educational needs when he was 11 years old:

> Colin is a very good-natured boy who enjoys the company of his class-mates. He plays football and is very proud of being a member of the school quiz team. He has a great sense of humour... He is a lively, enthusiastic, friendly boy who can articulate readily and most competently his needs and opinions. He has made excellent progress in understanding spoken and written information. He has an excellent expressive vocabulary and uses it appropriately in his spontaneous language. His reading and thinking skills are well developed and he can use inference well... In school he contributes well to class debates and discussions. He has a wide general knowledge. He always listens well and absorbs the information presented. (Educational psychologist report 2002)

Lynne persuaded me to hold public talks to inform others about the techniques we had used. To cut a long story short, I ended up running classes in

ABA on a voluntary basis for about 40 sets of parents each month for about another year. Eventually we progressed to the formation of a formal charity that the parents decided to call Parents' Education as Autism Therapists (PEAT).

A theme that continues to rePEAT itself with every parent who has turned to PEAT is one of overcoming obstacles, obstacles that are either conceptual in nature or of a more practical nature, or a combination of both. 'Why didn't anyone tell us that something could be done, that *I* could do something?' These are words that continue to echo throughout the group. The effects of autism on the family are too many to list here, but there are a number of specific things that parents in the group had to deal with.

Diagnosis

First, there were emotional difficulties in coming to terms with the diagnosis of autism in their child.

Practical

Entwined with this were the emotional difficulties associated with not being able to help in a practical way as their child, and in some cases the entire family, slipped further and further away from their dreams and expectations.

Professionals

There were unintentional obstacles created by caring professionals who presented parents with a diagnosis but at the same time offered them no practical advice in the face of mounting difficulties.

It is not my desire to be contentious for the sake of it by raising this issue. I am merely reporting a shared experience of virtually all of the PEAT parents, an experience that chilled me to the bone when I first came across it and one that persuaded me to do whatever I could to help them.

Back to school

There were obstacles associated with the whole idea of studying again. Many if not all of the parents were desperate for a short-term fix that would return them from the nightmare that they were experiencing. The last thing they wanted was to have to pick themselves up and go back to school.

Gauntlet

Having run the gauntlet of all of these difficulties these parents rose to the challenge of organizing themselves into a registered charity. This was done for the benefit of others despite the extra work they had undertaken in the management of their children's learning. As word gets around about what we are doing, so PEAT expands. Currently there are about 100+ sets of parents in the group. Unfortunately we have only one full-time therapist, Stephen Gallagher, who visits parents across the whole of Northern Ireland doing a virtually impossible job. It is his compassion for the plight of the parents and children that helps to sustain PEAT in financially difficult times. At the time of writing this chapter money has run out for Stephen, which means that there is a potential crisis looming for the goals of the group.

One person who was central to establishing the movement in Ireland that PEAT began was Bobby Newman from the Association in Manhattan for Autistic Children. Before PEAT there was no ABA for children with autism anywhere in Ireland. With Bobby's help we ran workshops for parents that helped to push the boat out even further. Ken Kerr, who worked with PEAT initially, also promoted science-based treatments in the Republic of Ireland. He ran numerous workshops to introduce parents to ABA and he eventually opened up a school. Also there to lend a hand was Dermot Barnes, who brought over Doug Greer from the University of Columbia. Doug has since opened up two CABAS schools (Comprehensive Application of Behavior Analysis Schools). Currently there are about 12 ABA schools catering for about 200+ children in the Republic and numerous parent groups across the country. Interestingly, and I say this with a heavy heart, there are as yet no ABA schools in the North where it all began!

For me personally, both as an academic and as a father, it has been a humbling experience to have been involved with a group of individuals who battled hard to transform their love for their children into practical skills, skills that are tempered by the rigours required by a science of behaviour. On the positive side, we are now in a position where applied behaviour analysis is discussed in public meetings (Moffat 2003), both North and South of the border. Before this, behaviour analysis in Ireland was something that existed only for a small number of professionals or in the closed books on university shelves, to be opened in the event of an essay being needed for a course mark.

In spite of the progress we have made, for me the politics of it all is the most unexpected and stressful part of the journey. The setting up of a new group is always bound to annoy others who thought they were the only ones who had the right to be in the driving seat. I refer here to the establishment in its many guises, from other autism charities and their links with the Department of Education, to heads of special schools, to educational psychologists and psychiatrists. There wasn't much I could do about that. I was asked by parents to teach them what others were not teaching them. My personal commitment to continue hinged on the fact that the children always came first. But the politics don't just exist in the day-to-day affairs of community groups. In the heartlands of academia the situation for behaviour analysts is even more cut throat. This is something that I'll come back to later for it is crucial that parents understand the obstacles that impede the uptake of ABA. Suffice to say, at times academics may need help from parents to promote ABA in the community.

What parents are being taught

Before I outline briefly some of the essential features of ABA that guided me in my work with Lynne, I think it might be appropriate at this point to highlight some of the recommendations ABA has received elsewhere.

- 'Thirty years of research demonstrated the efficacy of applied behavioral methods in reducing inappropriate behavior and in increasing communication, learning, and appropriate social behavior' (Surgeon General 2000, p.5).

- The California Department of Education (1997) concluded that: 'research has shown that intervention and educational programming based on the principles and practices of applied behavior analysis can produce rapid, complex, and durable improvements in cognitive, social-communication, play, and self-help skills. Application of behavior-analytic principles are very effective in replacing and/or reducing maladaptive behavior' (p.67).

- The New York State Department of Health (1999) issued guidelines for the treatment of young children with an ASD stating that early and intensive behavioural intervention is at present the only appropriate treatment.

Statements like these are not made lightly, especially in view of their financial implications. Personally, I still marvel at what Lynne and I achieved and what others are achieving through ABA. So what lies at the heart of ABA in relation to autism?

Acknowledging the life of an individual to be a continuous stream has enormous implications for treatment designs. In a home programme, for example, it translates into the practice of teaching a parent to shadow the developing child (keep in mind the image of the behavioural stream) in such a way as to be able to monitor very closely the changes in choreography that make up the fine detail of the child's interaction with his/her physical and social environment. When this choreography is in need of change, then practical steps are taken to see how this can be achieved. The parent essentially is a guide in the truest and deepest sense of the word, someone whose role is 'to lead somebody in the right direction' (Encarta 1999).

The questions that arise usually for parents and therapists include which aspects of the choreography to start with, and what to do next. Not surprisingly, behaviour analysis has developed and continues to develop guidelines to address these questions (Bondy, Tincani and Frost 2004; Harris and Weiss 1998; Lovaas 1981; Maurice, Green and Foxx 2001; Maurice, Green and Luce 1996; Newman *et al.* 2002). All the while, there is an air of research and investigation in the evolution of an educational programme. Because an ABA programme is tailored to the individual it must evolve with the progress of the individual. This means that one has to adopt almost a 'suck it and see' approach. In other words, within the sophisticated application of general principles of behaviour, fixed treatment recipes are avoided and instead data-based decision making steers the evolving programmes. Putting it another way, through data collection one is able to determine whether or not a particular programme is effective. If it is not effective, data on the progress of your child will tell you and the programme must be adjusted to enhance the learning opportunities for the child. Data collection will tell you also when the child has mastered the material in a particular programme, when you should move on to another programme, or how you should adjust your programme to facilitate generalization.

The research conducted by behaviour analysts and parents in devising educational programmes hinges on methodology that most professionals in the UK and Ireland are not taught – that is, single-system (or single-case) research methodology (Johnston and Pennypacker 1980, 1993; Sidman 1960). Again, this methodology is not restricted to the study of autism but its relevance to autism can be seen from the following quotation by Anderson and Romancyzk (1999):

> One of the important characteristics of children on the autistic spectrum is uneven learning ability and skill levels. Thus, individualiza-

tion of intervention cannot be overstated. The specifics of programmes will be different for different children and must be sensitive to the child's needs. Thus, an important aspect of ABA is the introduction of procedures to quantify the child's behavior that can be used to create and evaluate individualized interventions. (p.165)

Many of the parents in PEAT and in other groups throughout Ireland and the UK now know about the need for evidence-based practice (Dillenburger 2004) and the value of experimentation. They know how to collect data on the educational programmes they use with their children and they know how to assess the effectiveness of these programmes. Although many parents are not entirely consistent in the application of their new science, they still have a better understanding of principles of behaviour than many students who graduate with a degree in psychology and, sadly, many professionals who consider themselves knowledgeable or even expert in autism.

So what does a home programme look like? Table 1.2 provides a snippet of an ABA programme for various behaviours that may be targeted for change.

It is difficult to imagine the kinds of demands placed on parents who commit to an ABA home programme. It is not unusual to find, for example, that over the course of about three years up to 500 different behaviours can be targeted for change. Quite apart from the practicalities involved in planning and implementing the programme, parents are taught a new perspective in the management of behaviour. Whatever the extent of the changes produced with their children, parents are empowered with basic scientific skills.

To conclude this section, there is one outstanding issue that needs to be addressed. I touched on it earlier when I talked about people drawing premature conclusions in their search for an explanation of behaviour. Let's look at this issue more closely. The most common mistake of this type of premature conclusion is called a 'category mistake'. Throughout the years I have been teaching behaviour analysis this is perhaps the one issue that is most difficult to deal with. I reckon it also lies at the heart of much of the mis-representation of behaviour analysis (Keenan and Dillenburger 2004; Morris 1985; Nye 1992; Skinner 1977, 1985; Wyatt 1990). My solution to teaching about it has been to use an animated cartoon character in a multimedia tutorial (Keenan and Dillenburger 2000). The character, Adam, walks across the screen towards the image of a girl who turns her eyes to look at him briefly. Adam then begins to bounce a ball and at one point he burps. The girl beside him admonishes him for this rude behaviour and he blushes, and stops what he is doing for a moment before continuing to bounce the ball.

Table 1.2 Educational curriculum
for a child on the autistic spectrum*

Skills/ Behaviours	Basic	Intermediate	Advanced
Attending skills	Child sits in chair independently. Child makes eye contact in response to name.	Child asks 'What?' when their name is called.	Child makes eye contact during conversation and group activities.
Imitation skills	Child imitates gross motor, fine motor and oral motor skills. Child imitates actions with objects.	Child imitates a sequence of actions or sounds.	Child imitates peer play.
Receptive language	Child follows one-step instructions. Child identifies objects and pictures.	Child identifies rooms. Child identifies emotions. Child follows two-step instructions.	Child follows three-step instructions. Child discriminates concepts.
Expressive language	Child imitates sounds and words. Child labels objects and pictures.	Child labels objects based on function. Child labels gender.	Child labels categories. Child retells a story.
Pre-academic skills	Child matches identical pictures. Child matches identical objects. Child undresses.	Child initiates for bathroom. Child washes hands. Child puts on some clothes.	Child brushes teeth. Child buttons clothes.

* Adapted from Gallagher (personal communication).

He burps again and is admonished again. After a moment he walks off the screen and returns with a flower, which he gives to the girl. The animation finishes with them both smiling. As far as animations go this is not exactly Oscar material. Parents are asked to jot down the words they feel are appropriate to this character called Adam. Typically, the words that parents use include cheeky, rude, immature, attention seeking, charming, shy and extravert. Once we have written down the words used by parents, I show the animation again, this time with the words that were used by a class of 100 undergraduate psychology students who did the same exercise. Now, the animation is designed so that these words appear on the screen to coincide with the behaviour being referred to.

More often than not the range of words obtained by the students matches the words used by the parents. At this point, all the words are placed on the left-hand side of the screen under the heading 'Descriptions' (see Figure 1.3). That is to say, it is acknowledged that these words indeed are used correctly as descriptions of behaviour.

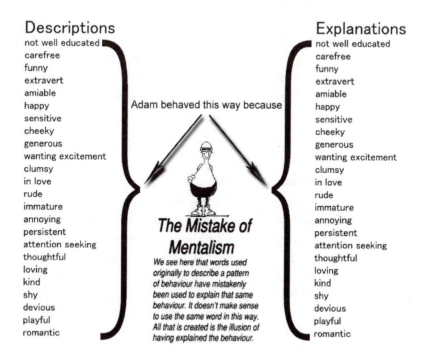

Figure 1.3: The mistake of mentalism

The mistake of 'mentalism' is demonstrated by moving the words across the screen and placing them under the heading 'Explanations'. In this way, the animation shows that the mistake of mentalism occurs when the words that correctly describe behaviour are simultaneously used to explain behaviour. A circular argument is mistakenly invoked giving the illusion of having supplied an explanation. Thus, for example, 'attention seeking' is a term used to describe Adam's behaviour. Usually if we are asked for an explanation for his behaviour (i.e. for his attention seeking) we tend to say 'he is doing this *because* he is attention seeking'. Does this ring a bell with you? Have you ever made such a mistake when you have explained someone's behaviour?

There is an advantage in using a cartoon character in this instance. In a further twist of the animation Adam's head is opened up to reveal an empty space, not even a brain. Parents are taught that their use of words to explain his behaviour is an indication of how their own education deceived them into devising false explanations. In a sense the exercise is a mirror showing how their education has led to a language trap that results in the illusion of an explanation (see Holth 2001 for a more detailed analysis of mentalism and category mistakes). Perhaps the most striking experience for parents, in this context, is the realization that the word 'autism' itself often is used incorrectly as an explanation. It is a descriptive label for a variety of behaviours and that's all! It does not explain the behaviours. A child does not engage in unusual behaviours *because* s/he has autism. S/he engages in those behaviours *and* the best we can do is lump them all together into one category and call it 'autism'. This term provides a useful reference for talking in generalities about the child. Nothing else!

Education authorities and ABA

Time and time again you may read in the media, and in numerous websites devoted to autism, statements which say that ABA (the applied branch of the science of behaviour analysis) is simply one of a number of therapies for autism. As we have seen, it is not! It is a fully-fledged science of human behaviour that has produced remarkable results in a wide variety of areas, autism being one of them; for a good overview of the applications of ABA see Cambridge Center for Behavioral Studies (2005). Parents put this best when they remark that neither of the two 'A's stand for autism!

There is no denying the need for behaviour analysts in Northern Ireland (BBC News 2003) and elsewhere in the world. Unfortunately, though, there are no comprehensive programmes for teaching ABA to professionals and neither is it taught as a core component of undergraduate courses in psychology or allied disciplines at any of Northern Ireland's universities. Consequently, a number of misconceptions about ABA have hindered its uptake in the community. This is a serious problem because learning about ABA involves more than just learning a few recipes for behaviour change (Walsh 1997) or attending a few short courses (Behavior Analyst Certification Board (BACB) 2005). Currently, if it were left up to psychologists who are not trained in behaviour analysis to indicate the essential features of behaviour analysis you would undoubtedly see something like this:

> Though vast in quantity, the great majority of behavioural findings tell us little of worth about ourselves. In a sense, having denied the importance of subjective data, their findings appear limited, alien, even 'soul-less'. (Spinelli 1989, p.175)

> Behaviourism also embodied the positivism of the Cartesian (from Descartes)-Newtonian tradition, in particular the emphasis on the need for scientific rigour and objectivity. Human beings were now being conceptualized and studied as 'natural phenomena', with their subjective experience, consciousness and other characteristics, which had for so long been taken as distinctive human qualities, being removed from the 'universe'. There was no place for these things in the behaviourist world. (Gross 1995, p.239)

> …my experience is that ABA is mainly about food and toy reinforcers, and not much in between. (Ginestet 2004)

Comments like these have found homes in many departments of psychology in the UK and elsewhere. However, they seriously misrepresent behaviour analysis. Indeed such is the misrepresentation of the field generally that there are few psychology departments in the UK who make adequate provision for the teaching of ABA despite its proven record in dealing with a wide range of social problems apart from autism and learning difficulties (e.g. Grant and Evans 1994; Hudson and McDonald 1991; Martin and Osborne 1980; Martin and Pear 2001; Mattaini and Thyer 1996; Nietzel et al. 1977; Sanders and Dadds 1993; Sidman 1989; Sulzer-Azaroff and Mayer 1991; West and Hamerlynck 1992).

Parents usually persist with ABA programmes for their kids because they hold no *a priori* assumptions about the philosophy of science underlying behaviour analysis. Rather they see with their eyes the developments their children make. Figure 1.4 graphically represents the argument being made regarding the way behaviour analysis is viewed within many psychology departments. In the picture you see me with one of my daughters. I prefer to see myself in the image on the left. Those who caricature behaviour analysis would see me in the image on the right.

Figure 1.4: Behaviourism views people as 'black boxes'

The contrast between the perspective of parents and the perspective of professionals fed on a diet of misrepresentation is unfortunate and it is one of the reasons why I used the word 'shame' in an address to the British Psychological Society (Keenan 2003). It is a shame that misrepresentation of behaviour analysis is so rife in psychology departments in the UK and Ireland. It is a shame that its developments are prevented from being shared with students who have an interest in helping others. It is a shame that parents of children with autism have to bear the brunt of funding decisions that are based on misinformation on ABA.

In my presentation, I gave two examples of how psychologists think about autism and how equality of opportunity for children with autism can be unintentionally impeded. I present them here again because I think they reveal to parents just how far off the mark many psychologists are when it comes to understanding behaviour analysis and autism. That old celestial sphere feeling comes to mind!

A student interested in working with children with autism for her undergraduate dissertation produced a research proposal based on research on video modelling (Nikopoulos and Keenan 2002). Her proposed experimental design is shown in Table 1.3.

Table 1.3 A video modelling procedure for teaching skills

Condition A	Condition B	Return to Condition A
Assess self-help skills in child with autism.	Show a 30-sec video of someone engaged in those self-help skills that are not in the child's repertoire.	Assess the effects of the self-help skills shown in the video, i.e. determine if the child has learned these new behaviours.

Her psychology departmental ethics committee did not give permission for the study because they decided that 'it constituted an intervention' and that therefore they could not grant approval (UK undergraduate students are not allowed to engage in clinical interventions). They demanded that the research proposal be submitted to the main university research ethics committee for approval. In other words, they decided that a procedure designed to *teach* new skills to a child should be considered a clinical intervention instead of a practical in applied learning or education and that they were not able to decide if it was ethical to do this. Thus a team of psychologists preferred to rely on the opinion of central university committees (non-psychologists) for a decision, thereby delaying the project so much that the student had to do something else in order to be able to complete her dissertation before the hand-in date. The child would not have been taught the skills had it not been for the student's personal commitment to help on a voluntary basis in her own time. I wonder if a similar decision would have been made if the proposal had been designed to use video modelling to educate a typically developing child?

The second example also involves a proposed undergraduate dissertation that was viewed as a clinical intervention rather than education or a description of learning, consequently not permitting the student to do the work. The aim of this study was to teach a child with autism to follow a specific schedule for his morning routine. The student thought that the work could have the added bonus of reducing disruptive behaviours that tended to occur because there was no morning routine. Permission was not given for this study. Consequently, the student redesigned her study so that now the parents were to be taught how to teach their own child instead of the student teaching the child. The psychology ethics committee also did not permit this study because teaching the parents was deemed to be a 'clinical intervention by proxy'. Need I say more? It really is a sad day for psychology when procedures designed to enhance a child's self-help skills cannot be seen for what they are, opportunities for learning. Ironically, what this means is that parents who know how to apply the principles of behaviour are considered 'clinicians' rather than parents, simply because they are skilled at creating opportunities for learning!

Unfortunate as it is, parents need to be familiar with the range of obstacles that are likely to impede the uptake of ABA in the community. Parents who diligently carry out their home-based programmes usually are bewildered by the reactions of professionals who either do not believe the data they have collected, or dismiss the video evidence as changes that would have happened anyway. Even stranger still is the total lack of interest by some professionals into exactly what kinds of educational programmes the parents have implemented. Clearly there is a vast discrepancy between those who perpetuate negative myths about behaviour analysis and those who use ABA in a compassionate way to facilitate meaningful changes in the lives of their children and others.

Politics

To show you what happens when misrepresentation is perpetuated by people in positions of authority I would like now to address some of the politics experienced by families in the PEAT group. Initially, in my naivety, I thought that the Department of Education would support the work that is being done by PEAT. To-date contacts have not been encouraging. Here is an extract from their response nearly a whole year after I first wrote to them outlining the scientific evidence supporting the effectiveness of behaviour analysis in the education of children with autism:

> This department is mainly concerned with the education of children in school, although it is entirely possible for home tuition to be provided by teachers for children unable to attend school for a variety of reasons, mainly medical. Applied Behaviour Analysis methods, on the other hand, appear to be practised outside the education system by people other than teachers and this again might tend to suggest that they fall outside this Department's area of responsibility. (Department of Education in Northern Ireland, letter dated 24 August 2000)

But there are no teachers with the skills to set up ABA programmes! Nor are there any courses at a university level where they can receive the appropriate training. It was shortly after I received this response that we decided to hold the first ABA conference in Ireland. One of our keynote speakers was Gina Green. Gina is a past president of the Association for Behavior Analysis (ABA 2005) and, at the time of the conference, she was Director of Research at the New England Center for Children and *Psychology Today* magazine nominated her as mental health professional of the year in the US. The US Secretary of Education Richard W. Riley named the New England Center for Children as a recipient of the US Department of Education's National Award for Model Professional Development. Citing efforts to improve teachers' expertise and raise student achievement, Riley stated: 'These award winners exemplify what can be done to give teachers the best skills and knowledge' (Press Release 2000).

A representative from the Department of Education in Northern Ireland was invited to the conference by PEAT. However, although he did attend the conference he did not approach Gina to be a consultant. The Department of Education still has not contacted her despite the seemingly obvious benefits that could accrue from having her involved in a consultancy basis for ABA development in Northern Ireland.

For a time I wondered if the obstacles I was encountering were merely over-interpretations stemming from paranoia on my part. However, in reality many families in PEAT struggle against a wall of misinformed and prejudicial views about ABA held by many professionals. This occurs to the extent that successful home programmes for children are jeopardized because professionals at various schools refuse to embrace these achievements and engage in partnership with parents who are developing skills in ABA. Currently, parents are being forced to use the courts to gain funding for their home programmes and to gain access to schools by independent observers to assess the provision being offered for their children. This is a drastic step for anyone to take but the parents have been left with no alternative. In addition the parents have managed to stimulate the production of two TV documentaries on their struggle. They even managed to set up a public meeting in parliament buildings in Belfast in 2003 (Moffat 2003). This event was particularly significant given the political crisis that has existed for some time in Northern Ireland; over 200 people were present, including members of the Northern Ireland Assembly, representing nearly all the political parties, and parents and professionals from ABA schools in the South. During the meeting it was revealed that the then Education Minister, Jane Kennedy, had been misinformed by her civil servants about the extent of the training educational psychologists received in ABA. She had been told that all educational psychologists received training in ABA techniques. However, a phone call to Queen's University in Belfast where the training took place revealed that this amounted to just a few lectures!

Similar struggles have been fought by parents in other countries. As a result of actions by parent groups in British Columbia, Canada, the Supreme Court made the following statement: 'It is beyond debate that the appropriate treatment is ABA [Applied Behaviour Analysis] or early intensive behavioural intervention' (The Supreme Court of British Columbia 2000, p.64).

My most basic response to these 'autism wars' (Freeman 2003) is to wonder what professionals are so worried about. Parents are delighted in their newfound skills and in the achievements made by their children. There is something seriously wrong when progress like this is not nourished. Perhaps it is simply a case that sincere people are protecting parents from the ghost of their own illusions that are generated by misinformation. That possibility means that not only kids but professionals too are victims of misinformation.

When governments in the North and South of Ireland set up task groups to look at provision for autism (Task Group 2002), ABA professionals were excluded from participating. Numerous letters of protest were delivered. In the North, the only way the PEAT group could get a response from the Department of Education, as to why ABA professionals were not included, was through the help of a local group of politicians called the Women's Coalition. They raised the issue on the floor of the Northern Ireland Assembly. The answer that came back was the following: 'For manageability reasons, this Group was kept small.'

Yet the Task Group included members of two other voluntary organizations who work in the area of autism but who have no expertise in ABA. The argument that manageability was the major reason for excluding an ABA representative is particularly disconcerting because a relatively large proportion of the report was given over to commenting on ABA, and getting it wrong. The views expressed in the report do not accurately reflect the current standing of ABA worldwide. Indeed the views expressed in the report may be harmful to budgeting decisions regarding the development and quality of ABA training in the community. They may impact also in a detrimental way on the support PEAT parents receive from professionals not trained in ABA.

One comment for which there is no evidence at all is found in Section 3.25 of the Task Force's evaluation.

> Local professionals who work with young children suggested to Task Group members that they would have grave reservations about being involved in subjecting such young children to such an intense behavioural programme for fear of causing some kind of psychological damage. (Task Group 2002)

It seems to us that this statement is based on personal views and preconceived ideas of people unfamiliar with ABA. The parents of the PEAT group were sickened by the suggestion that they would knowingly bring harm to their children. ABA-trained parents know that to be effective, learning must be fun. Since when has intense and playful fun been considered damaging to a child?

It is ethically imperative that practitioners who claim to offer ABA services can provide evidence of competency in this discipline. The report makes no mention of this crucial aspect of quality assurance either. Potentially this omission opens the floodgates for people briefly acquainted with ABA to offer training that does not meet agreed international standards. Unfortunately, this is already happening to some extent in our community. To counteract this state of affairs globally, an international certification programme in ABA that protects the rights of children and other clients has been set up (BACB 2005).

Parents in the PEAT group were outraged by references in the Task Group report to the use of aversive procedures for dealing with difficult behaviours. As presented, the report services as a warning to professionals not familiar with ABA to be wary of it because of potential damage to children. There are no grounds for this position and none was offered.

However, it would be difficult for a parent to criticize this view without being seen as someone who will opt for anything, even potential damage to their children, as long as there was a glimmer of hope. To put the issue of aversives in perspective Sallows (1999) notes the following:

> the reader may be interested to know that aversives were a generally accepted practice during the 1960s and 1970s. TEACCH, for example, also advocated the use of aversives at that time. In their training manual, Schopler *et al.* (1980), describe the use of 'aversive and painful procedures' such as meal deprivation, 'slaps or spanks on the bottom', or 'electric shock, unpleasant tasting or smelling substances' as appropriate interventions if positive methods are ineffective. (p.48)

Had an ABA representative been on the Task Group a more informed debate could have taken place and misrepresentation would not have appeared in a government-sponsored report. This is a particularly serious issue because the goal shared by all professionals is the welfare of children who are relying on unbiased discussion about scientifically validated treatment. This point is made all the more poignant by the Task Group's reference to comments by a parent, Catherine Maurice, which gives the impression that she is opposed to ABA. Maurice (1993) wrote a highly influential book called *Let Me Hear Your*

Voice in which she described the amazing progress her children make thanks
to ABA. It is difficult to reconcile the impression created in the report with the
views she really holds. Maurice recently addressed the Autism Advisory Board
of the Cambridge Center for Behavioral and said the following:

> There is widespread misunderstanding and distortion of the approach.
> Dozens of pseudo-scientific books and articles out there describe it as
> child abuse, a squelching of the spirit, a crushing of the soul. Treating
> the symptoms and not the 'root cause,' whatever that might be; a denial
> of the self, cruel, manipulative, dehumanizing, punishing, controlling;
> etc. etc. Moreover, even when people do not attack behavior analysis,
> they make glaringly ignorant statements about it, like 'Oh yes, that's
> where they do discrete trials for forty hours a week.' Or, 'behavior man-
> agement is for really low functioning kids.'
>
> And then gradually, I began to understand ABA more and more. I
> started to understand what it was: Not some dehumanizing control of
> people through a cynical manipulation of rewards and punishments,
> but rather the light of scientific exploration brought to bear upon
> behavior, and upon learning... What I do know, what I have seen with
> my own eyes, is the significant difference that Behavior Analysis is
> making in other children's lives, and in the lives of adults as well. What
> convinces me to keep speaking out is not even that I know some other
> children who have achieved normalcy. Rather, it is knowing that
> Behavior Analysis continues to help those that do not recover. As time
> goes on, I have seen many different rates of progress in children who are
> receiving behavioral intervention. (Maurice 1999)

The support that Professors Newman and Green and many other international experts in ABA have shown, and continue to show, for the development
of ABA in Ireland and in other countries was ignored by the Task Group.
Instead, they relied extensively on the writings of one individual English professional, who coincidentally appears to be no fan of ABA as evidenced when
she described the whole discipline of ABA as intellectual nonsense. Another
curious fact is that the PEAT book was personally given to members of the
Task Group and, although it has received international acclaim, it was not
even referenced in the report.

The report makes a case also about the expense involved in ABA. While
cost-benefit analyses (US) were given to the Task Group (Jacobson, Mulick
and Green 1998), no mention of these can be found in the section on ABA.
Each of the cost-benefit studies showed the substantial savings to be made
when long-term care is no longer needed for children who have benefited
from ABA. The conclusion from one of them was as follows:

> The principal conclusion from this preliminary cost-benefit analysis is that the cost savings substantially exceed the early intensive treatment cost for a candidate 3-year-old child with autism or ASD. This conclusion holds for a wide range of cost assumptions and discount rates. (Columbia Pacific Consulting 1999)

Parents for the Early Intervention of Autism in Children (PEACH) also conducted a cost-benefit analysis for behavioural intervention versus traditional provisions (in special schools) for children with autism in the UK in 1997. Their findings showed that a typical home-based intensive behavioural programme was estimated to cost approximately £17,000 per annum covering a 50-week period. In comparison a National Autistic School (NAS) placement cost between £22,500 and £23,500 per annum covering a 38-week period. And even if ABA were to be more expensive than an NAS school place, if teachers were properly trained in ABA, there would be no additional expense at all, because the children would receive 5 × 5 hours of ABA per week in the school and home-based programmes would not have to be anywhere near as elaborate as they are at the moment. A bumper sticker I saw once on a car summed it up: 'If you think education is expensive, try ignorance!'

The Peter Principle

The obstacles described above for Northern Ireland have uncanny parallels with obstacles experienced by parents in other countries (e.g. Freeman 2003). One might suppose that obstacles based on misinformation could be easily dissolved with straight talking and by making available evidence from peer-reviewed research articles. At the very least one might suppose that professionals would be able to discriminate commercial packages that incorporate some of the principles of behaviour (e.g. Treatment and Education of Autistic and related Communications Handicapped Children; TEACCH) from the basic science itself. Again one might suppose that professionals would acknowledge the overwhelming evidence favouring the use of basic scientific practices to guide decision making in the education of children, or that they would avoid so-called eclectic practices that cannot be justified on the basis of existing research (Howard *et al.* 2005). With every new autism project that is set up in Northern Ireland without regards to the existing evidence for ABA, one could imagine that explanations are available as to why money is wasted on reinventing 'the wheel'. Maybe some day, also, professionals will stop referring to PECS (the Picture Exchange Communication System) and ABA as interventions for autism when, in fact, ABA is the science from which the technology of PECS was derived (Bondy and Frost 1994). All these suppositions are, however, pipedreams at present. With each tribunal another family is driven to despair and more public money is wasted instead of investing it in training in ABA. I know that if I were a parent with a child with autism I would probably have handcuffed myself to the railings outside the town hall to make public the deplorable treatment visited upon distraught parents and helpless kids. Direct action has its moments but it would be better still to brush up on how experienced behaviour analysts have presented the case for ABA in courts (Baer 2005). The only problem is that there are too few of them around to call upon for such help.

One idea that I feel gives some insight into what it is we are dealing with in this whole affair comes from a book called *The Peter Principle* (Peter and Hull 1994). In their book the authors describe two scenarios that bear a striking resemblance to the difficulties faced by parents of children with autism:

> **Probation-teacher C. Cleary's** first teaching assignment was to a special class of retarded children. Although he had been warned that these children would not accomplish very much, he proceeded to teach them all he could. By the end of the year, many of Cleary's retarded children scored better on standardized achievement tests of reading and arithmetic than did children in regular classes. When Cleary received his dismissal notice he was told that he had grossly neglected the bead stringing, sandbox and other busy-work which were the things that retarded children should do. He had failed to make adequate use of the modelling clay, pegboards and finger paints specially provided by the Excelsior City Special Education Department.

> **Miss E. Beaver, a probationer primary teacher,** was highly gifted intellectually. Being inexperienced, she put into practice what she had learned at college about making allowances for pupils' individual differences. As a result, her brighter pupils finished two or three years' work in one year.

> The principal was very courteous when he explained that Miss Beaver could not be recommended for permanent engagement. He knew she would understand that she had upset the system, had not stuck to the course of studies, and had created hardship for the children who would not fit into the next year's programme. She had disrupted the official marking system and textbook-issuing system, and had caused severe anxiety to the teacher who would next year have to handle the children who had already covered the work.

In explaining these cases the authors note that in most hierarchies 'super-competence is more objectionable than incompetence'. And it is objectionable *'because it disrupts the hierarchy,* and thereby violates *the first commandment* of hierarchal life: *the hierarchy must be preserved'* [emphasis in original] (Peter and Hull 1994, pp.44–5).

Parents all over the world, who struggle for support in using not just science-based practices, but science-based practices with a huge research base, are struggling against the many effects that come under the heading of the Peter Principle. What tends to happen is that professionals not trained in ABA are usually trained in an anti-ABA perspective, with no evidence to support this stance. Their rhetoric is so predictable it is almost robotic. This in itself is ironic given that one of the misrepresentations of ABA is that it churns out robotic kids. These professionals usually are fairly well established within their hierarchies and they don't take kindly to parents who dare to challenge their years of service. And so the conflict begins. In Northern Ireland the new mantra of the educational hierarchies is a call for 'eclecticism'. But this is a call based on self-preservation and, as was said earlier, it is not one based on any scientific evidence. ABA professionals and parents familiar with ABA ask: 'Why eclecticism when we already have the research evidence about what works?' Jacobson, Foxx and Mulick (2005) summarized the problem in the following way.

> Many allied health and human services disciplines do not emphasize scientific training in the preparation of practitioners and professionals. Unfortunately, over time many of these individuals rise to become influential managers in human services. As a result the developmental disabilities field, like other human services fields, is pervaded by the delivery of services and design of supports that are less effective than they could be, and sometimes even damaging. Treatments often are provided based on unvalidated or even disproven models of human behavior or methods of intervention. Sometimes people with developmental disabilities may receive services that actually conflict and undermine effectiveness of care. These types of problems are not limited to adult human services. The education of people with developmental disabilities has been affected by the same forces. Expenditures for the education of children with special needs have continued to grow to the point where school districts budgets are stretched thin. Yet, many of these costs are for programs that are ineffective, poorly designed, and inappropriate and that actually retard student progress, or which are selected by practitioners (e.g., special educators, principals) based primarily on their endorsement or marketing by authorities or well-known professionals in education. (p.xii)

What is intriguing about these comments is that they came from people living in the US and not from the UK, showing that the issues cross international boundaries.

Conclusion

ABA is a science of behaviour, which, when applied to autism, empowers parents with the skills to harness principles of behaviour for bringing out the best in their children. Results produced when ABA is implemented correctly are quite remarkable and that is why parents persist despite the hard work involved. Sometimes the changes in the children who benefit from ABA are so extensive that they cause all sorts of problems for the establishment not familiar with ABA. For example, bureaucratic boundaries between education and health authorities are rendered meaningless when significant improvements in a child's overall health and well-being are brought about by educational procedures. If everyone cares, then these bureaucratic boundaries need to be dismantled so that resources are marshalled in an efficient and cost-effective way.

Those authorities who refuse to fund ABA programmes are saying in effect that science does not have a role in decision making. This state of affairs will change but in my experience, and as is the case in other countries, it will only change with parent power. One word of advice from the Executive Director of Greenpeace, USA, makes a lot of sense in the struggle needed to effect this change: 'We know that unless a politician feels real pressure, or a chief executive senses a threat to his market, everything else is just talk' (Passacantando 2004, p.4).

The philosopher Schopenhauer once said, 'All truth goes through three stages. First it is ridiculed. Then it is violently opposed. Finally, it is accepted as self-evident.' How far is my community along this path? Personally, I shudder when I consider the answer for I know that my community is so structured that there is little accountability for some decision making. But a wave in Ireland that is powered by informed parents with love on their side will change this state of affairs. A similar wave is gathering momentum in New Zealand, as you will see from the various chapters in the remainder of this book.

References

Anderson, S.R. and Romancyzk, R.G. (1999) 'Early intervention for young children with autism: continuum-based behavioural models.' *Journal of the Association for Persons with Severe Handicaps 24*, 162–173.

Association for Behavior Analysis (ABA) (2005) *Leadership*. http://www.abainternational.org/ (accessed 29 April 2005).

Autismspeaks (2005) *What is Autism?* http://www.autismspeaks.org/autism/menu/about.asp (accessed 14 March 2005).

Baer, D.M. (2005) 'Letters to a lawyer.' In W.L. Heward, T.E. Heron, N.A. Neef, S.M. Peterson, D.M. Sainato, G. Cartledge, R. Gardner III, L.D. Peterson, S.B. Hersh and J.C. Dardig (eds) *Focus on Behavior Analysis in Education: Achievements, Challenges, and Opportunities* (pp.3–30). New Jersey: Pearson Education, Inc.

BBC News (2003) *Shortage of Child Behaviourists* (29 May). http://news.bbc.co.uk/1/hi/northern_ireland/2945182.stm (accessed 29 May 2003)

Behavior Analyst Certification Board (BACB) (2005) *Consumer Information*. http://www.bacb.com/consum_frame.html (accessed 01 January 2005).

Bondy, A. and Frost, L. (1994) 'The Picture Exchange Communication System.' *Focus on Autistic Behavior 11*, 1–19.

Bondy, A., Tincani, M. and Frost, L. (2004) 'Multiply controlled verbal operants: an analysis and extension to the Picture Exchange Communication System.' *The Behavior Analyst 27*, 247–261.

California Departments of Education and Developmental Services, Collaborative Work Group on Autistic Spectrum Disorders (1997) *Best Practices for Designing and Delivering Effective Programs for Individuals with Autistic Spectrum Disorders*. Sacramento, CA: California Department of Education (July).

Cambridge Center for Behavioral Studies (2005) *Autism and ABA*. http://www.behavior.org/ (accessed 15 March 2005).

Christopher, K. (2003) 'Autistic boy killed during exorcism – News and Comment.' *Skeptical Inquirer*, Nov–Dec.

Cogan, J.F. (1995) *Demon Possession Handbook for Human Service Workers. Part 1: Demon Possession Defined and Explained*. http://diskbooks.org/part1.html (accessed 29 April 2005).

Columbia Pacific Consulting (1999) *Cost-Benefit Analysis*. Prepared for Harper Grey Easton, Barrister and Solicitors. 1550–650 West Georgia Street, Vancouver, B.C. V6B 4NB (7 December).

Cooper, J.O., Heron, T.E. and Heward, W.L. (1987) *Applied Behavior Analysis*. New York: Macmillan Publishing Company.

Dillenburger, K. (2004) 'Evidence-based practice in Northern Ireland.' In B. Thyer and M. Kazi (eds) *International Perspectives on Evidence-based Practice in Social Work* (pp.97–112). Birmingham: Venture Press.

Dillenburger, K. (2005) *Bereavement and People Affected by Violence: A D.I.S.C. Analysis*. Victims and survivors conference. Community Relations Council, Templepatrick, NI (7–8 March).

Encarta (1999) *World English Dictionary*. Microsoft Corporation. Bloomsbury Publishing plc.

Freeman, S. (2003) *Science for Sale in the Autism Wars: Medically Necessary Autism Treatment, the Court Battle for Health Insurance and Why Health Technology Academics are Enemy Number One*. Lynden: SKF Books USA, Inc.

Friman, P.C. (2002) *Psychopathological Interpretation of Common Child Behavior Problems. A Critique and a Related Opportunity for Behavior Analysis*. Video Tutorial. https://apps.abainternational.org/onlinestore/desc.asp?tid=86 (accessed 29 April 05).

Ginestet, C.E. (2004) Letter in response to Keenan, M. (2004) 'Autism in Northern Ireland: the tragedy and the shame.' *The Psychologist 17*, 187.

Glenn, S.S. (2004) 'Individual behaviour, culture, and social change.' *The Behaviour Analyst 27*, 133–151.

Grant, L. and Evans, A. (1994) *Principles of Behavior Analysis*. New York: HarperCollins College Publishers.

Green, G. (2003) *Making Sense of Autism Treatment Research*. Video tutorial. https://apps.abainternational.org/onlinestore/desc.asp?tid=78 (accessed 29 April 2005).

Gross, R. (1995) *Themes, Issues, and Debates in Psychology*. London: Hodder and Stoughton Educational.

Harris, S.L. and Weiss, M.J. (1998) *Right From the Start – Behavioral Intervention for Young Children with Autism. A Guide for Parents and Professionals*. Bethesda, MD: Woodbine House.

Holth, P. (2001) 'The persistence of category mistakes in psychology.' *Behavior and Philosophy 29*, 203–219.

Howard, J.S., Sparkman, C.R., Cohen, H.G., Green, G. and Stanislaw, H. (2005) 'A comparison of intensive behavior analytic and eclectic treatments for young children with autism.' *Research in Developmental Disabilities 26*, 359–383.

Hudson, B.L. and McDonald, G.M. (1991) *Behavioural Social Work: An Introduction*. Hampshire: Macmillan Education Ltd.

Jacobson, J.W., Foxx, R.M. and Mulick, J.A. (eds) (2005) *Controversial Therapies for Developmental Disabilities*. Hillsdale, NJ: Erlbaum.

Jacobson, J.W., Mulick, J.A. and Green, G. (1998) 'Cost-benefit estimates for early intensive behavioral intervention for young children with autism – general model and single state case.' *Behavioral Interventions 13*, 201–226.

Johnston, J.M. and Pennypacker, H.S. (1980) *Strategies and Tactics of Human Behavioral Research*. Hillsdale, NJ: Erlbaum.

Johnston, J.M. and Pennypacker, H.S. (1993) *Readings for: Strategies and Tactics of Behavioural Research*. Hillsdale, NJ: Erlbaum.

Keenan, M. (1997) 'The A, B, C of litter control.' *Irish Journal of Psychology 17*, 327–339.

Keenan, M. (2003) *Autism in Northern Ireland: The Tragedy and the Shame*. The British Psychological Society annual conference. Invited address for the Award for Promoting Equality of Opportunity.

Keenan, M. and Dillenburger, K. (2000) *Behaviour Analysis: A Primer* [computer software]. New York: Insight Media.

Keenan, M. and Dillenburger, K. (2004) *Why I'm Not a Cognitive Psychologist. A Tribute to B.F. Skinner* [computer software]. New York: Insight Media.

Keenan, M., Kerr, K.P. and Dillenburger K. (eds) (2000) *Parents' Education as Autism Therapists*. London: Jessica Kingsley Publishers.

Kirk, S., Kutchins, H. and Rowe, D. (1997) *Making Us Crazy: DSM – The Psychiatric Bible and the Creation of Mental Disorders*. New York: Free Press.

Lovaas, O.I. (1981) *Teaching Developmentally Disabled Children: The Me Book*. Austin, TX: Pro-Ed.

Martin, G.L. and Osborne, J.G. (eds) (1980) *Helping in the Community: Behavioral Applications*. New York: Plenum Press.

Martin, G. and Pear, J. (2001) *Behavior Modification: What It Is and How to Do It* (7th edn). New Jersey: Prentice Hall.

Mattaini, M.A. and Thyer, B.A. (1996) *Finding Solutions to Social Problems: Behavioral Strategies for Change*. Washington, DC: American Psychological Association.

Maurice, C. (1993) Let Me Hear Your Voice: A Family's Triumph Over Autism. New York: Ballantine.

Maurice, C. (1999) *Address to the Annual Board Meeting of the Cambridge Center for Behavioral Studies.* Palm Beach, Florida. www.behavior.org (accessed 5 December 1999).

Maurice, C., Green, G. and Foxx, R.M. (eds) (2001) *Making a Difference: Behavioral Intervention for Autism.* Austin, TX: Pro-Ed.

Maurice, C., Green, G. and Luce, S.C. (eds) (1996) *Behavioral Intervention for Young Children with Autism: A Manual for Parents and Professionals.* Austin, TX: Pro-Ed.

Moffat, C. (2003) 'The human right we won't name: education for autistic children.' *Fortnight Magazine 420*, 22–23.

Morris, E.K. (1985) 'Public information, dissemination, and behavior analysis.' *The Behavior Analyst 8*, 95–110.

Moynahan, L. (2001) 'Relatio ergo sum – a spontaneous commentary upon Dillenburger and Keenan.' *European Journal of Behaviour Analysis 2*, 162–174.

National Autistic Society (NAS) (2005) *How Many People have Autistic Spectrum Disorders?* http://www.nas.org.uk/nas/jsp/polopoly.jsp?d=299anda=3527 (accessed 29 April 2005).

Newman, B., Birch, S., Blausten, F. and Reinecke, D. (2002) *Graduated Applied Behavior Analysis.* New York: Dove and Orca.

New York State Department of Health, Early Intervention Program (1999) *Clinical Practice Guidelines: Autism/Pervasive Developmental Disorders, Assessment and Intervention for Young Children (Ages 0–3 Years).* Albany, NY: Author (May).

Nietzel, M.T., Winett, R.A., MacDonald, M.L. and Davidson, W.S. (1977) *Behavioral Approaches to Community Psychology.* New York: Pergamon Press.

Nikopoulos, C.K. and Keenan, M. (2002) *Construction of an Activity Schedule for Children with Autism: The Effectiveness of Video Modeling.* Experimental Analysis of Behaviour Group annual conference, London (March).

Novak, G. (1996) *Developmental Psychology: Dynamical Systems and Behavior Analysis.* Reno: Context Press.

Nye, R.D. (1992) *The Legacy of B.F. Skinner: Concepts and Perspectives, Controversies and Misunderstandings.* California: Brooks/Cole.

Passacantando, J. (2004) *New Scientist*, 28 August.

Peter, L.J. and Hull, R. (1994) *The Peter Principle: Why Things Always Go Wrong.* London: Souvenir Press Ltd.

Press Release (2000) *National Award for Model Professional Development. Schools and school districts recognized for outstanding professional development* (Sept. 18). http://www.necc.org/news/national_award_press_release.asp (accessed 31 December 2000).

Sallows, G. (1999) *Educational Interventions for Children with Autism in the UK: Comment on the Jordan et al. June 1998 Final Report to the DfEE.* http://trainland.tripod.com/glen.s.htm (accessed 30 March 2005).

Sanders, M.R. and Dadds, M.R. (1993) *Behavioural Family Intervention.* London: Allyn and Bacon.

Schopler, E., Reichler, R.J. and Lansing, M. (1980) *Individualized Assessment and Treatment for Autistic and Developmentally Disabled Children. Vol. 2: Teaching Strategies for Parents and Professionals.* Austin, TX: Pro-Ed.

Sidman, M. (1960) *Tactics of Scientific Research.* New York: Basic Books.

Sidman, M. (1989) *Coercion and its Fallout.* Boston: Authors Cooperative, Inc., Publishers.

Skinner, B.F. (1953) *Science and Human Behavior.* New York: Free Press.

Skinner, B.F. (1977) 'Why I am not a cognitive psychologist.' *Behaviorism 5*, 1–10.

Skinner, B.F. (1985) 'Cognitive science and behaviorism.' *British Journal of Psychology 76*, 291–301.

Spinelli, E. (1989) *The Interpreted World.* London: Sage Publications.

Sulzer-Azaroff, B. and Mayer, G.R. (1991) *Behavior Analysis for Lasting Change.* New York: Holt, Rinehart and Winston, Inc.

The Supreme Court of British Columbia (2000) *Docket C984120* (July 26).

Surgeon General (2000) *Mental Health: A Report of the Surgeon General*, 21 March www.surgeongeneral.gov/library/mentalhealth/chapter3/secb.html#autism (accessed 04 December 2001).

Task Group (2002) *Education for Children and Young People with Autistic Spectrum Disorders.* Report of the Task Group on Autism Northern Ireland Department of Education (April) www.DENI.gov.uk (accessed 24 December 2002).

Tavris, C. (1999) 'Disorderly conduct.' Review of *Making Us Crazy: DSM – The Psychiatric Bible and the Creation of Mental Disorders* by S. Kirk, H. Kutchins and D. Rowe. *Times Literary Supplement*, October, 29, p.6.

Thompson, T. (2003) 'Council to pay up for autistic boy.' *The Scotsman*, 3 March. http://thescotsman.scotsman.com/index.cfm?id=261152003 (accessed 3 March 2005).

Walsh, P. (1997) 'Bye-bye behaviour modification.' In K. Dillenburger, M.F. O'Reilly and M. Keenan (eds) *Advances in Behaviour Analysis* (pp.91–102). Dublin: University College Dublin Press.

West, R.P. and Hamerlynck, L.A. (eds) (1992) *Designs for Excellence in Education: The Legacy of B.F. Skinner.* Longmont: Sopris West, Inc.

Wyatt, W.J. (1990) 'Radical behaviorism misrepresented: a reply to Mahoney.' *American Psychologist 45*, 1181–1183.

CHAPTER 2

Where are We Now in New Zealand?

Mary Henderson

Autism has different meanings to different people depending on their age, the country in which they grew up, whether a family member has autism, whether they are academics, doctors, are employed by the government to deliver services for those with autism, or whether they have seen the movie *Rain Man* or more recently *Mercury Rising*.

Prior to the 1970s when Lovaas conducted and published his 'Young Autism Project' I would imagine that autism presented one face, that of being institutionalized, and with an emphasis on the teaching of toileting-hygiene-dressing skills, prevention of self-injurious behaviour, handling sleep issues, eating disorders, and generally keeping such persons as safe as possible so that they did not harm themselves or others. Within all countries there are still many individuals diagnosed with autism spectrum disorder (ASD) whose lives are viewed in these terms.

The history of autism and its treatment (or lack of treatment) is easy to trace and become familiar with. Below is a list of books which I recommend parents read so they can make sense of how we got to 'where we are now'. It seems that because autism is a syndrome and not a medical disease, its treatment and care are extremely varied and largely dependent on how individual countries have allocated funding and what theories were popular at the time. There are, among its history, exceptional stories of persons with ASD across the spectrum who have made remarkable progress. However, what is glaringly obvious to parents of children with ASD is that across the decades the professionals in the field of ASD who are charged with influencing the views and decision making of public bodies, government, other professional bodies, and parents by and large simply are not correct in the treatment methods, views and care of persons with ASD. Children in these stories do well because parents go beyond and above the norm to provide for their children. In the process they become people within the history of autism who have moved hundreds of other families to action by sharing their experiences with the result that there is a change in the accepted picture of ASD. These are all important documents, and governments, academics and parents should spend time with them. Not to do so is to assume that in this day and age we have 'righted all that was wrong'. As we say in New Zealand, one is definitely 'wise to the present' by discovering the history and taking heed when making decisions that affect so many.

- *A Thorn in My Pocket* by Eustacia Cutler (2004) – this was written by the mother of Temple Grandin, and it gives a good overview of institutions in the US during the 1960s and 1970s.

- *The Siege: A Family's Journey into the World of an Autistic Child* by Clara Claiborne Park (1967).

- *Turn Around, Bright Eyes: Snapshots from a Voyage Out of Autism's Silence* by Liane Gentry Skye (2002).

- *Let Me Hear Your Voice* by Catherine Maurice (1993).

- *Congratulations! It's Asperger Syndrome* by Jen Birch (2003), New Zealand adult autobiography.

- *Autism: From Tragedy to Triumph* by Carol Johnson and Julia Crowder (1994).

All of these books outline systems that continually commit the same errors in dealing with this population. All highlight issues around the amount of time to diagnosis, the lack of funding available, and the lack of appropriate treatments once a diagnosis is established.

What these books do for parents, of course, is to inform them that as things stand today it is up to the family to source and provide treatment. Sadly, for families that are unable to do this, or who choose not to, their child is more than likely destined to be the victim of erroneous treatment methods – there is no evidence to suggest that this decade of treatment and care provided by governments is improved over what was provided two to three decades ago.

Figure 2.1: Our son

As a parent of a ten-year-old child with ASD who has received intensive intervention since he was two years of age (most of which has been paid for privately), we know that the life our child lives today is a direct result of us deciding that he would only have appropriate therapies for his development. We also know that in making that decision we could not include him in government-funded special systems that are second rate and outdated. With that decision we took on a big financial burden. What we have experienced is a government simply not prepared to give families a say in choosing a therapy based on available scientific evidence and not wanting to pay for it.

The struggle for families to provide what is going to make lifetime changes for their child with ASD is not a unique or lone struggle. Within New Zealand many communities tell comparable stories. One struggle that always strikes me as very similar involves children who are deaf. Their parents fought for cochlea ear implants and now many children receive such treatment. At one time, though, in this country the thought was to isolate this population and create a separate community for them to live in. With respect to autism, not providing early intervention to enable a child to be mainstreamed is like not enabling a deaf child to access cochlea ear implants or not providing a physically disabled child with a wheelchair.

What our government says of course is that any child with ASD can enter mainstream schooling. However, they take no responsibility in terms of provision to enable this to happen. It seems to me it is like promising to install an entrance for a physically disabled person but not providing the equipment for them to move about the school.

In New Zealand two reports, one by Professor Werry (1998) and one referred to as 'The Curry Report' (Curry 1998), have been published that highlight the areas of concern with ASD and make specific recommendations. Professor Werry's report was written based on an inquiry after the death of a 17-year-old girl with ASD called Casey Albury-Thomson (Matthews 2003). The system failed the family and the child miserably. Neither report, however, has resulted in any changes at a family level. Rather, small changes occurred within existing systems such that there was a small injection of money for special projects which was then removed after a couple of years.

After the Albury-Thomson case, a group of us were given an injection of money to run a school for a couple of years. Our research was written up (Ministry of Education 2003) but it is now merely a fond memory of what could have been. At the end of the day it was considered too expensive! At present we have another programme up and running for sports and recreation. Again this is a two-year project, but at the end of the project I anticipate that after the reports are written it will succumb to the same fateful comments: 'too expensive!'. I am not aware of any research that shows what cost is involved in parenting a child with ASD, or any disability. In New Zealand, all out-of-school activities cost more for a child with ASD than for a typical child. Why? To participate, a child with severe or moderate ASD will need a support person. A child with Asperger's may be able to share a support person with others. All of this adds up quickly. Funding from the government does not cover participation in the community. It gives the impression that it does in the New Zealand Disability Strategy (Office for Disability Issues 2001) or the Progress in Implementing the Disability Strategy report (Office for Disability Issues 2004). The reality, however, is that our funding is based on family need versus the needs of the child with ASD to participate in community life. Up until 2002, our Disability Strategy included all ages; in 2002, it was split into those over 65 and those under 65. Hence it has been largely focused on our elderly and their physical needs. Funding for our children with ASD ends up being spent so parents can have a 'time-out', which is important of course; however, there is nothing left for the 'community life' of the child with ASD. In real terms, there are no programmes to enable participation; families don't have the money to provide the support individually or privately in order for their child with ASD to participate. Bright Sparks (www.bright-sparks.co.nz) is a disability project, sports and recreation programme, which is a parent-driven initiative. This means that a group of parents, who wanted sports and recreation for their children with ASD, ran it out of their own funds for a year. They then applied for funding, and got it on a three-year contract. The families use some of their own funds or their disability funding. Some children use it as a stepping-stone to mainstream sport and recreation; others simply benefit physically and socially by participating. Families benefit by having places to go and things to do after school with their child with ASD. In areas of Auckland of lower income, children do not participate; in middle-income areas participation is for a limited time. Once again, then, we have a programme that is not fully funded and therefore excludes, rather than includes, children with ASD in the community. The irony of our Disability Strategy is that it promotes community involvement, yet totally lacks the practical strategies on how this might happen. Bright Sparks is an example of what is simple enough to set up, offer and make happen, yet due to 'funding issues' it cannot be maintained.

Another case that featured in New Zealand over the last couple of years is the Daniels case (Daniels 2003). The government had taken away funding from moderate needs children, or changed the system around, with the result that those children lost one-on-one supervision and teaching in mainstream schooling. This affected many Asperger's and high-functioning children with ASD. After going through the High Court the Department of Education is now charged with putting in place what is appropriate for these children. Nevertheless, many of our Asperger's and high-functioning children are ending up in Special Schools.

Special Schools, as Smith, Lovaas and Lovaas (2002) show, for high-functioning persons with ASD, are not where the children benefit most. Why is that? The research shows that children with ASD need to model behaviours of typical peers not atypical peers. In other words, as any parent and non-academic person can figure out, if unusual and/or stereotypic behaviours are learned and maintained through practice and the observation of others, then it is likely to be more difficult to discourage them in a Special School.

The irony of funding 'appropriate educational practices' is most apparent with children who have had early intervention provided and funded privately within mainstream schooling. When their education is 'appropriate to their needs' they learn. What we are seeing now is the first batch of children coming through who have had some form of early intervention. For example, one of the parents of two children who attended the Autism Action Inc. Precision Teaching Centre (AAPTC) has spent thousands of dollars on providing skilled people – aides/therapists trained in applied behaviour analysis (ABA) practice and methodology, either via the AAPTC or the Center for Autism and Related Disorders (CARD 2000–2001) – to work with her children in mainstream school and at home. One of the children is now considered high functioning and now does not qualify for any Ministry of Education (2005) Ongoing and Reviewable Resourcing Schemes (ORRS) funding. However, the family has gone to arbitration, because even though the child now needs less help than in the early years some help is still needed at mainstream school. However, this different type of specialized help is not catered for in the ORRS application form. In summary, we have a situation where 'appropriate education', when made available to a child, results in real progress. However, because those charged with providing 'appropriate education' persist in their myopic practices to the detriment of the child, parents have to step in to rescue their child. 'How can the largest group of special needs children be simply left out of funding?' After a while this seemingly sensible question transforms into a rhetorical question when parents eventually understand the extent of the system's resistance to implementing evidence-based practice.

Within our education system it happens time and time again that children with ASD lose funding. This is because the main funding criteria are based on behaviour, hygiene and physical skills, which of course are issues for all our severe/moderate ASD kids. However, when these kids improve through intervention so, by definition, does their profile. What then happens is they no longer meet the criteria for funding. So what happens to them? Simple – either their parents continue to pay for any extra help they may need or they are left in mainstream until they no longer cope. Usually some sort of incident occurs and they are then manoeuvred out into a Special School, or are schooled at home! Typically, a high-functioning child or an Asperger's child will have deficits in comprehension and social skills. These skills are not necessary to pass the school curriculum or exams, but are essential for 'passing' the other aspects of schooling which are all to do with the playground, with friendship or with self-esteem. For the child who is not adequately prepared we see frustration at not quite getting what is going on. This frustration manifests itself in behaviours that result in them harming either themselves, their peers or their teachers. Although this sequence of events is fairly predictable, the ORRS funding application form doesn't concentrate on these skill deficits. Hence what we have is what I call a 'knockout system'. It is a system that is guaranteed to succeed, where success is defined with respect to the child as a 'knockout' and they hit a brick wall with regards to funding. Appropriate curriculum content and training for social skills and social comprehension isn't available in mainstream. Parents have to provide it using their own therapist/aides and there is no choice but to continue. Should they not continue their child would go into a Special School where his/her needs for social skills and social comprehension would not be met. From there it is a slide down a slippery slope. And of course for kids who start out with a diagnosis of high functioning or Asperger's, their main deficits do not become obvious until they are about seven years old. When these deficits show up there are no suitably trained professionals to manage the appropriate programmes in schools and so the children are 'knocked out' of the system into Special Schools.

The criteria for funding both in health and in education are determined within what is called 'a needs-based system'. Neither body recognizes international standards and criteria for diagnosing ASD. Instead, they both view ASD as a disability to be lumped in with all disabilities, a practice that does nothing to enhance or give respect to the uniqueness that is ASD.

As a family we have been fortunate to live in New Zealand and Western Australia. When our ASD child was five years of age we moved to Perth for a year. I want to share the view of our experience within a different system and draw some comparisons with the amount of time and energy we spend within New Zealand just in managing our child's funding within health and education.

Learning about and manoeuvring your way through the public system with an ASD child in New Zealand, in time commitment alone, is equivalent to taking on another job or a small business. Once a parent decides that they do want effective intervention and that they do want their child in mainstream life with the family, community and schooling, the work and the time input begins.

In New Zealand a child can be categorized generally as 'having difficulties', at which point one simply calls on special education or health authorities to access funding. In contrast, in Western Australia each child with ASD is required to have a formal diagnosis before any taxes are spent (this was in 1999). At first glance, the system in New Zealand compared with that in Western Australia seems better to the outsider and to the new parent, as it appears more proactive. However, over time, what appears more proactive in New Zealand is its inherent weakness. Why? In both health and education, attention appears to be to crisis and change. This might translate into 'something is not right, send in the experts' or 'the child's behaviour is deteriorating, send in the experts' etc. It all appears proactive, but after the initial flurry of recognition when the child is first suspected of being ASD, most encounters are reactionary. Our family experience has been that our child benefited more by having a diagnostic team of speech-language therapy (SLT), cognitive testing and the DSM-IV outline and detail of his specific strengths and weaknesses, and a programme based on that, as we experienced in Western Australia.

Western Australia required that our child was formally diagnosed. This involved six hours of assessment with a speech pathologist, six hours of cognitive assessment with a psychologist, and an appointment with a paediatrician. All diagnosing was written up into reports that were then used in accessing funding and programming within health and education. In New Zealand diagnosis is not required to involve a speech pathologist or cognitive assessment. The person who has the most input is a paediatrician. The documentation that is given out is not standardized and therefore could not be used in other countries to access funding and services. The diagnosis and documentation is not then used by health or education to determine services and funding. At this point 'needs assessors' are brought into the picture; to my knowledge these folk are not qualified to any set criteria that are recognizable in academia. 'Needs assessment' seems to simply follow its own in-house rules that change depending on how many children with ASD are applying for funding and what the assessor is 'seeing'.

In Western Australia, formal diagnosis determined (in 1999) each child's funding. There are very clear definitions of what the funding is and why it is at that level. Why is this important? Well, if I am talking to another family who has a child with the same diagnosis then I would find that we are receiving the same funding package. Currently this is not the case in New Zealand. Across the country, within suburbs, from child to child, there is no standard. There is case upon case of some children receiving large amounts and others receiving small amounts and yet the children present as the same within the ASD spectrum. This happens within health and education. Not only does this system not work, it has high levels of dissatisfaction with parents; it is costly, prejudicial and open to abuse. What families want is an even playing field so they can plan. We all want to know the rules; however, as long as we are under a 'needs-based' system with the focus being on the family not the child, then the drama and playacting and negativity of parents will continue to shine through, for at the moment it is the only way to get funding.

By the time we had gone through the diagnostic process in Western Australia, we as a family were educated about ASD and how it affected our child, in both positive and negative ways. We could, then, simply pick and choose from a variety of private and public programmes and spend our funding with them. When his needs changed we simply gave notice and moved to different service providers. There was no paperwork, no need to employ people and (blessing upon blessings) it didn't eat into our family time, hence all of our 'spare time' was not taken up running his life and fighting for funding. All children take time and commitment; however, a child with ASD in New Zealand takes about the same time, commitment and stress as a new baby. In Western Australia, it was akin to having a four year old. The analogy is simple: 'the severity of ASD × ease of funding management = family level of stress'.

Compare this to New Zealand. Because the diagnosis has no professional value, every year we go through assessments and then we have to find appropriate people in order to spend the funding. They in turn have to be employed by government agencies because we cannot invoice them as in a normal business transaction. This means that if we want to make changes then we also have to address the whole employment act. Time and time again forms come back requiring explanations as to how we are spending our funding. If only New Zealand would take a feather out of Western Australia's cap and simply recognize the professional qualifications, then we would be able to spend funding with speech pathologists, occupational therapists, and Masters of psychology etc. The term 'carer support' sends shivers down parents' backs, as it simply represents hours and hours of jumping through hoops without knowing the value of the hoops and where the deal changes every year based on the judgements of the assessors. Stress levels for parents in New Zealand are very high as they deal with health and education assessing and personnel!

Western Australia (WA) presented many choices in terms of both private and public services. We employed the services of an ABA-trained speech pathologist. Our child attended an Autism of WA playgroup. The school was able to hire a teaching aide who was trained in appropriate therapies via an agency. We had a team of people that spent time with our child at the weekend – they were trained in social skills and play skills for ASD children. Clearly, when you make simple changes in a system you simply enable more people to participate. In New Zealand, by contrast, although we have a lot of folk who are more than qualified to work with our children, most are unable to because the fund holders simply do not recognize them. The fund holders in both education and health pay between $9 and $14 per hour to the people charged with one-on-one care of our children with ASD. No matter how good the programming, unless the carers are skilled and academically knowledgeable (i.e. come on board with a level of skill), then most time spent with the person with ASD has no future benefit in enabling the child – it is merely babysitting. Our children with ASD need intervention in the form of skilled staff so they can grow socially, physically and academically. We should not be able to have under-skilled persons with any child. When we do this to our children with ASD, we are disabling the child, not enabling. Perhaps the Disability Strategy would be better named the 'Enabling Strategy' – so that it at least has the semblance of heading in the right direction!

All things considered, the basic advice to all parents regarding ABA in New Zealand is to first know that it is not available via the Ministry of Education or the Ministry of Health. So be prepared for an exhausting struggle. But is it worth it? Is it worth going it alone? There can be no doubt that the answer is a resounding 'Yes!'. The government funding of ABA in California and New York State has only come about because of those who have gone it alone. Change seems to come when a sufficient number of ASD persons have experienced the benefits offered by ABA or when enough people in the community have a different experience of ASD because of ABA than is currently the case.

In business we call the process of change 'the theory of the 100th monkey' (Keyes 1984). It goes like this. On an isolated island lived some monkeys. One day, out of the blue, one monkey took his fruit and washed it. Quite at random, over time more monkeys washed their fruit. When it got to the 100th monkey it seemed as if every man and his monkey were washing their fruit.

Change in government policies regarding ASD does not appear to come about simply because of published research! It seems that when enough people are implementing ABA and showing results via improved and recovered children, and when they refuse to remain silent, then things start moving.

There is no common sense or justice in all of this but it seems to be the way in the world of ASD and politics.

At the moment in New Zealand, autism is like an elephant to a group of blindfolded individuals, each describing a different side and each sure that what they are describing is right. Those who can see the whole elephant know that others are only seeing a small piece of the picture.

As a parent this is very frustrating because you realize why bad decisions are being made. Some of these bad decisions include:

- offering mainstream schooling without changing the curriculum to suit ASD children

- offering mainstream schooling without offering the funding to support the child

- offering mainstream schooling but not catering for the deficits of ASD children by including something like 'social skills' in much the same way as reading deficits are catered for other children, or ramps are introduced for wheelchair access for physical deficits

- not allowing parents to spend government funding on specialist therapies of their choice

- not diagnosing using standardized international criteria

- not providing training in ABA for those in health or education who are charged with caring for children with ASD

- keeping wages in health or education at a minimum level and thereby discouraging those who are qualified to work with these kids

- ignoring the numbers of ASD children being diagnosed in other Western countries (California 1 in 165) and not questioning why and not preparing for the growth in New Zealand. In every other area of life, be it childhood obesity, type II diabetes, literacy levels or income levels, we compare and contrast to other Western countries. To not do so with the growing rates of ASD brings up visions of people with their heads in the sand, hoping that this is simply not a reality for New Zealand. And with no plans in place for effective intervention, this could potentially be a time when it's about as good as it's going to be. Why? Less people want funding!

- continuing with a needs-based assessment process both in education and health when the assessors are not qualified to make decisions regarding what is required for the ASD child and family – and wasting money on assessment after assessment until there is not enough money to fund what is recommended.

In Auckland we have organized a series of educational sessions for carers/ teachers/aides/parents/therapists, to up-skill in the methods and practice of ABA as it applies to children with ASD. The aim is to start building knowledge and practical experience from the ground up. Action in the form of education and more and more examples of successes and teaching methods are what are required. We are following the example of the PEAT group making ABA available to the general public, being taught by those who have the academic and practical experience in ABA and ASD.

Unfortunately, in the world of education and health it seems you are guilty until proven innocent. However, we can be educated together and we can keep evidence of how our children were and how they are now. This evidence can be amassed and presented to those who make decisions. We can make them accountable for their decisions when they refuse to acknowledge the evidence before them.

ABA is not a panacea and it would be fraudulent of me to suggest that it has been the only thing that we have implemented with our child. We had what I thought were simple goals for our child:

- for him to be a member of our family
- for his brothers to play with him
- for him to attend and be a part of mainstream school
- for him to enjoy sports
- for him to be able to read and comprehend and enjoy the world via books
- for him to be able to travel with us as a family
- for him to look me in the eye and enjoy it, to hug me and mean it, to smile and feel joy, to be able to converse via language.

All of these are being achieved, some are complete, some are in the process, but all are happening and all are being implemented via ABA principles. We have needed a good team of people so that our family is able to keep functioning and doesn't burn out with the stress involved with so much responsibility.

Alongside ABA we have used natural remedies that enable our child to regulate sleep patterns, overcome chronic diarrhoea, and manage headaches arising from mineral deficiencies. We make sure he is drug free, and engages in healthy habits and physical activity.

To conclude, at the moment in New Zealand we are thankful that there are private organizations that offer ABA – like the Center for Autism and

Related Disorders (CARD), and Intervention Services for Autism and Developmental Delay (ISADD 2005) – and many private individuals who are skilled in ABA. Auckland University now offers an ABA postgraduate course. This is a big step forward; however, the ripple-down effect of that for our ASD kids will not be immediate. In the meantime I encourage parents, teacher aides and carers to learn as much as you can and to implement what you can.

References

Birch, J. (2003) *Congratulations! It's Asperger Syndrome*. London: Jessica Kingsley Publishers.

Center for Autism and Related Disorders (CARD) (2000–2001) http://www.centerforautism.com/ (accessed 29 March 2005).

Claiborne Park, C. (1967) *The Siege: A Family's Journey into the World of an Autistic Child*. New York: Back Bay Books.

Curry, D. (1998) *Autism Services in New Zealand: A Report by the Interdepartmental Autism Services Project Team*. Wellington, New Zealand: The Ministry of Health (October).

Cutler, E. (2004) *A Thorn in My Pocket*. Arlington, TX: Future Horizons, Inc.

Daniels, L.S.A. (2003) Out of Court Settlement (22 August) between LSA Daniels and Others and the Attorney General in respect of the Minister of Education, the Secretary of Education, the Ministry of Education and the Crown in Right of New Zealand. See http://www.qpec.org.nz/ for more information (accessed 1 May 2005).

Gentry Skye, L. (2002) *Turn Around, Bright Eyes: Snapshots from a Voyage Out of Autism's Silence*. Otsego, MI: PageFree Publishing.

Intervention Services for Autism and Developmental Delay (ISADD) (2005) http://www.isadd.org/ (accessed 29 March 2005).

Johnson, C. and Crowder, J. (1994) *Autism: From Tragedy to Triumph*. Boston: Branden Publishing Company.

Keyes, K. (1984) *The 100th Monkey. A Story About Social Change* (2nd edn). Los Angeles: Devorss and Co (Txp).

Matthews, L. (2003) *Tragic End to Life of Beauty and Misery*. New Zealand Herald. http://www.nzherald.co.nz/index.cfm?ObjectID=3197236 (accessed 21 February 2003).

Maurice, C. (1993) *Let Me Hear Your Voice: A Family's Triumph Over Autism*. New York: Ballantine Books.

Ministry of Education (2003) *An Evaluation of Some Programmes for Children with Autistic Spectrum Disorder in Auckland: Opportunities, Contingencies, and Illusions. Report to the Ministry of Education*. Wellington, New Zealand: Auckland UniServices Ltd. http://www.minedu.govt.nz/index.cfm?layout=documentanddocumentid=7929&data=l (accessed 5 April 2005).

Ministry of Education (2005) *An Introduction to ORRS – the Ongoing and Reviewable Resource Schemes*. http://www.minedu.govt.nz/index.cfm?layout=documentanddocumentid=5322&data=1 (accessed 13 January 2005).

Office for Disability Issues (2001) *The New Zealand Disability Strategy*. http://www.odi.govt.nz/publications/nzds/index.html (accessed 1 May 2005).

Office for Disability Issues (2004) *Progress in Implementing the New Zealand Disability Strategy 2003–2004. Fourth Annual Report from the Minister for Disability Issues to the House of Representatives*.

http://www.odi.govt.nz/nzds/progress-reports/july03-june04/index.html (accessed 1 May 2005).

Smith, T., Lovaas, N.W. and Lovaas, O. (2002) 'Behaviours of children with high-functioning autism when paired with typically developing versus delayed peers: a preliminary study.' *Behavioral Interventions 17*, 3, 129–143.

Werry, J. (1998) *Extracts from the Report to the Director General of Health under s47 of the Health and Disability Services Act 1993 on Casey Albury.* Wellington, New Zealand: The Ministry of Health (November).

CHAPTER 3

Impairments, Disability and Autism: Making Sense of It All, Behaviourally

Eric Messick and Mary Clark

My son Ben

When he was aged six, our intellectually gifted son, Ben, was diagnosed with Asperger's syndrome. Over the years we found the diagnosis helpful in many different situations. It enabled us to better understand our son's behaviour (e.g. the overwhelming nature of lots of children in a playgroup situation which led to aggressive behaviour such as biting and tantrumming). Before the diagnosis we tended to blame ourselves as first-time parents and assumed that it was a result of our deficient parenting! After the diagnosis we understood that the behaviours were *not* due to deficient parenting, and began to devise strategies to cope with it, to teach him to cope with the social world, and to pass these newly acquired skills on to his teachers.

We also developed relationships with several professionals who helped us with his major areas of difficulty within the school system such as learning to socialize, getting on with his peers, and fitting into the classroom environment. When the time came for him to attend high school, we asked the psychologist to do a full, descriptive report to help the school and his teachers understand his somewhat perplexing behaviour and reactions to various common situations. Previous schools, and his teachers, had welcomed this and told us that they found it helpful.

The school he was to attend is a fairly traditional boarding school that is co-educational in the final two years, otherwise boys only. This meant that our son was going to have to fit into not only a new classroom situation, but also a boarding house with some 70 boys aged between 13 and 18 years old. We saw advantages in the boarding environment – namely routines, rituals and consistency – but there were also challenges from the intense social interaction. Our initial interview with the headmaster was not a success. He did not appear to relish the prospect of a student who would inevitably have some difficulties fitting in. However, the prospect of such an academically capable student prevailed and he allowed us a 'trial' period.

We spent some considerable time discussing him with the boarding housemaster and matron, both of whom were receptive and understanding. We described, in detail, the sort of behaviours that he may exhibit under certain circumstances. For example, he would likely find the robust chaos of the boarding house confusing and overwhelming and he would have little ability to retreat into a quiet space for time by himself as he sometimes did at home. He would probably not show understanding of his peers' difficulties and might appear uncaring and lacking in empathy towards them. He would find team sports unappealing and would become easily frustrated with others behaving in a way different to his expectations or his behaviour. But we also described the flipside: that he would find boarding house rituals such as wake-up bells, fixed homework sessions and the concept of rigid rules quite acceptable and even reassuring. We anticipated the classroom challenges to be much as they always had been, namely that he would believe that the teacher was there for his sole benefit (as a result of his egocentric view of the world) and that the other students would be seen as irritants, a notion which he would have no hesitation in verbalizing! He would have difficulty working productively in groups and would be easily frustrated by what he saw as others' inadequacies. We gave the school copies of the psychologist's report, which covered much of the same material we had covered with the headmaster, and invited them to talk with us about any problems, which we anticipated there would be!

For the first term the telephone was quiet. Ben was uncommunicative other than the occasional ring to say that things were OK. This was an unexpected change and we enjoyed the fact that we were not being called to school at least once a week with some sort of problem or issue. Nevertheless, we were not entirely convinced that all was sweetness and light, so we were nervous when the time came for the first parent–teacher conferences. Each teacher we visited sang our son's praises. He was, they said, a model student producing his work on time, doing far in excess of what was asked of him, and challenging the teachers themselves with enquiring questions and requests for further work in most areas. He was coming top of his year!

The last two teachers we spoke to were the only ones who commented on his (from their point of view) idiosyncratic behaviour in the classroom. They mentioned him not developing friendships, being isolated in the playground during school break times, engaging in inappropriate intolerant conversation within the classroom (e.g. putting other boys down, ridiculing their shortcomings), arguing during classroom group tasks, not enjoying or seeing any point in unstructured classroom time, and having difficulty tolerating any changes in what he anticipated was going to happen that day in the classroom. Because we thought they would have been better informed (the school had been given the psychologist's report), we were perplexed and told them that this behaviour was consistent with his diagnosis. But they responded that they knew nothing of that!

We followed this up with the housemaster who told us that he had decided not to tell Ben's teachers about the diagnosis, as he believed that every child should be taken as he/she appears and that a label did not give the child a fair chance to be seen and treated as one of the class. We were at first shocked by what we saw as a failure to give his teachers the full picture so that they could work with our son. But we came to see it, in retrospect, as advantageous because his teachers had not pigeon-holed him as 'trouble' in advance of meeting him, and had no preconceived ideas about what a boy with Asperger's would mean for them in the classroom.

As his school career has progressed, there have been occasional social difficulties, and teachers have been told of his diagnosis on a need-to-know basis. *Need-to-know* means that when he fits in and blends with the crowd (which he does increasingly often now) he is accepted for who he is without the label being known. But when the familiar difficult issues arise, we may use the label so that his behaviour is better understood and so that he can be helped to change his behaviour and gain greater insight and awareness of who he is as a developing person. This has given him the best of both worlds, being both accepted and understood.

Ben has flourished both academically and socially during his time in the school. He is now invited to parties with friends. Like most teenagers he has a mobile phone at hand and uses text messaging with alacrity. There are girlfriends, which he keeps a closely guarded secret from his parents, and offers to tutor other students who struggle in subjects that come naturally and easy to him. His housemaster repeatedly comments that the other students in the boarding house both accept him and enjoy his quirky sense of humour and unusual take on the world. They are proud that he is in their boarding house. Academically, he continues to come top of his year, even though he takes on new subjects each year, often without any former experience in them. He has had essays published in a newspaper, and this year will receive seven prizes at a school prize-giving. His dream is to receive a scholarship to study at Cambridge University once he finishes school next year.

Impairments

Ben is top of his year, a prize winner, a writer, a partier, and a teenager. In addition to these things, he is also an organist, a photographer, and maybe even a future geographer after passing the National Certificate of Educational Achievement scholarship exam for geography after never even taking a geography class! Oh, that's right, he also has Asperger's syndrome.

What if, instead of the above, mum and dad only conveyed that Ben has Asperger's syndrome. He goes to a residential school, has bitten, been aggressive, tantrummed, has difficulty developing friendships, is often isolated, engages in inappropriate conversation, argues and has difficulty tolerating changes. What would this dialogue do for him? Is it really useful to highlight one's impairments, as big or small as they may be, early on in a relationship? 'This is Ben, he has Asperger's.' 'This is Jo, he doesn't wake up until noon and he can't hold a conversation with anyone.' 'I'm Margaret, I wash my hands twenty times a day, I can't deal with dirty dishes, and sometimes I think the mob is after me.' Usually, introductions like these do not occur – or do they? Should they?

Most people would prefer to remain free from impairments of any sort, but impairments are part of life. Some impairments are temporary and minor, but others are more permanent and severe and require attention from others. This second type of impairment may be brought to the attention of appropriate professionals who, in turn, offer a medical or psychological diagnosis. The nature of diagnoses will be covered later but, loosely speaking, a diagnosis means that the impairment is professionally recognized and understood in at least some respects. If the community's care system is working well, then this diagnosis may act as a ticket to getting help.

If the diagnosis is chickenpox, pneumonia or another medical problem, then a medical practitioner may be involved in the helping process; if the diagnosis is an autism spectrum disorder (ASD) or another 'mental illness', then one or more of several different kinds of professionals may be involved. In both of these situations, help may come in various forms and in many levels of effectiveness and is probably more likely to occur for individuals who receive a diagnosis than for those who do not. So, if we encounter severe impairments in life, should we seek a diagnosis because it increases the chances of getting help? The answer is 'probably', but there may be unseen costs.

These costs are not financial. Rather, they are a price paid by those diagnosed when others respond inappropriately to the diagnosis or to the impairment that warranted the diagnosis. An important difference between the layperson and those professionals qualified to help a person with an impairment is that the layperson is probably less likely to be adequately informed about the impairment and its associated diagnosis and, consequently, less likely to make decisions that are in the best interest of those diagnosed. In the worst cases, a person with a diagnosis may be subject to prejudice and injustice; in the best cases, they can expect inclusion and an even playing field. Here, inclusion might mean accepting people as a whole person having both strengths and impairments (and not excluding them based on an impairment, say) and an even playing field probably means an environment that accommodates people through reducing the impact of their impairments or other struggles. Ben was included and, when necessary, Ben's mum and dad implemented their need-to-know policy to help achieve an even playing field.

Appropriately informing the public of ASD, then, is important so that inclusion and an even playing field are more likely than prejudice and injustice. Indeed, organizations around the world create various public announcements that are intended to inform the public about ASDs. But, really, what should this information entail? Perhaps it would be worthwhile to see how some ASD-oriented organizations around the world inform the public.

We entered 'What is autism?' into an Internet search engine to see what kinds of websites contained this question and how the question was answered. The search resulted in approximately 12,200 sites ranging from autism societies to health, education and disability-related organizations to various behavioural and psychological information sites and many others. We perused some of the sites and found common themes.

Several sites stated that ASD refers to any or all of the following five pervasive developmental disorders (PDDs): autistic disorder, Asperger's disorder, pervasive developmental disorder not otherwise specified (PDD NOS), Rett's disorder, and childhood disintegrative disorder. Many sites went further and referred to differences in the brain when describing autism. According to the Autism Society of America (2004), autism is 'the result of a neurological disorder that affects the functioning of the brain, autism impacts the normal development of the brain in the areas of social interaction and communication skills'. The Centers for Disease Control and Prevention (2004) in the US states that 'autism spectrum disorders (ASDs) are a group of developmental disabilities that are caused by an abnormality in the brain'.

Some sites identified difference in genetics. The National Alliance for Autism Research (2004) is 'the first organization in the US dedicated to funding and accelerating biomedical research focusing on autism spectrum disorders'. According to the Alliance, 'it is widely believed within the scientific community that there is a strong genetic component or pre-disposition to autism spectrum disorders'. Other sites were less specific in their definition. The National Autistic Society (NAS) in the UK says, 'autism is a lifelong developmental disability that affects the way a person communicates and relates to people around them' (NAS 2004). We found definitions similar to the NAS definition from Autism New Zealand (2004), the Autism Association of Western Australia (2004), and Autism ACT of Australia (2004). Autism ACT, though, added, 'Many people with autism also have an intellectual disability', and the Autism Association of Western Australia added, 'autism can occur by itself or in association with other disorders such as intellectual disability, learning disability, epilepsy, rubella, fragile-x syndrome etc.'. So the question remains – what is autism?

Confused? Who wouldn't be? At this point, we are not left with an answer, but with more questions. What is the difference between the five ASDs? What are neurological disorders and abnormalities of the brain? What is a developmental disability? Is there an ASD gene? What is intellectual disability and learning disability? And the questions continue. Let us postpone the answer to the original question until the end of this chapter.

Models of disability

It is important to make a distinction between *impairment* and *disability* because they are not necessarily equivalent, although they are sometimes treated as such. An impairment is a specific difficulty that a person might have and might be considered to be a physical, psychological or other kind of impairment. Disability is a restriction in independence or well-being that is brought upon people with impairments. The source of disability differs depending on one's orientation. Just as different people can adhere to different religions, philosophies or other ways of being, people can adopt different orientations when it comes to understanding impairment and disability. It is common to see at least two models (orientations) of disability discussed in psychology textbooks and elsewhere: the social model and the medical model. Of these two models, the social model is typically identified as being the more preferred.

The social model identifies disability as hurdles in the environment that disable individuals with medical, psychological or other impairments. That is, everyone has strengths and impairments; disability occurs when a community does not take into account the special needs of people with certain impairments. For example, a person's legs may be impaired due to a spinal injury but, according to this model, the person is not disabled. Rather, the lack of wheelchair, ramps and wide doors disables the person. Likewise, a person with impairments in communicating, socializing and playing creatively is not disabled; the community's lack of knowledge about the impairments (and how to accommodate these people's special needs) disables the person. This model differs from the medical model in that it considers disability to be separate from the impairment and, instead, places it in the environment. We tend to agree with this model, but acknowledge the difficulty of achieving such an accommodating community. As described earlier, organizations do attempt to inform the public in an effort to nurture an accommodating community, but it is a large task over which most of us have little or no control. We will later support an extension of this model so that disability may be attacked from both sides – the community side and the impairment side.

The medical model, on the other hand, suggests that individuals with impairments suffer in some way or another and that the impairments disable the individual. It often implies that a community's aim should be to alleviate the suffering caused by the impairments, but that the disability is in the person (and may always be in the person). Implicit in this model is the distinction between those who suffer and those who do not. It can effectively create a separation that is probably not beneficial to individuals with impairments. At worst, it creates a group of people viewed as *disabled* and another group of people that are considered *normal*.

As its name suggests, the model addresses medical impairments, but we will see later that it is also used to understand 'psychological' or behavioural impairments. The following terms prevail in this model: illness (disease, disorder), symptom, pathology, diagnosis, aetiology, prognosis, treatment and cure. *Illness, disease* and *disorder* are general terms for poor health and consist of *symptoms* of some underlying cause. *Pathology* refers to the specific anatomical or physiological differences that occur when someone is ill. If a medical practitioner is available, they may offer a *diagnosis* that describes the features of the illness. From the diagnosis, the practitioner may then describe the *aetiology*, or cause, of the illness as well as a *prognosis*, a prediction of how the illness will develop over time. Some illnesses can be *cured*, or completely removed via certain *treatments* such as medication or surgery; other illnesses may not be cured, but decreased in severity – both outcomes might be considered good medicine. Here, the model suggests that the impairment is the illness (disease, or disorder) and it is the illness that disables the person. The medical-model solution to disability, then, is to eliminate or abate the illness so that the person is no longer (or at least less) disabled. The model works for medical problems, as exemplified below, but there are problems applying it to problems that are often considered 'psychological' or behavioural.

If someone experiences a cough and some congestion (symptoms), they may state that they have an illness and visit a medical practitioner. After an examination and some blood tests (or other appropriate tests), the practitioner may diagnose the illness as pneumonia and the aetiology of the disease as a bacterial infection that spread to the lungs via contact with the bacteria elsewhere. They may offer a prognosis that suggests that the situation will worsen with time and that further congestion, fever, muscle and chest pain, and difficulty breathing may follow unless a treatment is put into place. In this case, the disease may be cured with antibiotics that eliminate the bacteria and the symptoms may be temporarily alleviated with over-the-counter remedies such as cough syrup and pain relievers. Following the course of antibiotics the cough, congestion and other pathology may disappear and the illness may be considered cured. In short, the cough, congestion, fever, muscle and chest pain, and difficulty breathing (pneumonia) are symptoms of an underlying problem (bacterial infection) that can be treated (cough syrup and pain relievers) and/or cured (antibiotics).

In an introductory psychology textbook, Weiten (2004) writes, 'the medical model proposes that it is useful to think of abnormal behaviour as a disease...we'll take the position that the disease analogy continues to be useful, although one should remember that it is *only* an analogy' (p.561). Regardless of whether or not the model rests on an analogy, it suggests that disability is still caused by a disease or illness (abnormal behaviour, in this case) within the individual and that the illness should be eliminated or reduced in order to reduce the associated disability. This model is probably the model that characterizes the views of the majority of people in the Western world; however, the model may be misleading.

In New Zealand, the medical model has manifested itself in TV advertising campaigns called *Like Minds, Like Mine* (2004). In 2000, the Ministry of Health launched these campaigns in an effort to lessen the stigma associated with *mental illness* (this term is often used interchangeably with *psychological disorder* or *mental disorder*). The adverts show short segments of accomplished New Zealanders who have also been diagnosed with certain 'mental illnesses'. They are portrayed in a jovial and dignified manner and brief dialogue corroborates each person's manner and highlights that they have a 'mental illness' and are doing well despite the fact. For example, Mahinarangi Tocker, a singer and songwriter, says, 'I thank the day I learnt to accept that I have a mental illness and that I can say "I have a mental illness"; it's a huge release and a relief.' Paul Holmes, a broadcaster, speaks with Denise L'Estrange-Corbet, a designer with depression, and says, 'We are terribly judgemental of mental illness and we should not be because it's just an illness and the greatest thing we can do is talk about it. I understand her now; I wish she'd told me ages ago.' The message, here, is clear – it's just an illness. But is it?

The 'mental illness' concept certainly follows the medical model in that it places the disability within the person, albeit as a result of a 'mental illness' within the person. A strength of this concept as well as the campaign described above is that it teaches the public to point to a 'mental illness' as an explanation for and cause of disability instead of pointing to a person. Resultantly, people may be less likely to point to a person and say things like, 'she is just an antisocial and mean person'. Instead, perhaps they would say, 'she is a great person, she is just struggling with a "mental illness"'. The two statements would probably have a much different effect on the community and perhaps statements like the second increase the chances of inclusion and an even playing field.

But a problem is that pointing to a 'mental illness' easily gives rise to statements like 'his autism is inhibiting his communication' or 'his Asperger's syndrome makes it difficult to make friends'. Some years ago in the States I worked with a boy diagnosed with attention deficit/hyperactivity disorder (ADHD). I met with him one morning and he repeatedly tapped his pencil on the desk. I kindly asked the boy to stop tapping his pencil and he said, 'I can't, Eric, it's my ADHD!' The problem with the medical model in this respect, the conceptualization of disability being caused by 'mental illness', and the resulting statements described above, is that the model misleads people in their search for causes of and solutions for disability. If ADHD is causing the problematic pencil tapping, then people may be misled into searching for a solution to the problem by looking for and addressing the ADHD somehow. But where is the ADHD and how can it be addressed? Similarly, where are ASDs and how can they be addressed?

If it really is useful to think of abnormal behaviour as a disease (Weiten 2004), then we should be able to offer a parallel example of how the medical model works with a 'mental illness' such as an ASD. If an individual experiences difficulty communicating, socializing with others and engaging in creative play, then someone close may identify these difficulties as symptoms of an underlying problem and may seek the advice of a psychologist to ascertain the possibility of a 'mental illness'. Following an assessment, the psychologist may then put forth a diagnosis of an ASD. The prognosis might be that these difficulties will continue across the person's life span and may even get worse, but the practitioner would not be able to offer a precise account of what these difficulties would be. Unfortunately, the aetiology of ASDs is unknown, so the practitioner would not be able to offer any information regarding the causes of ASDs. The claims that leaky gut, other aspects of the digestive system, MMR (measles, mumps and rubella) vaccinations, mercury, etc. cause ASDs have not been scientifically validated and should not be cited as the aetiology of ASDs (although these possibilities should continue to be thoroughly investigated). As a quick aside, we are not saying that there is no biological, neurological or genetic influence to ASDs, only that these factors are currently poorly understood, so we cannot confidently identify any of them as contributing to ASDs. We may not fully understand the aetiology, then, but what about treatment? A treatment may be prescribed by the practitioner, but the specific treatment (if it is to be effective) would vary substantially from person to person, just as the prognosis would vary. But can the practitioner cure ASDs? In short, no! Why? Because this question is misleading in that it identifies ASD as an underlying problem that can be cured in the same way that a medical problem is cured. There is a big difference between *curing autism* and *curing pneumonia*. In the latter case, there is a physical thing (the bacteria) that is causing the pneumonia and the elimination of this thing is the important part of the cure. In the former case, the cause of the ASD cannot be pinpointed to a specific thing like bacteria. So the idea of curing or treating autism in the sense of eliminating or reducing its 'underlying cause' is a snafu. (For a very thorough and technical discussion of the problems of 'treating' underlying pathologies, see Goldiamond 2002.) Further, in situations where someone loses their ASD diagnosis, where has the ASD gone?

We cannot detect 'mental illness' with a blood test or other medical test, see it under a microscope, and identify it in parts of the brain or in any other part of the body (like we can with bacteria or viruses), measure it like other things, and generally it does not fit any criteria for existing in our physical world. Yet 'mental illness' is often identified as a cause of disability (i.e. of behavioural excesses or deficits) and is talked about as if it were a thing – this child *has* an ASD and that's why he has difficulty playing. The model can trick people into identifying a *non-thing* as the cause of behaviour. This non-thing further misleads people in their attempts to find a solution. The logic may go something like this: ASD is making it difficult for this child to play with others. We, therefore, need to eliminate the ASD so that the child can play more easily; in other words, we need a treatment that will eliminate (cure) or decrease (treat) the ASD. If we follow this line of reasoning, we may be as fruitful in our search for a thing to cure as someone searching for a gremlin.

The word *gremlin* is said to have been coined by the Royal Naval Air Service some time during World War I and made known by a children's book called *The Gremlins: A Royal Air Force Story* written in 1943 by Roald Dahl. According to the story, a gremlin is a small creature that causes mechanical problems in aircraft. Since 1943, gremlins were blamed (jestingly, it is hoped!) by allied aircraft personnel for various mechanical and engine problems during World War II and the term is still used today in contexts broader than the aeroplane industry. If we take statements like 'a gremlin keeps causing my car to run poorly' seriously, then we are in a bit of trouble when it comes to solving the car problem – we would need to find the gremlin and get rid of it.

There are no documented gremlin captures, no photos of gremlins, no information on what they eat or how they might be enticed into a trap, and no evidence for their existence except for the apparent vehicle impairments they cause. We may be tempted to understand gremlins by looking at the various impairments that they allegedly cause. Perhaps we suggest that there are in fact two species of gremlins: *Gremlinus Irelandus* and *Gremlinus Zealandii*. The former may be responsible for electrical impairments and the latter for mechanical impairments. We could engage in lengthy, scholarly discussion about which species cause a certain problem. We may even 'discover' a new species of the variety *Americanus* which causes fuel-related impairments and we may debate further as to which of these gremlins is really responsible. Perhaps there are even cases where two or even all species are responsible.

But a good mechanic doesn't worry about gremlins. Instead, they would do some tests in order to find the specific engine component that is causing the problem (the impairment) and then they would fix the problem component directly. Perhaps it might be a dirty carburettor, a lack of transmission fluid or a worn bearing. These are things that mechanics have known to cause engine problems and they are readily addressable through appropriate maintenance and repair. If the same engine components have difficulties in many other cars, then perhaps some engineers need to go back to the proverbial drawing board.

We hope, by now, we've persuaded you that there are no such things as gremlins! The lesson to be learned from these species of gremlins is that a mechanic cannot address an engine problem by addressing the gremlins allegedly causing it. A mechanic can, however, address the problems directly, without any reference to gremlins, and engineers can understand the cause of the problems by directly researching the physical and mechanical properties of the problematic engine components. If the technology and research reach a certain point, the engine components might be redesigned in a way to avoid the impairments arising in the first place. Do we then say that we got rid of the gremlins? Of course not!

In a similar way, no one has ever found an ASD. Plenty of people have been diagnosed with ASD, but no one has ever found a thing called ASD. There is often debate as to what a person's diagnosis is. Is it autism or is it Asperger's? Is it autism and mental retardation or just autism? We may notice certain impairments that fit all or some of the rubrics of autism, Asperger's syndrome and mental retardation and we may debate as to which of these diagnoses is 'actually' the case. In a way, we are arguing between the doings of *Gremlinus Irelandus* and *Gremlinus Zealandii*, but where did this argument get us with our car problems? Maybe when we point to a 'mental illness' to explain impairments we are in fact creating gremlins and making it even more difficult to explain impairments. Instead, maybe we should gain an understanding of the biological, neurological and genetic factors (nature) as well as the behavioural factors (nurture) that contribute to impairments and disability. Just as the old nature versus nurture debate never really results in one or the other as the sole determinant of behaviour, ASDs cannot be considered to be a manifestation of only one or the other.

What is autism, really?

It would be incorrect to say that *ASDs* refer to those currently unidentified biological, neurological or genetic factors that might influence those with ASD diagnoses. It would also be incorrect to say that those with ASD diagnoses 'simply' have some learned behaviour problems. What is autism, really? Autism is a label for a collection of behaviours, full stop! Specifically, the label *autism* is given by a trained professional (usually a psychologist) when the person engages in some of the behaviours specified in the fourth edition text revision of the *Diagnostic and Statistical Manual of Mental Disorders* (DSM-IV-TR) published by the American Psychiatric Association (2000) or the tenth edition of the International Statistical Classification of Diseases and Related Health Problems (ICD-10) published by the World Health Organization. The DSM editions began as a variant of the ICD-6 in 1956 and the most current editions of the two manuals are comparable.

The DSM editions describe 'mental disorders' and the ICD editions describe both medical and 'mental disorders'. The DSM-IV-TR seems to be the more commonly used system, so we will focus on this publication.

Figure 3.1 shows the diagnostic criteria for autism as specified in the DSM-IV-TR (American Psychiatric Association 2000, p.75). The criteria state that a diagnosis can be given if a total of six or more of the listed behaviours occur; if delays or abnormal functioning in social interaction, language or imaginative play occur prior to age three years; and if the difficulties are not better described by another disorder. The listed behaviours fall into three general categories: impairment in social interaction (e.g. 'failure to develop peer relationships appropriate to developmental level'); impairment in communication (e.g. 'delay in, or total lack of, the development of spoken language (not accompanied by an attempt to compensate through alternative modes of communication such as gesture or mime)'); and restricted repetitive and stereotyped patterns of behaviour, interests and activities (e.g. 'apparently inflexible adherence to specific, nonfunctional routines or rituals'). Quite literally, if an individual does enough of the above behaviours within each of the three categories and if these behaviours severely impact their day-to-day living, then they may receive a diagnosis of autism or another ASD. The diagnosis only conveys what the person's behaviour looks like; it does not lead to an understanding of the cause of the behaviours described by the diagnosis and it does not immediately give rise to solutions. The same is true for any 'mental disorder' in the manual. The DSM-IV-TR doesn't claim to offer anything beyond a classification and makes the following important statements:

> although this manual provides a classification of mental disorders, it must be admitted that no definition adequately specifies precise boundaries for the concept of 'mental disorder'... DSM-IV is a categorical classification that divides mental disorders into types based on criteria sets with defining features. This naming of categories is the traditional method of organizing and transmitting information in everyday life and has been the fundamental approach used in all systems of medical diagnosis... In DSM-IV, there is no assumption that each category of mental disorder is a completely discrete entity with absolute boundaries dividing it from other mental disorders or from no mental disorder. There is also no assumption that all individuals described as having the same mental disorder are alike in all important ways. (APA 2000, pp.xxx–xxxi)

(I)   A total of six (or more) items from (A), (B), and (C), with at least two from (A), and one each from (B) and (C)

(A)   qualitative impairment in social interaction, as manifested by at least two of the following:

1. marked impairments in the use of multiple nonverbal behaviors such as eye-to-eye gaze, facial expression, body posture, and gestures to regulate social interaction

2. failure to develop peer relationships appropriate to developmental level

3. a lack of spontaneous seeking to share enjoyment, interests, or achievements with other people (e.g., by a lack of showing, bringing, or pointing out objects of interest to other people)

4. lack of social or emotional reciprocity (note: in the description, it gives the following as examples: not actively participating in simple social play or games, preferring solitary activities, or involving others in activities only as tools or 'mechanical' aids)

(B) qualitative impairments in communication as manifested by at least one of the following:

1. delay in, or total lack of, the development of spoken language (not accompanied by an attempt to compensate through alternative modes of communication such as gesture or mime)

2. in individuals with adequate speech, marked impairment in the ability to initiate or sustain a conversation with others

3. stereotyped and repetitive use of language or idiosyncratic language

4. lack of varied, spontaneous make-believe play or social imitative play appropriate to developmental level

(C) restricted repetitive and stereotyped patterns of behavior, interests and activities, as manifested by at least two of the following:

1. encompassing preoccupation with one or more stereotyped and restricted patterns of interest that is abnormal either in intensity or focus

2. apparently inflexible adherence to specific, nonfunctional routines or rituals

3. stereotyped and repetitive motor mannerisms (e.g. hand or finger flapping or twisting, or complex whole-body movements)

4. persistent preoccupation with parts of objects

(II) Delays or abnormal functioning in at least one of the following areas, with onset prior to age 3 years:

(A) social interaction

(B) language as used in social communication

(C) symbolic or imaginative play

(III) The disturbance is not better accounted for by Rett's Disorder or Childhood Disintegrative Disorder

Figure 3.1: Diagnostic Criteria for 299.00 Autistic Disorder (DSM-IV-TR, p.75; reprinted with permission from the Diagnostic and Statistical Manual of Mental Disorders, Copyright © 2000 American Psychiatric Association.)

The diagnostic criteria for Asperger's disorder, PDD NOS, Rett's disorder and childhood disintegrative disorder are similar to autism, but differ in some ways. Asperger's disorder differs in that communication impairments are not present. PDD NOS is a diagnosis given to individuals who meet some, but not all, of the criteria for autism or the other ASDs. A diagnosis of Rett's disorder is given to people who develop as expected for the first five months but then show difficulties in the three general categories described above and who show a deceleration of head growth during the next four years. Finally, childhood disintegrative disorder describes some of the same behaviours in the three general categories, but these behaviours must occur after at least two years of normal development but before age ten. Similarly, labels such as *intellectual disability, learning disability* and *developmental disability* have defining features, but are still only labels.

So, what is the difference between the five ASDs? All of these ASDs (or PDDs) label difficulties in the areas of social interaction, communication and/or creative play and differ in time of onset and in other subtle respects. All five diagnoses label collections of behaviours, not underlying causes. It may very well be the case that genes, brain structure or function, and/or some other physiological conditions or environmental events predispose people to behave in ways that warrant an ASD label (or other 'mental-disorder' label), but any assertions involving such a predisposition are still only assumptions. More research needs to be done to test these assumptions (and perhaps to address ASD at this genetic, neurological or physiological level), but we do not need an understanding of genes, brains or physiology to understand the behaviours that are described by ASDs.

We are not saying that these things are not important, only that we do not fully understand how they contribute to ASD. We certainly recommend that families and professionals gain an understanding of all areas of ASD, but the domains of genetics, neurology and physiology are beyond the reach of most people. There is, however, a wealth of easily accessible information relating to the behaviours of people categorized within ASDs and, in some parts of the world, practitioners who are competent in the understanding of behaviour of all sorts, including the behaviour of people with ASDs. The name of the science of behaviour is behaviour analysis and when this science is applied to change behaviour, it is called applied behaviour analysis (ABA). We suggest that an understanding of ABA is the best starting point for anyone who is interested in helping someone with ASD to improve their life.

Revisiting the car analogy, the behaviour analyst is akin to the mechanic in that the impairments were identified and addressed directly, without the need for gremlins or even a full understanding of why the engine component may have had problems in the first place. The scientist researching genetics, neurology and physiology is analogous to the engineer who researched the cause of the problematic engine component and redesigned the part so that problems no longer occurred. In the world of ASDs, practitioners and researchers can operate in ways similar to mechanics and engineers, respectively. Practitioners should identify impairments and address them directly through ABA and researchers should continue their work in understanding the biological, neurological or genetic factors that might accompany diagnoses of ASD so that maybe, some day, the impairments might be addressed at these levels even before diagnoses occur.

What is ABA?

ABA is the application of the principles of behaviour to understanding and addressing behavioural impairments. It is the most effective method of improving the lives of people with ASDs and the field spans far beyond ASD into parenting and child management; education; severe problems; clinical behaviour therapy; self-management of personal problems; medical and health care; gerontology; behavioural community psychology; business, industry and government; sport psychology; and behavioural assessment (Martin and Pear 2003). The behaviour-change process often begins with an identification of goals. What behaviours should be occurring if the process is successful? These behaviours are often called target behaviours.

When behaviour analysts and families select target behaviours and design ways of achieving target behaviours, behaviour analysts call the change process a *programme*. Israel Goldiamond (2002) was a behaviour analyst who advocated a constructional approach to solving behaviour problems. That is, for individuals with behavioural impairments (which might be labelled a 'mental illness'), the best approach is to teach the person new skills – to construct behavioural repertoires. The idea is based on the fact that aberrant behaviour often occurs because a more appropriate, less costly, similarly functioning behaviour is not in the person's repertoire. If, for example, we rewind time to when Ben was young and occasionally tantrumming when preferred items were withheld, the tantrumming might be seen as a strength because he has learned to interact socially, albeit inappropriately. Tantrumming might be decreased by teaching him to ask for objects and to teach others to only give objects following appropriate asking. Here, the impairment is really the absence of an *asking* repertoire; it is not excessive grabbing and not an ASD. This constructional approach is in stark contrast to approaches derived from the medical model where the approach is often to eliminate the impairment in order to decrease disability. Following the medical model, then, one might be tempted to address excessive tantrumming (the alleged impairment) by decreasing it through, say, some kind of reductive procedure each time a tantrum occurs. This procedure may be quite successful at decreasing tantrumming; however, the real impairment would continue to be a lack of verbal skills. A procedure that decreases tantrumming will not automatically result in increased asking. In fact, Ben would probably have learned other inappropriate behaviours that function in the same way as tantrumming. Further, as discussed previously, there is no procedure to eliminate ASDs because ASDs are not things.

Perhaps a better way to address impairments directly, then, is to replace the notions of *diagnosis, treatment* and *eliminate*, with *current relevant repertoire, programme* and *construct*, respectively (see Goldiamond 2002 for a detailed account of his constructional approach and the elements of a behavioural programme). Instead of spending a lot of time on a diagnosis, practitioners should identify an individual's current relevant repertoire: the part of the person's repertoire that can be built upon. Succinctly, what can this person do right? For example, early babbling and perhaps echolalia might be relevant for learning vocal imitation which can then turn into word imitation. Echolalia, in this light, is not an impairment to be eliminated; it is a strength because it might be the first step towards language. At this point, the practitioner can then create an ABA programme that involves a terminal repertoire (or target repertoire) and a sequence of steps that bridge the current repertoire to the terminal repertoire. These steps might involve any ABA technique including, but not limited to, discrete-trial teaching (Lovaas 2003), precision teaching (Johnson and Layng 1992), direct instruction (e.g. Engelmann, Haddox and Bruner 1983), functional communication training (Mathews 2003), incidental teaching (Fenske, Krantz and McClannahan 2001) and pivotal-response training (Koegel and Koegel 1999). The steps might also involve temporary, progress-maintaining reinforcers ranging from edible items to toys to activities. The purpose of the programme is to construct a repertoire that can occur in a person's normal environment without the need for further intervention or progress-maintaining reinforcers (or at least with less intervention than was previously necessary). A behaviour analyst, then, would not attempt to treat or eliminate an ASD. Rather, they would design a programme to construct the behaviours that are required for language (e.g. saying letter sounds), social interactions (e.g. eye contact) and creative play (e.g. playing with toys appropriately). In this respect, disability may be tackled by addressing the impairments directly.

ABA and the social model of disability

In identifying the difficulty of describing ASDs and other 'mental disorders' as illnesses and suggesting instead that 'mental illnesses' ought to be viewed as labels for collections of behaviours, by no means are we suggesting that the problems of people with 'mental illnesses' are any less severe. We are suggesting that conceptualizing certain kinds of behaviour as symptoms of underlying 'mental illnesses' will be less likely to result in a useful solution because it leads people away from the causes of behaviour over which they actually have influence – the nurture bit, not the nature bit. With a good understanding of ABA and perhaps some professional help from a behaviour analyst, the nurture bit can be fine-tuned to address impairments well. We suggest, then, that disability should be reduced or eliminated by addressing it from the community's side (via the social model) and from the impairment side (via ABA).

Earlier, we suggested that the social model is preferred over the medical model because it places the onus of disability in the community, not in the person. We discussed the medical model and criticized its use when conceptualizing 'mental illnesses' because it places the disability in the person (caused by a 'mental illness' within the person) and, further, misleads people in their search for solutions to disability. In advocating the social model, we suggested that public educational initiatives are good so long as they result in a community that makes efforts to even the playing field (i.e. decrease disability). The specific way in which disability may be reduced depends on the disability, but the general approach is probably to educate the public in ways that change the behaviour of the community. Through education, communities may better include people with impairments so that disability is less likely to occur and may even the playing field by advocating for government spending to decrease disability by providing necessary technology and human resources.

If disability is a result of barriers created by a community that does not cater well for people with impairments, then it follows that decreasing impairments may be another approach to decreasing disability. For people with an ASD, impairments are generally behaviours that occur either too much (e.g. talking obsessively about a favourite television show) or not enough (e.g.

saying complete sentences). If a community is not well educated with respect to ASDs, then they may disable these people by responding inappropriately to the impairments, perhaps by staring, making rude comments or avoiding the person. Ideally, the community should be educated, just as the key personnel at Ben's school were, but at the same time, these impairments can be addressed directly by applying the principles of behaviour analysis so that disability is less likely to occur. Given the right resources and ABA personnel, people with ASDs can learn to talk about a variety of topics, initiate conversation, play with toys, maintain eye contact, discriminate facial expressions, and do just about any other behaviour you can think of.

Unfortunately, ABA is not readily available in all parts of the world, so some people are born into communities that, perhaps unknowingly, disable them from birth by not offering provisions for ABA services and/or educating the community. Others, particularly in some states in the US, are born into communities that quickly address their impairments by providing ABA services and community education. In other parts of the world, gross injustices occur when communities or governments misunderstand ABA and dissuade communities from using it or make it difficult for qualified behaviour analysts to practise. ABA is not easy and practising ABA effectively and ethically requires a level of training comparable to medical practitioners and psychologists. Yet in most parts of the world there is no way for communities to identify competent professionals; even worse, individuals with no training in ABA or with training in a different field such as psychology can practise ABA inappropriately without consequence to themselves, but with detrimental consequences to the field of ABA. The exception to this identification problem is the Behavior Analyst Certification Board (2004) in the US (www.bacb.com). The Board is the only organization in the world that certifies people who are competent to practise ABA, at least according to their standards. The benefit to the public, then, are competent practitioners who are more easily identifiable. Some professionals outside of the US hold the Board's highest qualification, Board Certified Behavior Analyst (BCBA), but it will be some time before the qualification is well recognized internationally. There are individuals without this qualification who are quite competent though. So we urge anyone seeking ABA services to consider carefully the experience and qualifications of the person who is to deliver the services. We also suggest that people seeking ABA services search the Board's free online registry that lists names and locations of people who have received certification.

Final considerations

Would Mary's story be different if Ben's peers and teachers were informed of his diagnosis from his first day at school? Would he have enjoyed more or less friends, success or independence? We'll never know. We do know that disability was not evident in his life at that time – he did flourish academically and socially. The disability was not avoided by addressing his impairments through ABA, as is the case for some other people. It was, however, avoided through careful disclosure (or non-disclosure) of his diagnosis on a need-to-know basis (i.e. appropriately informing and educating the community) and through attention to his strengths rather than his impairments. We are not necessarily advocating against revealing a diagnosis; instead, we suggest that it is important to consider the effect on the community's behaviour towards the person with the diagnosis.

A clever study illustrates the effect that a label can have on people's judgement of those labelled. Langer and Abelson (1974) showed a video of a man being interviewed to two groups of 20 clinicians. One group was told that the interviewee was a job applicant; the other group were told he was a patient. Approximately half of each group were of a traditional psychological orientation and the other half of each group were of a behavioural orientation. So, all 20 clinicians representing both orientations saw the same exact video. The only difference was how the interviewee was labelled by the experimenter introducing the video: job applicant or patient. When the video finished, each clinician completed a questionnaire relating to the interviewee, his gestures, attitudes, and other aspects of his outlook on life. These questionnaires were then analysed by the experimenters and a score on a scale of 1 (very disturbed) to 10 (very well adjusted) was given to summarize each questionnaire. The questionnaires were then averaged for each orientation within each group. Figure 3.2 shows the results of the study.

The figure shows the mean (average) adjustment rating given to the interviewee by the traditionally-oriented and behaviourally-oriented clinicians in each group. The dark bars show that behaviourally-oriented clinicians rated the interviewee similarly (approximately six out of ten) regardless of what the label was while the light bars show that traditionally-oriented clinicians rated the interviewee differently. Although the average rating given by the job-applicant group was also approximately six out of ten, the average rating given by the patient group was almost half of this rating! So, simply changing the label of the interviewee from *job applicant* to *patient* was enough to substantially alter the judgement of the traditionally-oriented clinicians. It is clear

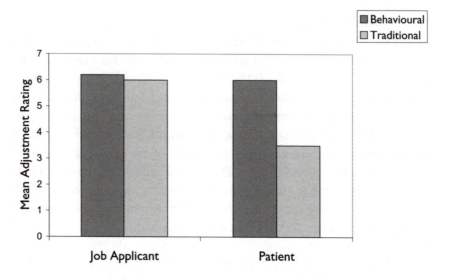

Figure 3.2: Mean adjustment ratings given by behaviourally-oriented and traditionally-oriented psychologists for each interviewee label (job applicant and patient). Data are re-plotted from Langer and Abelson (1974).

Figure 3.3: Illustration by Gösta Dillenburger. What caused the cup of juice to spill onto the floor? It may be convenient to say that a child did this because if his autism; however, this reasoning is much like pointing to a gremlin as the cause of the spilled juice. Autism and gremlins are not things and therefore cannot cause behaviour. If a child regularly spills juice onto the floor, the cause of this behaviour lies in the antecedents and consequences of juice spilling. Perhaps throwing juice onto the floor results in the withdrawal of mum's mealtime demands such as 'drink this' or 'eat this'.

where the disability resides in this case. We do not mean to imply that all people of a traditional psychological orientation will be swayed in this manner. We are only showing that if a label can alter the judgement of a trained professional who is supposedly able and non-biased in the area of clinical judgement and educated with respect to impairments and disability, then a label might also alter the judgement of others.

We suggest that the focus of discussion for any person who is at risk of being the subject of disability ought not to be on labels, but on the behaviours that are described by the labels (see Figure 3.3). Referring to people as *high functioning* or *low functioning* is much less informative and less helpful than a description of what they can do and what they are still learning how to do. Spending a lot of time and money on diagnoses or other labels is not as fruitful as spending time and money on assessments and interventions that begin a path to decreased disability – either through addressing impairments through ABA or through educating communities. Finally, we encourage communities to promote ABA and ASD awareness and to seek government funding to level the playing field for people with ASDs so that disability may become an issue of the past.

References

American Psychiatric Association (APA) (2000) *Diagnostic and Statistical Manual of Mental Disorders, 4th Edition, Text Revision* (DSM-IV-TR). Washington, DC: American Psychiatric Press, Inc.

Autism ACT of Australia (2004) *What is Autism?* http://autism.anu.edu.au/whatis.htm (accessed 16 April 2005).

Autism Association of Western Australia (2004) *Some Frequently Asked Questions Concerning Autism, and Their Answers.* http://www.autism.org.au/faq.htm (accessed 16 April 2005).

Autism New Zealand (2004) *What is Autism?* http://www.autismnz.org.nz/autism.php (accessed 16 April 2005).

Autism Society of America (2004) *What is Autism?* http://www.autism-society.org/site/PageServer?pagename=whatisautism (accessed 16 April 2005).

Behavior Analyst Certification Board (2004) *Consumer Information.* http://www.bacb.com/consum_frame.html (accessed 16 April 2005).

Centers for Disease Control and Prevention (2004) *About Autism.* http://www.cdc.gov/ncbddd/dd/aic/about/default.htm (accessed 16 April 2005).

Dahl, R. (1943) *The Gremlins: A Royal Air Force Story.* New York: Random House.

Engelmann, S., Haddox, P. and Bruner, E. (1983) *Teach Your Child to Read in 100 Easy Lessons.* New York: Simon and Schuster, Inc.

Fenske, E.C., Krantz, P.J. and McClannahan, L.E. (2001) 'Incidental teaching: a not-discrete-trial teaching procedure.' In C. Maurice, G. Green and R.M. Foxx (eds) *Making a Difference: Behavioral Intervention for Autism* (pp.75–82). Austin, TX: PRO-ED, Inc.

Goldiamond, I. (2002) 'Toward a constructional approach to social problems.' *Behavior and Social Issues 11*, 2, 108–197.

Johnson, K.R. and Layng, T.V.J. (1992) 'Breaking the structuralist barrier: literacy and numeracy with fluency.' *American Psychologist 47*, 1475–1490.

Koegel, L.K. and Koegel, R.L. (1999) 'Pivotal response intervention I: overview of approach.' *Journal of the Association for the Severely Handicapped 24*, 174–175.

Langer, E.J. and Abelson, R.P. (1974) 'A patient by any other name…: clinician group difference in labeling bias.' *Journal of Consulting and Clinical Psychology 42*, 1, 4–9.

Like Minds, Like Mine (2004) *Like Minds Advertising Campaign 2002.* www.likeminds.govt.nz (accessed 16 April 2005).

Lovaas, O.I. (2003) *Teaching Individuals with Developmental Delays: Basic Intervention Techniques.* Austin, TX: PRO-ED, Inc.

Martin, G. and Pear, J. (2003) *Behavior Modification: What It Is and How To Do It* (7th edn). Englewood Cliffs, NJ: Prentice Hall.

Mathews, B. (2003) 'A picture's worth: PECS and other visual communication strategies in autism.' *Journal of Intellectual and Developmental Disability 28*, 311–312.

National Alliance for Autism Research (2004) *What is Autism?* www.naar.org/aboutaut/whatis.htm (accessed 16 April 2005).

National Autistic Society (NAS) (2004) *What is Autism?* www.nas.org.uk/nas/jsp/polopoly.jsp?d=211 (accessed 16 April 2005).

Weiten, W. (2004) *Psychology: Themes and Variations* (6th edn). Belmont, CA: Wadsworth/Thomson Learning.

CHAPTER 4

Starting an ABA Programme

Erika Ford and Judith Petry

This chapter focuses on the application of the principles of behaviour to early intensive intervention for children with autism and it describes how these principles have been used to teach one young boy effectively (Gordon, not his real name) with a diagnosis of autism. The chapter outline is in three parts. Parts 1 and 3 are written by Judith, Gordon's mum, and Part 2 by Erika, the CARD Supervisor (Center for Autism and Related Disorders), on the development and implementation of the programme.

Part 1 – Judith (Gordon's mum)
A summary of Gordon before diagnosis
Gordon's differences were apparent to me almost from the very beginning of his life. The word 'different' would gradually shift in its reference point over time. But at this early point, he was different to the only other baby I had known intimately well. That is my daughter Kiara, born four years earlier. From the time that Gordon was around four weeks old I began to notice a subtle difference in the intensity of the connection that I felt with him – compared, that is, to what I had experienced with Kiara.

It all started with the onset of his first developmental milestone, the smile. Whereas Kiara had first smiled to us at four weeks old, all of our family's love and attention did not achieve the same result with Gordon. As an accurate prediction of things to come, his first visit by the Child Health Nurse at six weeks old recorded his communicative development in the negative – that is, in terms of what he could not do: 'Responds to voice and startles. Not smiling yet' (six-week Child Health Check).

We waited patiently for that first smile to happen, for him to begin to communicate to us. (All the while commenting and even mildly apologizing when my family and friends sought to interact with him: 'Sorry, he doesn't smile yet,' I would casually say.) When eventually the smile did happen (not at four, five or six, but finally at seven weeks old), it was to me a quietly disappointing and confusing experience. Gordon did not share his first precious smile with me. Or even with another member of his family for that matter. It was with a family friend – but to Gordon that friend was a virtual stranger, someone with whom he had spent no time, someone with whom he had no relationship.

That all important mother–child connection did not seem to effect the same 'magical' bond with Gordon. Not in the way that it had with my first child, my daughter. By the time she was six weeks old I had felt like our 'bond' was 'special', 'incredible', 'magical'. But with Gordon at the same age, I couldn't even manage to get him to smile. I felt confused, sad and bewildered – emotions that are still strongly cemented in my memory today, almost five years later. This delayed and different smile was not an incident in isolation. It accurately reflected a pattern of behaviour that would follow from that point on: Gordon's communicative development would have little to do with the effort that I put in.

More 'little' things like this carried on throughout his first year. Niggling away at me. Irritating me. Not being able to make sense of them. In the smile, the eye contact, the facial expressions – the entire repertoire of non-verbal baby communication skills – they were less intense with Gordon. Often this was reflected in his baby photos. He always looked like such a serious little boy. Getting him to smile for a photo was a reflection of real life; it just seemed to take longer and require a lot more effort in order to get just a little communicative reaction.

By the time that Gordon was four months old, our connection problem had manifested itself in my mind as a serious bonding issue, one that I couldn't keep a secret any longer. I decided to talk to my husband about it. But, despite my emotionally expressed concerns that 'I feel like something special is missing between us (Gordon and me)', Andrew, unfortunately, could not see it. Everything was just fine in his eyes. And so began the process of other people denying the problem that I felt but could not identify. For the next two years I would live with two problems, each compounding the other. First, there were the actual day-to-day difficulties in parenting Gordon, and second, the difficulty in trying to make sense of what was happening.

Gradually the little things turned into bigger things. That delayed and different smile experience as a newborn was presenting itself as an 'absence of personality' and a 'difficulty to define his character' by his first birthday. Although written in a light-hearted tone, these were the exact words that I used to describe him in my diary notes: '...Gordon is lovely. It is difficult though to yet describe his personality! I guess we will start to see his character unfold more now, as he gets older' (Diary notes – Gordon's first birthday).

As Gordon became more mobile and moved into the toddler period my concerns with him shifted from what I had perceived as a bonding issue, to more of a teaching issue. My daughter had started at school, so it was now just Gordon and I at home for much of the day and at this point it became apparent that I literally just did not know what to do with him, not even for a few minutes at a time. Each day began with a sense of 'dread', wondering how I was going to spend six hours alone with him, one-on-one. Finding activities that we could do together for any sustained length of time was challenging. No, make that virtually impossible. However, to contradict everything that I 'felt', appearances were deceptive. In every physical way he looked like a normal, happy, healthy and active child. It was only in regard to that invisible and indefinable connection issue that I continued to feel a sense of unease.

By the time that Gordon was 14 months old, I had serious doubts about my ability to be a competent parent to him. At this point you could describe him as a child who just did what *he* wanted to do. He had become what we referred to as our 'difficult' one. The only way to get him to stop and stay relatively still was to put a video on. And then he would just sit, glued to it. At video times it was as if people didn't exist. When we spoke to him he didn't acknowledge us. In fact, even shouting his name didn't result in him turning his head to look at us – such was the mesmerizing effect of the video, which successfully captured his complete and full attention.

It was at this time that I made my first attempt to discuss Gordon's behaviour within the public health system. After reading an article in a woman's weekly magazine discussing the MMR–autism link and noticing some similarities between the description of the three-year-old autistic child in the article and in 14-month-old Gordon (references about eye contact, attention span, communication and behaviour all rang an eerily similar bell), I approached my GP and directly asked her if she thought that Gordon might have autism. My GP's short answer to this was 'No'.

At the scheduled 15-month Child Health Check (Table 4.1) Gordon was described by the Child Health Nurse as 'active and social'. However, in the section titled 'Does your child hear well?' (my alternative interpretation: 'Can your child communicate well?'), Gordon only passed four out of the seven criteria.

Table 4.1 Fifteen-Month Child Health Check – Gordon received 'Yes' or 'No' ticks to the following questions

	YES	NO
Can your child…		
copy or repeat simple words or sounds?	✓	
try to talk?	✓	
use their voice to get attention?	✓	
say two or three words?	✓	
Do they…		
point to people and things they know when asked to?		✓
understand things like 'come here'?		✓
listen when people talk?		✓

I have no idea whether these results fall within normal limits for a typical 15-month-old child as the Child Health Nurse gave no significance to his score on this simple evaluation. I do suspect, however, that this pattern may well accurately reflect the typical development of an ASD child.

When Gordon was 16 months old I felt strangely compelled to write four long pages of diary notes detailing his every bit of development. Writing diary notes about him had become a way for me to cope with a situation that I could not make sense of. An attempt to unscramble the confusion that was swirling around in my head:

...Keeping Gordon stimulated, entertained and happy is and has been a real challenge over the past 6–8 months, mainly since he became mobile. We have moved a lot of toys permanently into the lounge, but for the most part he is not interested in them...Gordon does not initiate getting into his toys, but will play with a toy if initiated by an adult – e.g. stacking rings, pull along toys, barrels. He likes to play with the TV buttons – the on/off, volume and channels buttons, but this can be a real pain! (Diary notes – Gordon at 16 months)

Gordon was 23 months old when I gave birth to my third child, a boy named Sean. However, to a large extent my experience with Gordon had left me with a loss of confidence in myself as a parent – to boys. (I and everybody else figured that his gender must have been in some part contributing to my so-called parenting difficulties with him, as my daughter Kiara was doing absolutely fine.) Subsequently, I enrolled Sean and myself in the Parents As First Teachers (PAFT 2005) programme. I knew that somehow I was failing Gordon and I didn't want this to happen with my third child. I hoped that this programme would give me some advice on how to be a better mother to Sean, and perhaps to Gordon.

At home, things went from bad to worse. The amount of videos he was watching had become excessive and his behaviour sometimes unmanageable. There were tantrums happening every day, often for reasons I could not understand. His most extreme frustration had resulted in him headbanging the walls or the floor. While this only happened a few times, when it did I felt utterly heartbroken. I wanted to do anything that would prevent him suffering this much. This wasn't attention-seeking behaviour. In fact, he didn't care whether I was watching him or not. So, for as much as possible, I had resorted to giving him whatever he wanted. And mostly what he wanted was videos. From the time that he woke up until the time that he went to bed, Gordon's preferred choice of activity was watching videos. On the positive side, videos promoted his language skills. He learned many of the names of the characters in his videos and could label them accordingly.

I was constantly aware of the need to get Gordon out of the house, primarily motivated by the need to get him away from the 'dreaded' videos and towards a place where he would occupy his time more productively. With a newborn baby to juggle at the same time, this was not easy. It had to be a venue where I could get safely from the car to the building without risk of losing Gordon, who was liable to run in the opposite direction and never obey any verbal instructions. Simple things like 'come here' or 'stop' didn't work. I often had to physically pick him up when I wanted him to do things 'my' way.

It was not uncommon to see me with one arm pushing Sean in the buggy, and one arm holding Gordon, who might be tantrumming at the time. Going to an unfenced park by myself with the two boys was sometimes akin to giving Gordon a ticket to the hospital emergency department because he was likely to run out onto the road if I was not within arm's reach of stopping him. Similarly, going to a shopping mall was only worthwhile if I didn't want to actually achieve anything myself. I learned to ignore the rude comments and glances of other shoppers while I struggled with his tantrums, which could occur for the simplest of non-compliance issues, like not going in the direction he wanted to.

Things were a bit more manageable when we went out to a fully enclosed building or playgroup (one where he couldn't escape) and preferably one where there were no demands placed on children by other adults. In other words, informal and unstructured activities like playgroups were 'in' and formal and structured venues like childcare, private kindergarten and pre-school sporting activities were 'out'. In any case, I had pretty much figured out the best way on how I (or any adult for that matter) should be with Gordon and this involved following him around (wherever he wanted to go) and talking to him as much as I could. That was how things worked best between us.

One of my most distinct memories is of talking to him while he was drawing on a chalkboard at a local playgroup. I can still vividly remember the conscious realization that not only did I now not expect Gordon to reply to me when I spoke to him, I now didn't even expect him to look at me. Nevertheless, I resolved to keep following him around and to keep talking to him. And so I did. I talked and talked. The more I talked to him, the sooner this struggle with communication would all be over. Eventually, I assured myself, we would stop having these non-stop, all day long, one-sided conversations.

At this point I still attributed a lot of the unease I felt about Gordon's development to my perceived poor parenting skills (unable to identify the problem, I was blaming myself), but I was also blaming government policy for allowing children like Gordon (I figured that there must be more children out there like him – somewhere) to 'fall through the cracks'. I felt that Gordon was not getting an adequate early childhood education. He certainly wasn't getting it with me (and the videos at home) and he wasn't getting it out in the community either. His inability to participate properly at structured activities and my lack of confidence with him in public had in effect left us more socially isolated.

Society expected parents to be fully equipped to develop, care for and educate their children, but in Gordon's case I was not equipped. However, neither was any place within the early childhood industry, which I had thoroughly exhausted in my search to help him. While medical science recognized the critical importance of the first three years of development, it did not seem to be matched in terms of any effective systems or processes to ensure that the mental health and development of our 0–3 year olds was on track.

In June 2002, I took Gordon to the Child Health Nurse for his Two-Year Child Health Check (Table 4.2). He was two years and two months old at this appointment. I was desperately eager to talk to an 'expert' about his language development. At this stage he had quite a few words, although unfortunately I have no record of how many. The Child Health Nurse recorded in Gordon's book: 'Not speaking in simple sentences. Single words only' (Two-Year Child Health Check). Additionally, under the checklist 'Can your child hear well?' (my translation: 'Can your child communicate well?'), Gordon now only received two 'Yes' ticks, from a total of eight questions: a 25 per cent pass rate.

Table 4.2 Two-Year Child Health Check – Gordon received 'Yes' or 'No' ticks to the following questions

	YES	NO
Do they…		
know lots of words?	✓	
like being read to?	✓	
Do they…		
do two things when asked, like 'get the ball'?		✓
repeat what you say?		✓
point to a picture when asked, e.g. 'show me the baby'?		✓
use the name for themselves?		✓
use the names of people and things they know?		✓
have a name for themselves?		✓
say simple sentences like 'milk all gone'?		✓

However, the Child Health Nurse treated neither the results above nor my expressed concerns regarding his delayed language development with any seriousness whatsoever. Her quick and casual feedback was that speech and language therapy didn't start until children were three years old anyway, so there was nothing to do until then! Her comments were recorded as 'Review speech at next appointment'. The next scheduled Child Health Check would have been ten months later, when he was three years old.

In July 2002, during a visit with the GP, Gordon's behaviour was as usual difficult. He was doing what he always did at other places. Touching everything that he shouldn't (like the doctor's equipment) and nothing that he should (like the toys in the basket), and never listening to a thing I said. He didn't respond to me when I said, 'don't touch' or 'get down'. So, finally, I spoke out, though not with any predetermined objective; it was simply from the sheer frustration, desperation and embarrassment of that moment (and all the others before it): 'Gordon just never does what I tell him. He doesn't listen. He doesn't obey commands.' The GP listened to me and took this seriously. It was from this point on that the formal process of diagnosis and professional involvement began.

Process of diagnosis

My 'accidental' comments at the GP's office had resulted in her advising that Gordon have his hearing tested and, failing that (if no hearing problem was identified), to consider the possibility of attention deficit/hyperactivity disorder (ADHD). One month later, two different hearing tests had confirmed that his hearing was normal, and my research on ADHD had concluded that that didn't fit either, so in my confusion I once again turned to my diary notes and wrote my last description of him prior to his diagnosis of autism, which came two months later. Unknown to me at the time, my notes that night would almost precisely match the description of autism as it is applied to diagnosis in early childhood:

> Gordon's development is of concern to me. Of most concern is his speech and language. He rarely speaks and if does, only says one (single) words – nouns/objects – e.g., fish, horse, etc. He doesn't often respond when being spoken to, not even with eye contact – but we are working on this. He does not 'engage' in communication – or very minimal. (Diary note – Gordon at two years four months)

While the formal process of diagnosis commenced when Gordon was aged 2.3 years at the GP's office with her acknowledgement of a problem, the real process of diagnosis spans his entire life up until that point. For over two years nobody else could see, let alone identify, the problem; the subtle differences that were apparent to me when he was a newborn baby and had increased over the next two years. Although I was often confused about our connection, as well as my inability to teach him or to manage his behaviour, I constantly adjusted my own thought processes in response to other people's opinions and reactions; all people that I trusted, ranging from my husband, to my friends, family and various professionals within the community.

I believe that Gordon's example clearly demonstrates that existing New Zealand health policy has plenty of scope for improvement in regard to mental health services in early childhood. At 14 months I had directly asked my GP if Gordon had autism and this had failed to be identified at this point. Child Health Checks at 15 months and 2.2 years had shown his hearing and hence communicative development to be initially veering off track, and subsequently severely off track. But the Child Health professionals charged with the interpretation of these important, indeed crucial, screening devices had failed to correctly interpret their results. (In fact, their attitudes had reflected no cause for concern whatsoever.) It was not until Gordon was 2.3 years old that professionals within the health and then education systems finally acknowledged the existence of a 'problem', albeit defined incorrectly initially. In essence, the 'formal' process of diagnosis was preceded by a much longer informal and formal process of both misdiagnosis and failure to diagnose (Table 4.3).

Events leading up to the ABA programme

Finding my way to ABA was relatively straightforward, compared to the process of diagnosis. I had already visited Autism New Zealand one month prior to our appointment with the paediatrician and had received a standard Parent Pack. (My telephone conversation with an Early Intervention Teacher from Group Special Education in September had suggested that we consider autistic spectrum disorder and my Internet search that evening had confirmed that her suggestion was almost certainly correct.) Inside the Parent Pack was a huge amount of information about autism and what could be done. But there was one thing that impressed me the most and that was an extract by Temple Grandin titled 'Teaching tips for children and adults with autism' talking about the necessity of good teaching in early childhood. It became quickly evident that early intervention was the key to success.

Table 4.3 Process of diagnosis

Gordon's age	Month	Status
2 years, 3 months	July	Advised by GP to get hearing tested and to consider ADHD.
		Pre-school teacher agreed that Gordon should have hearing tested and suggested that the teachers do written observations and get Group Special Education (GSE) to assess if still concerned.
2 years, 4 months	August	Two different hearing assessments showed that Gordon's hearing was normal. Both recommended speech language therapy (SLT) assessments.
		Judith lodged self-referral for SLT screening assessment with GSE.
	September	Parents As First Teachers (PAFT) teacher visited the home for younger sibling. After observing Judith's attempts to manage Gordon's behaviour and subsequently become very upset she advised that 'something is wrong' (with Gordon) and recommended contacting GSE.
2 years, 5 months	September	Judith phoned GSE and spoke to an Early Intervention Teacher (EIT). The EIT suggested that they consider autistic spectrum disorder. Judith was advised to contact a paediatrician, and Autism NZ, and to attend the screening assessment with GSE.
2 years, 6 months	October	Screening assessment with GSE. The report described Gordon as '…presenting with significant communication challenges. His development is not typical of his peers and presents as a disorder rather than a delay.'
		One and a half hour appointment with the paediatrician. Received diagnosis of autism. No in-depth assessment given, no advice for intervention and no information of prognosis. They were referred to Autism NZ and to GSE.
2 years, 11 months	March	Received second appointment with paediatrician.

I was now on a race against time to get Gordon help and to get it quickly. Although I had digested the Parent Pack fairly quickly, the information on the Internet was overwhelming. With all of the therapies available and the organizations administering them, there seemed to be no end to the job ahead. I made myself a lengthy 'to do' list the day after his diagnosis, which at that point was in no particular order in terms of priority of effectiveness. At this point it was impossible to know what help was the most important and how to tie everything together. A lot of hours were spent acquiring information – on the telephone, the Internet, and reading. Talking to professionals suddenly became a big part of my life in trying to unravel the best way forward for Gordon.

The last thing on my 'to do' list was 'investigate private autism pre-schools'. Not that I knew if any actually existed! In other words, I wanted to find people who knew how to teach kids with autism. I hadn't heard about ABA or the concept of a home programme at that point. I referred back to my Parent Pack and went searching for anything to do with teaching ASD pre-schoolers. One of the most impressive brochures was from an organization called CARD (Center for Autism and Related Disorders). The next day, I phoned their Auckland office. Erika answered that first phone call and she has been in constant contact with our family ever since.

Gordon started his ABA home programme six weeks later. When CARD started working with him on 9 December 2002, he had an excellent programme, an excellent programmer and an excellent therapist. It was as if an angel had fallen straight from heaven into the palm of our family hand. The torturous existence of raising a child with autism alone and without support had come to an end and finally we had what I had thought previously to be non-existent – we had help to teach Gordon.

Because Gordon's autism had manifested itself in my mind as an inability to learn in the way that normal children did, I was instinctively desperate for someone or something that could teach him in a way that he responded to. I had never felt that he couldn't learn; in fact in some ways he was extra smart. For example, he could identify all of the various species of animals depicted in the visually taught Reading Master program (The Parent Company 1997), and even sight-read almost all of the words. He could do interlocking puzzles, he liked going on the computer (to watch the Reading Master on CD-ROM!). He did have some interests and abilities.

Up until this point I had relied on advice from staff at the Autism Auckland office to help me with the questions that arose as I had navigated my way around the autism and special needs industry. It was not until I attended an introductory talk on the UK National Autistic Society (NAS) EarlyBird course in the November, just prior to him starting his already organized ABA programme, that I met other parents of children with autism. While there, one mum gave me the most valuable piece of advice that I ever got – to read a book called *Let Me Hear Your Voice* by Catherine Maurice (1993).

Well, that book became my hope, my dreams, and my guidebook on implementing an ABA home programme, all in one. If I had one 'ray of light' in this dark time, this was it. Just looking at that book reminded me how positive Gordon's future could become. Although I have never met Catherine Maurice, she did more for me (and Gordon, of course) than our entire public medical or educational system put together at that point. It was her who beautifully illustrated how incredibly successful ABA could be – by demonstrating how effective and powerful the tools of modelling, prompting and reinforcement could be when applied correctly and consistently to a child's programme in the natural environment. Life was, after all, filled with learning opportunities and Gordon's life was about to turn into one big therapy session. For as much as possible, I would use the language in his ABA programme and apply it as natural teaching opportunities arose.

Part 2 – Erika (CARD Supervisor)

The intervention model

The intervention programme received by Gordon was based on that recommended by CARD. With an ABA foundation, his therapy consisted of both discrete-trial training and natural environment training, taking place primarily within the home setting. At treatment initiation, Gordon's therapy took place in his bedroom and was conducted at both the table and on the floor. Generalization training took place around the house and in the garden. While a minimum of 20 hours per week of therapy was recommended by CARD, Gordon received between 10 and 15 hours of therapy per week during the first two years of intervention. Therapy sessions were two to three hours in duration and clinic meetings were conducted on average every two weeks. Clinic meetings provided an opportunity for Gordon, his mother and his team of therapists to meet with the programme supervisor to update and troubleshoot the programme.

Curriculum content

The CARD curriculum is comprised of eight content areas that have been thoroughly researched and are based on typical child development. Each child's programme is individualized to their particular strengths and weaknesses. The content areas include: language, play, theory of mind, social skills, executive functioning, self-help, motor skills and school skills (see Figure 4.1).

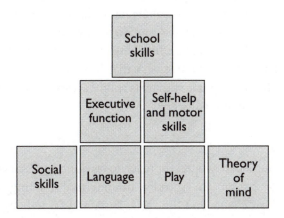

Figure 4.1: The CARD curriculum content areas

While Gordon's programme has included aspects from each curriculum area, the primary concern for Gordon's parents was his delay in language development and this will be the focus of the chapter.

Language curriculum

Initially, ABA language programmes for children with autism were based on a linguistic model, divided into the sections of 'receptive' and 'expressive' language. In curricula that use this type of framework it is common to teach the child to hand over an object when presented with the instruction 'give me (object)' or to respond vocally with the name of the object '(object)' when shown the object and asked 'what is it?'. It is easy to assume that when a child can identify an item both receptively and expressively, they have learned the 'meaning' of the word and will use it in many contexts without further training. With many children on the autism spectrum this is not the case. Teaching a child to receptively and expressively identify 'cookie', for example, does not mean that the child will now be able to respond given other antecedent conditions. In other words, there is no guarantee that when he is hungry/wants a cookie, and there's no cookie to be seen, he will respond appropriately when asked 'what do you like to eat?'. Similarly, it is not inevitable that when he sees a cookie, he'll point and say 'cookie'. It is therefore necessary to go beyond the receptive/expressive framework and analyse language according to function. In his 1957 book B.F. Skinner provided a functional analysis of verbal behaviour that extended operant conditioning to verbal behaviour. In this analysis Skinner classifies language according to its functional properties and the environmental variables under which responses occur. Table 4.4 provides a brief description of how language can be classified from a behavioural perspective (Sundberg and Partington 1998). CARD employs a verbal behaviour framework that is designed to ensure that each programme of the language curriculum is taught across all the language repertoires or functions described below.

Type of training

When considering a behavioural approach to teaching children with autism, it is common for people to consider discrete-trial training and applied behaviour analysis as one and the same. Discrete-trial training, however, is only one of many empirically validated behaviour analytic procedures that should be incorporated into a comprehensive programme (Sundberg and Partington 1998). Discrete-trial training (DTT) in this context involves teaching language in highly structured teaching environments. Discrete-trial training involves one-on-one direct instruction, where the stimulus items used for a particular task are chosen by the teacher. Complex skills and behaviours are taught by breaking the skill into its smaller subcomponents. DTT has been shown to be extremely effective (Lovaas 1987; Smith 2001).

Once the individual components have been acquired they are chained together to form the more complex target behaviour. DTT often involves the repetition of a target skill until the mastery criterion is met. DTT allows many learning opportunities within a teaching session and is an integral part of teaching basic compliance and communication skills. However, it does have its limitations and should be supplemented with other procedures. Specifically, DTT is primarily teacher directed and the reinforcers used to increase target behaviours are unrelated to the response, making generalization to natural contingencies unlikely without specific training. Natural environment training (NET) is a behavioural approach that has also been identified as an effective teaching method (Delprato 2001; Hart and Risley 1975; O'Dell and Koegel 1987; Koegel, McGee, Krantz and McClannahan 1985). The

Table 4.4 The behavioural classification of language

Verbal operant	Description	Example
Echoic	Repeating what is heard	Mum says 'Cookie' Child says 'Cookie' Mum says 'Fantastic'
Mand	Asking for reinforcers (preferred items) A request	Child is hungry Child says 'Cookie' Child gets cookie
Tact	Naming or identifying objects, actions, events etc.	Child sees a cookie Child says 'Cookie' Mum says 'That's right'
Intraverbal	Answering questions or conversations where your words are controlled by other words	Mum says 'What's your favourite food?' Child says 'Cookie' Mum says 'Yum, me too'
Receptive	Following instructions or complying with the requests (mands) of others	Mum says 'Give me the cookie' Child gives the cookie Mum says 'Thank you'
RFFC (Receptive by feature, function or class)	Identifying specific items when given some description of that item	Mum says 'What do you eat?' Child says 'Cookie'

teaching sessions are more loosely structured in comparison to that of DTT. The sessions are conducted in the child's typical environment and are directed by the child who initiates a teaching opportunity by indicating a particular need or want. Natural environment training has the advantage of utilizing the child's motivation in the teaching process and minimizes the requirement for generalization training (Sundberg and Partington 1998). However, the acquisition rate may be slower due to the reduced number of training opportunities and specific targets can only be taught if they arise within the natural environment. Any language programme for children with autism should involve a combination of the two procedures. The type of instruction that takes place will depend on the skill being taught, with manding (requests) and more complex skills such as emotions or problem solving being taught using NET. Discrete-trial training was used in the initial stages of Gordon's programme (with the exception of manding) and gradually gave way to natural environment training as he progressed to more complex skills.

Applied behaviour analysis and Gordon

At two years seven months of age Gordon was seen at the Center for Autism and Related Disorders (NZ) Ltd for an intake assessment. At this point in time, Gordon would not consistently imitate sounds or words, demonstrating a weak echoic repertoire. Additionally, Gordon did not engage in appropriate manding for desired items or information. That is, he would not request vocally for his needs and wants. Much of Gordon's maladaptive behaviour in the form of tantrums (yelling and crying) functioned as inappropriate mands. Gordon's receptive language (non-verbally following the instructions of others) was also delayed. During assessment, Gordon would not receptively identify an object upon hearing the instruction 'give me (object)'; however, he was observed to receptively identify some colours and shapes. Gordon's tact repertoire was the strongest, with a vocabulary of approximately 50 words at intake. However, many of these words were related to videos and were not used in context. He did not tact actions, adjectives or prepositions. Gordon was not able to correctly point to an item when it was described by its feature, function or class and presented with deficits in intraverbal skills, demonstrated by his inability to respond vocally to conversational questions. Gordon had been observed to imitate a specific action (gross motor) sequence learned from a video; however, he did not consistently imitate the actions of others at the initial intake. Gordon could independently complete interlocking and inset puzzles, thus exhibiting elementary matching-to-sample skills. At intake, he would not comply with requests to match three-dimensional objects to samples of those objects.

At time of writing Gordon had received two years of ABA intervention that focused on systematically teaching each of these verbal deficits. An exhaustive review of each of these programmes is beyond the scope of this chapter; however, the following section describes several of Gordon's programmes in relation to each of the verbal operants or functions of language, described in Table 4.4. Figure 4.2 provides an overview of the sequence in which skills were taught. Most programmes within the curriculum teach each

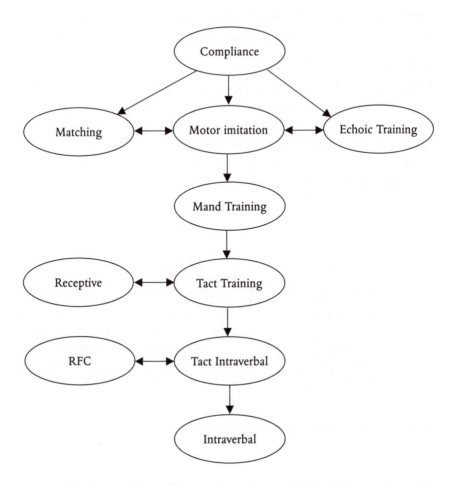

Figure 4.2: Skill development hierarchy

of the functions of language (e.g. echoic, mand, tact and intraverbal). Within some programmes the functions of language are taught concurrently, while in others they are taught sequentially in the order represented by the arrows. Compliance, matching and motor imitation are early learner skills that are a prerequisite to more advanced learning such as speech, play, self-help, fine and gross motor skills, and social skills. An echoic repertoire or verbal imitation is a prerequisite to mand training if the responses are to be vocal (as they were with Gordon). If, however, the child is unable to imitate and an alternative response form, such as picture exchange communication, were to be used for requesting, then echoic training (verbal imitation) is not a prerequisite.

COMPLIANCE

The first target within Gordon's programme was the development of compliance to simple instructions. During baseline, Gordon did not respond to simple instructions such as 'come here' and 'sit down'. Additionally, he engaged in inappropriate behaviour such as crying or screaming when such a demand was placed on him. This skill was targeted via discrete-trial training as represented visually in Figure 4.3.

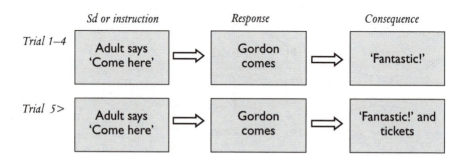

Figure 4.3: Sequence of steps in early DTT for compliance

A discrete trial can be thought of as a teaching sequence that consists of three components: an Sd (discriminative stimulus), a response and a consequence. The Sd is any stimulus (either non-verbal or verbal) that precedes a response. This may be in the form of an instruction, question or a gesture or it may be simply the presence of an item, activity or picture. The response is the child's behaviour following the Sd and the consequence is feedback for the child based on their response. In Figure 4.3, the consequence box represents the positive reinforcement provided to Gordon following a correct response. A reinforcer is any stimulus or event that follows the behaviour and increases the future frequency of that behaviour. It is one of the most widely used principles of behaviour (Cooper, Heron and Heward 1987). The selection of potential reinforcers (such as bubbles or tickles for Gordon) was achieved by asking Gordon's parents what were his preferred activities, by observing Gordon's choice of activities during his free time, presenting him with a choice of objects or activities, and by constantly sampling or exposing Gordon to novel items, noting which ones were preferred and making future presentations contingent upon the target behaviour.

The first target within the compliance programme was to teach Gordon to respond to simple instructions. The therapist presented the instruction 'come here' and during the first three trials physically prompted Gordon to respond by gently taking his hand and guiding him in the right direction. Following these 'prompted trials', reinforcement such as verbal praise was delivered. After the fourth trial the therapist probed to see if Gordon could respond independently; following a correct response, a higher level of reinforcement (verbal praise and tickles) was delivered. Over a number of sessions, the distance between Gordon and the therapist was systematically increased. Additionally, generalization training took place with other family members and within other locations around the house (e.g. kitchen, lounge, outside and between rooms). Once Gordon responded independently, an 'error correc-tion' procedure was used following a non-response or incorrect response. The error correction procedure provides the child with feedback on their response in the form of a mild 'informational' 'No'. After two non-responses or incorrect responses a prompt is given in order that the child experiences success. Once 'come here' had reached the mastery criteria of 90–100 per cent (i.e. once he had shown that he could respond correctly with an accuracy of 90–100%) over three consecutive sessions, 'come here' was maintained throughout every session and a new target 'sit down' was introduced.

MATCHING

Matching identical and similar objects and pictures is a fundamental skill that enables the child to attend to visual stimuli and to identify the similarities and differences between objects and events. The ability to classify objects by how they look, their functions or their category can provide a foundation for future language training. Gordon exhibited elementary matching-to-sample skills as demonstrated by his ability to complete simple puzzles. Non-compliance prior to intake had prevented further assessment of this developmental area. Matching was introduced into Gordon's programme once compliance to the instruction 'come here' and 'sit down' was established. Within this pro-gramme Gordon was taught to match identical and similar object-to-object, picture-to-picture, picture-to-object and object-to-picture respectively. Matching was taught using discrete-trial training (see Figure 4.4).

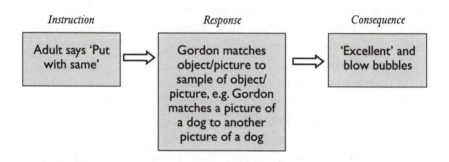

Figure 4.4: Sequence of steps in matching training

As with all programmes, one target was introduced at a time. Once mastery criteria of 90–100 per cent over two consecutive sessions were achieved a new target was introduced. Generalization probes were conducted throughout and teaching continued until Gordon could match novel stimuli at an accuracy of 90–100 per cent without prior instruction. Generalization probes involve the therapist periodically presenting untaught items to assess whether the child has mastered the concept or whether or not further teaching is required. Matching was also targeted within a number of other programmes such as categories, letters, numbers and emotions. For example, Gordon was not only taught to match similar objects within the objects labels programme but he was taught to match and sort items from within various category groups (e.g. animals, vehicles etc.) prior to moving on to more complex labelling (tacting) and questions related to categorization. Additionally, Gordon learned to match upper to lower case letters and to match faces depicting the same emotions (e.g. happy faces versus sad faces) prior to moving on to more advanced skills within these programmes.

MOTOR IMITATION

Imitation is an essential prerequisite to learning a variety of important skills. The development of an imitative repertoire helps to facilitate play skills, self-help, fine motor skills (small precise movements), gross motor skills (large, general movements), and social interaction. Through the imitation programme, Gordon learned to imitate object manipulation, gross and fine motor movements and multiple step action chains (see example below). Initial teaching was conducted using discrete trials and subsequently generalized within the play setting. The teaching sequence used to teach imitation is depicted in Figure 4.5.

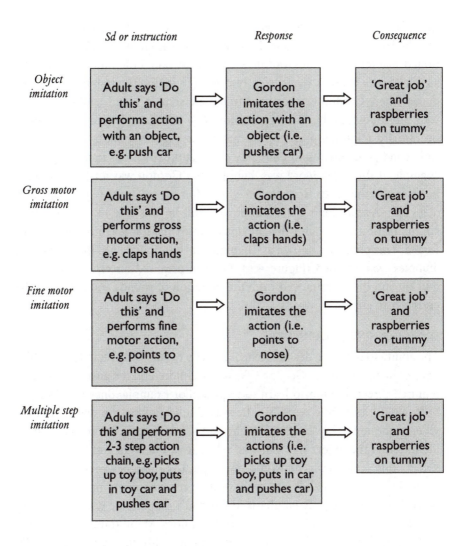

	Sd or instruction	*Response*	*Consequence*
Object imitation	Adult says 'Do this' and performs action with an object, e.g. push car	Gordon imitates the action with an object (i.e. pushes car)	'Great job' and raspberries on tummy
Gross motor imitation	Adult says 'Do this' and performs gross motor action, e.g. claps hands	Gordon imitates the action (i.e. claps hands)	'Great job' and raspberries on tummy
Fine motor imitation	Adult says 'Do this' and performs fine motor action, e.g. points to nose	Gordon imitates the action (i.e. points to nose)	'Great job' and raspberries on tummy
Multiple step imitation	Adult says 'Do this' and performs 2-3 step action chain, e.g. picks up toy boy, puts in toy car and pushes car	Gordon imitates the actions (i.e. picks up toy boy, puts in car and pushes car)	'Great job' and raspberries on tummy

Figure 4.5: Sequence of steps in imitation traininge

ECHOIC TRAINING

A child's ability to repeat the sounds and words of another person is central to the development of vocal communication. In order to increase the frequency of vocal behaviour a pairing procedure was utilized throughout initial therapy sessions. Therapists paired reinforcers with their own vocalizations so that the vocalizations would become conditioned reinforcers for Gordon. That is, if Gordon were to emit a new vocalization accidentally, it should have functioned as its own reinforcer and thus there would be an increase in the likelihood of it occurring again. For example, it was known that bubbles functioned as a reinforcer for Gordon, so therapists said 'buh, buh' and immediately blew the bubbles. Concurrently, a vocal imitation programme was introduced where Gordon was required to imitate sounds, blends and chains that were already within his vocal repertoire. New sounds and words were taught by initially reinforcing an approximation or slight variation on the target sound and gradually reinforcing only closer approximations to the target. For example, if the target word was 'bubbles' but Gordon was unable to imitate bubbles, the therapists first reinforced Gordon for the closest approximation (e.g. 'bu'). As Gordon's speech improved and he was able to imitate a new approximation (e.g. 'bub') the previous approximation was no longer reinforced. This process is known as 'shaping' and continued until the final target 'bubbles' was reached (Figure 4.6). Gordon acquired an echoic repertoire quickly and the focus moved from the imitation of sounds and chains to the correct articulation of words.

MAND TRAINING (REQUESTING)

The ability to request a desired item or activity occurs early on in typical child development. However, Gordon (like many children on the autism spectrum) required direct training to learn to request. For example, once Gordon had been taught an echoic repertoire he was able to imitate the word 'bubbles' when requested to say 'bubbles' and he had a small tact repertoire so he could identify that the object was 'bubbles' when it was held up and he was asked 'what's this?'. However, he would not request the bubbles vocally when he wanted them. This inability to request often resulted in crying and tantrum behaviour and thus early emphasis in Gordon's programme was on teaching mands (requests) for desired objects and activities. Mand training continued throughout the first two years of treatment, with the targets gradually becoming more complex. Mands are taught using natural environment training (NET) and involve contriving 'establishing operations' (i.e. creating a situation that is likely to result in the child wanting a particular object or wanting to engage in a particular action). To begin teaching Gordon to ask (mand) for bubbles the therapists would tempt Gordon with the bubbles by blowing them once and when it was obvious that Gordon wanted them again (e.g. he reached for them) the therapists would use an echoic prompt 'bubbles'. When Gordon repeated the word 'bubbles' (or an approximation of the word if the word was difficult) the therapists would blow the bubbles. Over several

	Sd or instruction		Response		Consequence

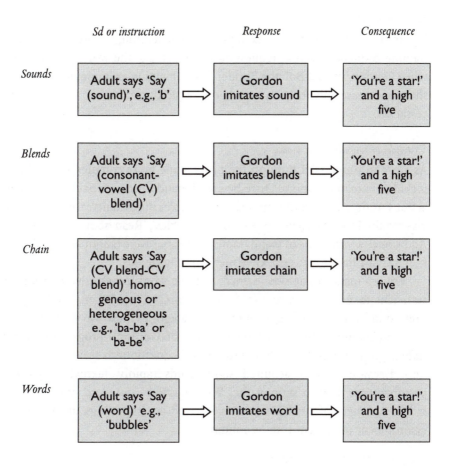

Figure 4.6: Sequence of steps in echoic training

sessions the therapists were able to fade the echoic prompt by using a delay, whereby they paused to give Gordon an opportunity to respond independently. If Gordon did not respond within three seconds, they would prompt with the beginning sound of the word. If Gordon still did not respond within three seconds a full echoic prompt was used. The targets used within mand training varied within and between sessions, with the therapists using whatever objects and activities were reinforcing for Gordon that day. Data were taken on the rate of requests per session that were prompted and the number of requests that were independent.

Example of early mands

Figure 4.7 demonstrates an example of each teaching phase in the early training of mands, such as requesting an object, e.g. the word spoken 'Bob' when Gordon wanted Bob the Builder. The remaining examples in Figure 4.7 show one phase only for early mands, e.g. requesting an action, assistance and cessation.

Examples of more complex mands

As Gordon progressed through the programme more complex targets were included in mand training. Once he could mand for a variety of objects and actions using a one-word response, the complexity was increased so that he was required to use two words, e.g. 'Blow bubbles', 'Read book', 'Open door'. Additionally, variations of mand frames or phrases were taught such as 'I want (__)', 'Can I have (__)', and 'Give me (__)' (Figure 4.8).

Once a mand frame was learned, a single word response was no longer sufficient to gain access to the desired item/activity. When Gordon progressed to learning colours, attributes and categories these too were included in mand training. During the second year of Gordon's programme mand training was utilized to teach him to ask 'Wh' questions to seek out information. Because Gordon acquired sight words rapidly, textual or written prompts were used to prompt the 'Wh' questions and were systematically faded. A variety of situations were contrived across settings in the natural environment to prevent rote responding.

TACT TRAINING (COMMENTING)

While Gordon had approximately 50 labels in his repertoire at intake, these were not typically used in context and because he did not demonstrate joint attention his tacting (commenting) was not used as a means of social interaction or for the sharing of information. Most of the tacting programmes began by teaching Gordon to respond to a verbal question such as 'what is it?' within the object labels programme, 'what colour?' within the colours programme, 'where is it?' within the prepositions programme, or 'what's happening?' within the actions programme. Once Gordon was able to respond to a particular question, the goal was to fade the question and have him spontaneously comment in the presence of the object/item/picture. Figure 4.9 demonstrates the procedure for teaching tacting (commenting). The fading procedures took place over a number of trials and with more complex programmes over a number of sessions.

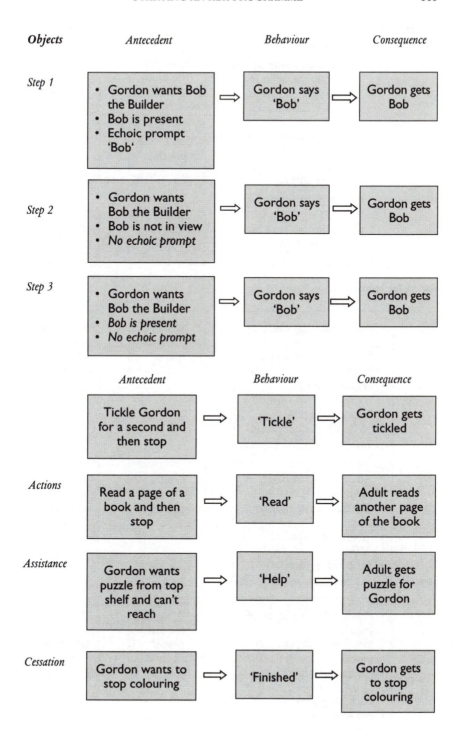

Figure 4.7: Sequence of steps in early mand training

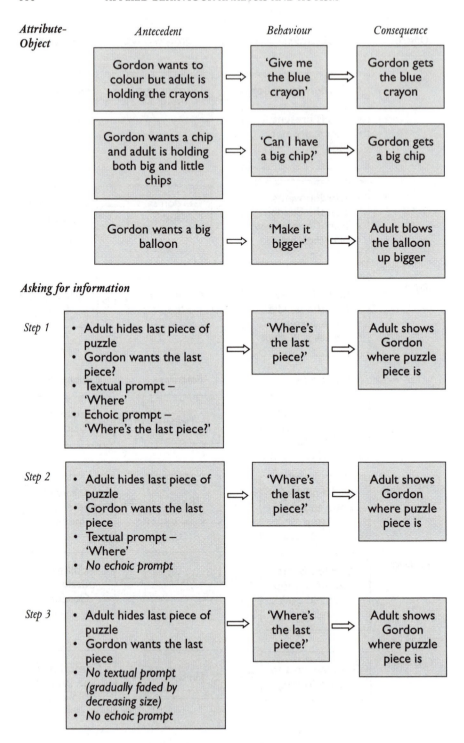

Figure 4.8: Sequence of steps in more complex mand training

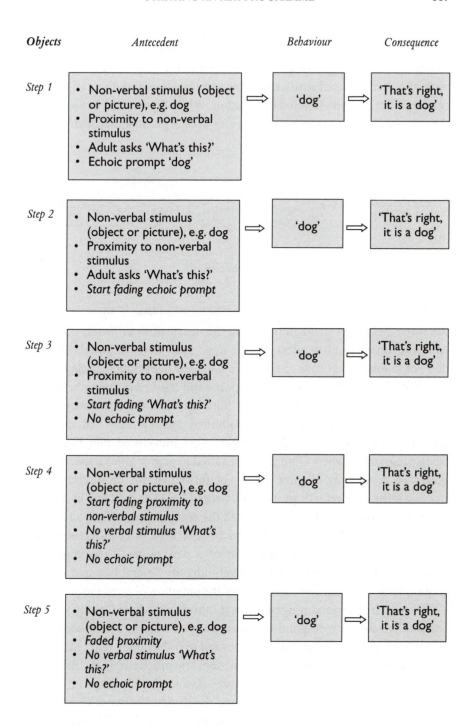

Figure 4.9: Sequence of steps in early tact training

Data were taken throughout on the level of prompting required and the rate of independent and prompted tacts per session. Once Gordon was consistently tacting (commenting) using one-word responses, the complexity of his responses was increased until he was able to integrate and combine all of those concepts that he had mastered in isolation. While Figure 4.10 demonstrates the same example increasing in complexity, at each phase stimuli were rotated to prevent rote responding.

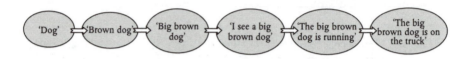

Figure 4.10: Sequence of steps in more complex tact training

RECEPTIVE/RECEPTIVE BY FEATURE, FUNCTION AND CLASS (FFC)

Receptive behaviour involves following the instructions or mands of others. At intake, instructions to select specific items (e.g. 'Give me book', 'Point to dog') or follow instructions to engage in a specific behaviour (e.g. clap hands, sit down) did not produce a correct response and resulted in crying behaviour when a response was prompted. Once initial compliance to the instructions 'come here' and 'sit down' was established and Gordon had mastered matching identical objects, these objects were introduced into the object labels programme, where Gordon was required to give or touch a specific item presented in an array of three items. For further details on discrimination training techniques refer to an article by Green (2001) on advances in stimulus control technology. As Gordon acquired the receptive identification of each new object, generalization was checked across at least three different objects and pictures prior to the introduction of a new target. This programme continued until Gordon could receptively identify several hundred objects. Additionally, once Gordon had mastered the imitation of gross motor actions a 'following instructions' programme was introduced where Gordon was systematically taught to respond to instructions to engage in one-step gross motor actions, two-step action sequences and to follow one-, two-, three- and four-step functional instructions. Functional instructions (e.g. 'Bring me shoes', 'Get the book', 'Give to mummy', 'Go to (location)') were initially taught within one room of the house and the distance between Gordon and the object/location/person was systematically increased until he was able to move all around the house in order to follow the instructions. The more complex instructions incorporate concepts mastered within other programmes such as colours, attributes, prepositions and locations (Figure 4.11).

In addition to teaching Gordon to receptively identify objects by their label or the name of the object it was necessary to teach him to identify the object by one of its features, its function or its class (category). A variety of individual programmes such as colours, function, categories and actions included components that targeted this skill. Figure 4.12 demonstrates the describe programme which taught Gordon to identify an object when given three descriptors for that object.

TACT-INTRAVERBAL AND INTRAVERBAL TRAINING

An intraverbal repertoire is essential for social interaction and engaging in conversation. It allows us to talk about things that are absent. The intraverbal repertoire is often the most difficult with children on the autism spectrum to acquire (Sundberg and Partington 1998). It is important that this repertoire is not taught until the child has acquired an extensive mand, tact and receptive repertoire. If intraverbal programmes are introduced before the child is ready, there is the risk that this repertoire will become rote and therefore not functional to the child. When teaching intraverbal behaviour it is common to prompt a response by presenting the child with a non-verbal stimulus (e.g. picture of the response). This helps provide context and meaning to the response and reduces the likelihood of rote responding that may occur if only a verbal prompt is given. When a visual stimulus is used to prompt an intraverbal response this is called tact-intraverbal behaviour. Because Gordon exhibited a strong textual repertoire and acquired sightreading rapidly, textual prompts were also used to teach him intraverbal behaviour. Intraverbal programmes taught early on in Gordon's programme involved responding to questions such as 'What colour is a (object)?', 'What do you (action) with?', 'What is a (object)?', 'Tell me some (categories)?' and 'Where do you go to (action)?' Gradually more complex interactions were taught where Gordon was required to respond to personal information questions, reciprocate the statements made by others, and respond to other persons' statements with an appropriate question. By chaining individual programmes Gordon was taught how to maintain a conversation and stay on topic for an increasing number of exchanges. Initially, many of these programmes were taught in a structured setting and then generalized across people and to different environments. Figure 4.13 illustrates how most intraverbal targets were taught using a non-verbal stimulus.

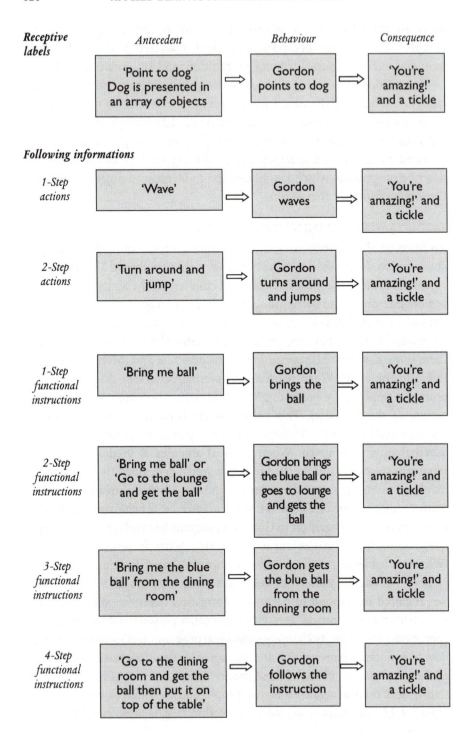

Figure 4.11: Sequence of steps in receptive and early receptive FFC training

Describe programme

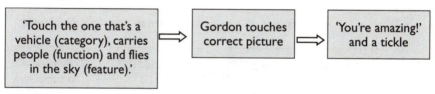

| 'Touch the one that's a vehicle (category), carries people (function) and flies in the sky (feature).' | ⟹ | Gordon touches correct picture | ⟹ | 'You're amazing!' and a tickle |

Figure 4.12: Sequence of steps in complex receptive FFC training

Two years down the track

At the time of writing Gordon was four years, nine months of age and had received two years of behavioural intervention. He had been attending kindergarten without support for 16 months and was expected to begin school without support within four months. He was cooperative with adults and would follow the kindergarten rules independently. He could sit and attend to an activity for extended periods of time. Gordon has a strong mand repertoire, using a variety of carrier phrases (e.g. 'I want…', 'Can I have…', 'Give me…' etc.) to request desired items, activities and information. Additionally, Gordon no longer exhibited excessive tantrum behaviour. Gordon demonstrates a large tact repertoire and comments spontaneously on his environment, often sharing information with his family and friends. He is curious about his environment and the people within it as demonstrated by the frequent asking of questions. Furthermore, Gordon now acquires new words and phrases from his natural environment without training. Gordon follows 3–4 step instructions presented at kindergarten and at home and can identify and describe a wide variety of items and actions according to their feature, function and class. His receptive and expressive language is appropriate for his age as demonstrated by his assessment results from the Pre-school Language Scale 4th Edition. This assessment was carried out in February 2004 when Gordon was three years ten months of age. At this point in time Gordon's age equivalence for auditory comprehension was four years one month (68th percentile), his age equivalence for expressive communication was three years eight months (47th percentile) and his total language age equivalence was three years ten months (61st percentile). Gordon interacts with his peers (both at kindergarten and during play dates at his home), has a 'best friend' and engages in group play. Gordon engages in age-appropriate functional pretend play, games with rules and socio-dramatic play. He is able to create and participate in play

Functions programme

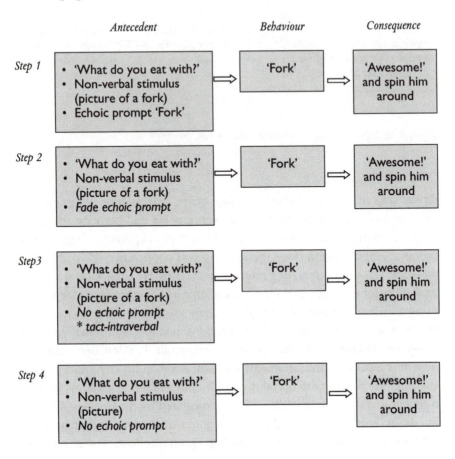

Figure 4.13: Sequence of steps in intraverbal training

scenarios that involve role-taking. Gordon understands and can explain cause and effect relationships and make inferences within the natural environment. He understands emotions and reads facial expressions and will respond to these appropriately. Gordon will hold a short conversation, maintaining the topic by making appropriate statements and asking questions. Conversation training, including the maintenance of longer conversations and topic initiation, is an ongoing target at the time of writing.

While Gordon has made excellent progress over the past two years there are several remaining areas of development yet to be addressed. Children with autism are frequently described as having a 'theory of mind' deficit or lacking the ability to identify the perspectives of others and respond appropriately. The next year of Gordon's programme will focus on the analysis of behaviours that may indicate a poor understanding of what other people 'know', their preferences, other people's 'beliefs' and 'false-beliefs', intentions and deception. Teaching strategies will be put in place to target these skills and progress measured by observing changes in Gordon's behaviour during social interactions. Many children diagnosed with an autism spectrum disorder present with deficits in executive functioning. Executive functioning refers to the skills mediated by the prefrontal cortex of the brain, including processes that underlie goal-directed behaviour. It includes a representation of the situation, objectives of the task (that is, the desired outcome), and the strategies or procedures to obtain the goal. Furthermore, it involves the ability to monitor progress towards goals and recognize when they have been achieved. Executive functions encompass a wide range of abilities, which include planning, organization, self-regulation, impulse control, and inhibition of pre-potent but incorrect responses, set maintenance and flexibility of thought and action. Future assessment will determine the need for programming within these areas.

Part 3 – Judith (Gordon's mum)
How Gordon's mum describes him now

Gordon is a very happy little boy who now enjoys a significantly improved quality of life compared to two years ago. His ability to experience and enjoy diverse and interesting environments has been one of the most significant improvements resulting from his increased language and cognitive skills. What I mean by this is that Gordon is now able to go out more because he is just easier to manage. In turn, this has resulted in a far better quality of life for him and also for every other member of our family. Family outings to friends' houses, the shopping mall, restaurants, the movies, the beach, and even boring stuff like the supermarket are now mostly (as much as three children allows!) an enjoyable experience for all of us. Our lives as parents have become a lot easier now that we can effectively manage Gordon (like our other children) through 'natural' language structures, and generally be 'in control' as opposed to 'being controlled' by difficult behavioural issues. Gordon is flexible, adaptable and generally easily able to be redirected.

At home, Gordon keeps himself occupied throughout the day using his own initiative. I no longer need to prompt him to engage him in an activity or

Figure 4.14: Gordon and Erika utilizing a textual prompt to assist Gordon with asking for information

in play – in fact, he now prompts me (or his sister/brother) to play with him! Nor do we need to leave the house in order to get him away from an obsession with videos and DVDs. He is too busy playing and enjoying life to be passively watching movies all the time! He loves to draw pictures – he is very age appropriate in this respect and he particularly loves drawing pictures of 'Spiderman' (he is currently mildly obsessed with Spiderman). In fact, the only thing he wanted for Christmas last year was 'a Spiderman costume. That's all mum. That's all I want!' He is able to write his first name, and will frequently ask me how to spell other people's names so that he can write them too. Gordon loves to play dress-ups, particularly in his Spiderman or Harry Potter costumes! He also enjoys playing computer games (he learns these with help from his sister), playing with his train set, creatively building animals from Lego, playing 'Snakes and Ladders' (he will cheat in order to win!), reading books, riding his bike, going to the park, watching movies (occasionally!) and all the normal stuff that four year olds do.

Has Gordon recovered from his autism? Is he normal? Aside from the lengthy issue of defining what is 'recovery' and what is 'normal', the honest answer to each of these questions is 'No'. While in many ways he can behave, appear and function 'normally', Gordon does still 'have' autism; there is still something essentially 'different' about him. At times, these differences are subtle, and at other times they are more obvious. Sometimes they are not present at all. In short, a massive transformation has taken place, which has resulted in him being a lot less autistic than he used to be and a lot more normal than before. He may not yet be fully recovered, but with the help of ABA, he is at least on the road to recovery. Prior to ABA Gordon spent a lot of time 'alone – in his own little world'. Thankfully, he is now very much 'with us – in our world'.

In socialization, while he has made huge progress, there still remains much work to be done. And it is exciting to see him beginning to embark on the CARD theory of mind and social pragmatics programmes to help him in this area. At times, he can and does appear indistinguishable from his peers, although this is often from a 'non-professional' point of view. His ability to hold a conversation very much depends on the complexity of language used and his interest in the topic at hand. His conversations with peers tend to consist of comments and questions pertaining to the 'here and now' – whether it be a play-based topic, or real life. In saying all of this, Gordon loves to play and interact with his siblings and with other children. He formed a genuine friendship with a (neurotypical) boy from his pre-school last year, and this extended to play dates at both of their houses, which have continued to this day.

One of the more interesting aspects of watching Gordon's development unfold through ABA has been observing just how much he does want, need, enjoy and even love socializing, despite his sometime differences in the appropriate pragmatics of this area. It is as much an intrinsic need in him as it is in 'normal' people. Our society, however, has yet to catch up with recognizing the value and critical importance of teaching socialization skills as being just as important as academics in determining quality of life and psychological well-being.

What Gordon's future has in store for him nobody knows. However, I do know one thing with absolute certainty. The outlook for his future is significantly more positive than what it might have been if he had not had ABA. Having witnessed on a daily basis the huge volume and precision of work involved in teaching him everything that otherwise comes naturally in typically developing children, I am astutely aware that he would not have achieved this massive accumulation of skills without an intensive ABA programme. ABA has been the 'connecting link' that enabled him to access his environment.

The highs and lows of managing an ABA programme

THE LOWS

The word 'low' is something that I would not associate with our ABA experience. However, a transformation of this magnitude does come with some 'costs', 'challenges' and 'sacrifices' so I'll stick to these as more accurately representing the difficulties encountered on our journey.

Our family was very fortunate to have a significant portion of Gordon's ABA therapy funded by the Ministry of Health through the needs assessment service. While the NZ government does not formally recognize ABA as the most effective intervention for autism (despite it being recognized as so in medical textbooks and literature) I was able to obtain approximately $16,000 per year, all of which has been used to fund his ABA therapy. This $16,000 comprises a mixture of funding types including the standard disability allowance, carer support days and an allowance (of 20 hours per week) of personal care (for Gordon). By becoming a 'contract client' the funding allocation of 20 hours per week was paid directly to me to redirect at my own discretion to fulfil his 'personal care' requirements. For obvious reasons, I chose ABA as the most optimum form of long-term personal care.

Nevertheless, even with a relatively high amount of funding every member of our family has still had to make financial sacrifices in order to fund the balance of the financial cost of the ABA programme and all of its associated costs. In addition, my own (unpaid) work and time commitment, coupled with the fact that I consciously placed Gordon's development as the top priority of my life (particularly over the first year of therapy), has also had an impact on my other children, my family and my own needs. A massively disproportionate amount of my time and energy has been allocated to Gordon and his ABA. Although this has become more normalized recently, the opportunity cost of what has not been channelled into my other two children's needs and development is impossible to measure. I only hope that the lifelong benefits of reducing the severity of Gordon's disability now will in some way make up for the lost time and effort allocated to his siblings during this relatively short period of their life.

One of the biggest time factors in managing Gordon's therapy programme has been the overseeing of the therapy process and all of the many variables contained within it. Keeping his rate of learning at a fast pace has required a commitment to continually review all of the elements within the programme, delivery of the programme and of behaviour management. Issues crop up between formal clinics and my role as Gordon's mum has played a part in helping to fine-tune this process. ABA is after all simply good teaching practice, but it relies on absolute precision to implement successfully. It has been helpful at all times, to understand exactly what was working, what wasn't, and if possible to be able to help to figure out a solution.

Helping to ensure that the ABA programme was successful for Gordon's 'whole' life – that is, ensuring that all skills were generalized outside of therapy – has also been a large but rewarding responsibility. In order to do this it has been necessary to keep up with every detail of his ever-changing programme and performance. This has involved constantly reviewing the written data in his folder, talking to therapists before and after each session, being actively involved at clinics, and occasionally (over the first 18 months of therapy) watching video recordings of his therapy sessions. Every moment in life is a teaching opportunity and having an ABA programme has enabled me to precisely match my language to his exact cognitive abilities and to know exactly how to ensure that Gordon achieved the targeted response by prompting and modelling if necessary.

Implementing an ABA programme becomes a different way of life for a family not only as you adjust to the workload, but to the constant stream of therapists who now work in your home (almost) every day. Therapists are not just robots who walk in, deliver 'Sd's, and write down data. They are people and as such they form a relationship with your child through every little aspect of their own behaviour. Relationships impact on therapy. Two different therapists can deliver the exact same programme in quite different ways due to the individual style and personality that they each bring to the session and therefore the child. One of the more prevalent day-to-day issues in managing the programme has been the constant and ongoing assessment of Gordon's happiness and well-being as a function of these factors. This was something that I could observe at a distance with our open-door policy to therapy sessions. The therapists that have worked with Gordon knew that I took a slightly fanatical obsession in regard to his emotional well-being in therapy, although this is something that I personally regard as the more difficult aspect of ABA. Having high quality therapists who I can trust and am confident in has been a crucial component to this process.

It has undoubtedly been easier to oversee the programme while Gordon was in a period of long-term, consistent and high quality therapy. It takes time for any therapist to become familiar with the child, their programme and their behavioural intervention plan, and to synchronize all three together in a way that is fun and productive for the child. It has been frustrating for both

Gordon and me during periods of inconsistent therapy, due to a high turnover and a shortage of therapists. This is an issue that is relevant to the entire industry at present.

Behaviour management is an aspect of Gordon's programme that I sometimes found particularly difficult to accept. In order to reduce tantrum behaviour, behavioural principles such as extinction from escape were used when tantrum behaviour was maintained by task avoidance. This would involve the therapists ignoring the tantrum behaviour and continuing with the task at hand. The rationale for this being that if tantrum behaviour allowed Gordon to leave a non-preferred activity then that tantrum behaviour would be reinforced and the future likelihood of it occurring again would increase. On the whole, therapy sessions were fun and enjoyable for Gordon. However, when tantrums did occur, I sometimes found it extremely difficult to listen to his crying and therefore to accept the behavioural principles being applied. However, additional strategies were also utilized that focused on the prevention of 'problem' behaviours in general. For example, providing more reinforcement, more prompts and more visual structure are all ways to help sessions run more smoothly. In addition, I have gradually adapted my own views on behaviour management in order to allow the therapists and myself to manage Gordon's behaviour more effectively. It is important to note that while behavioural principles such as extinction from escape have been appropriate for certain situations, they are not a 'one size fits all' approach to managing all of Gordon's behaviour throughout all therapy sessions. It is essential that the function for the behaviour is determined prior to the implementation of behaviour management strategies. Good therapists know when to apply the formulas and when to utilize their own creativity in order to effectively manage and enhance a child's emotional and psychological well-being.

The only real 'low' that I would assign to our ABA experience is that pertaining yet again to government policy – taxation to be precise. One of my biggest issues of contention is that while ABA remains in the private sector, the government does in fact profit from this treatment by charging GST (Goods and Services Tax). To date, our family has paid approximately $4000 in GST to the government for the 'privilege' of accessing this service. I find it absolutely immoral that a government would seek to profit from an autistic child who is receiving what I can only describe as a therapy that allows a child to experience one of the most basic of human rights – to allow their brains to learn.

Freedom of speech is, after all, only possible when you have a voice to speak with and a brain that enables you to make a voice. I have personally witnessed such a transformation in my own child. I know it is possible to turn one autistic child's life around.

THE HIGHS

The overall massive transformation that has taken place in terms of Gordon's ability to 'think' – as evidenced by his behaviour, his ability to connect to his environment through language, play and socialization – is undoubtedly the biggest 'high' of all. Gordon was a child with few skills and a severely impaired ability to learn, and (I can only imagine) was often bored and frustrated. He now has so many skills. Skills that enable him to communicate, think, play, plan, learn, socialize, and generally live and enjoy life. These are the precious life skills that the CARD ABA home programme has given him. Autism is defined as a pervasive developmental disorder and, accordingly, Gordon has and is being taught a comprehensive early childhood developmental curriculum, using scientifically validated applied behaviour analysis teaching techniques.

We have been extremely fortunate to have an exceptionally high quality of programming throughout the past two years and this has resulted in (for the most part) a consistently high rate of skill acquisition. Virtually daily, Gordon has increased his skills, little by little, and each time this happened, it also increased his cumulative skill level, often in an exponential way. It has been a miracle of sorts to watch these 'hidden treasures' unfold from within him. The ABA home programme perfectly suited his learning style and learning needs. With ABA he learned to connect to his environment and to the people and objects in that environment. All of those connections to his environment, and therefore within his brain, could happen when we knew how to facilitate this process.

Another mum of a child with ASD gave me a really useful piece of advice. She said that she regarded herself as her child's 'Therapist for Life', and I think that that was so wise and so true. Parents can teach their child a lot. I personally found that becoming involved in Gordon's ABA programme has been a wonderful way not only to erode but also to reverse the sense of personal frustration and failure that had developed in me (as his parent) before implementing the ABA home programme.

Siblings can help a lot too. A good therapist can incorporate them into the therapy for a part of the session with ease. When Gordon commenced his ABA programme it was during the summer school holidays, so my then six-year-old daughter Kiara had plenty of opportunities to be involved in a small portion of the therapy sessions right from the very beginning. Without any formal teaching, she intuitively picked up on Gordon's current level of programme and was, as she always so proudly put it, important in her role as a 'junior therapist'. She continued to help Gordon to learn outside of the therapy sessions by using the simple and reduced language of his programme in real life.

As I type tonight Gordon approaches me and starts a simple conversation. He wants me to play with him. He normally plays with his siblings, but his older sister is presently staying with her grandparents, and his younger brother is now asleep, so I guess tonight I've been promoted from number 3 to number 1 on the playmate list! He recently received some toy money for Christmas and has organized a 'shop' in his bedroom with his 'toys' for sale. This is not a play situation that he has been taught either in therapy or by myself. I wonder whether his older sister Kiara taught him, or perhaps he has just picked it up from real life shopping...

Gordon:	Mum, I've got a shop in my room!
Mum:	Have you, really?
Gordon:	Yeah. Come and play with me. It's got money!
Mum:	OK then, hang on a minute.
Gordon:	What are you going to do?
Mum:	I'll just do some more typing.
Gordon:	OK. Write my name. It's 'G O R D A N'. (He tells me each letter individually.)
Mum:	OK. (Mum types 'Gordon'.)
Gordon:	Mum, Anthony is asleep on the sofa. Can you type slowly? (He really means 'quietly'.)
Mum:	Hang on. (I'm actually retyping our whole conversation very fast.)
Gordon:	Now write 'Gordon and Mum'.
Mum:	OK, I did it.
Gordon:	Yeah! Come on mum. Let's go and play in the shop!
Mum:	OK, let's go! This'll be fun!

...We move to the bedroom and play 'shop' for ten minutes or so, exchanging money for various toys, and receiving 'change'.

(Conversation between Gordon and Mum, January 2005)

When Gordon learns new skills we celebrate. It has been and always will be a celebration (in my mind at least) of all of the things that he has learned, that he is learning, and that he will continue to learn. But, most of all, I celebrate in the knowing that now he can learn.

A last word

I am thoroughly indebted to all of the people that have been involved in Gordon's life over the past two years. People who have contributed in ways big and small, directly and indirectly, to help make him the person that he is today. That age-old African proverb 'It takes a village to raise a child' is an understatement of sorts when referring to a child with autism; there are just so many people who are crucially involved with your child! First and foremost, however, I would like to take this opportunity to acknowledge the hundreds of hours of work contributed by the ABA therapists, the unsung heroes in our battle against autism. Thank you to: Susan, Denise, Suzanne, Kate, Wendy, Jackie, Maia, Rachel, Sayaka, Josie and Janine. Your work is priceless.

I would also like to acknowledge the direct contribution made by people from the following organizations – Group Special Education, Gordon's pre-school teachers, Autism New Zealand, the NAS EarlyBird teachers. Lastly, thank you Erika for making it all possible.

References

Cooper, J.O., Heron, T.E. and Heward, W.L. (1987) *Applied Behaviour Analysis.* New York: Macmillan.

Delprato, D.J. (2001) 'Comparisons of discrete-trial and normalized behavioural language intervention for young children with autism.' *Journal of Autism and Developmental Disorders 31*, 3, 315–325.

Green, G. (2001) 'Behavior analytic instruction for learners with autism: advances in stimulus control technology.' *Focus on Autism and Other Developmental Disabilities 16*, 72–85.

Hart, B. and Risley, T.R. (1975) 'Incidental teaching of language in the pre-school.' *Journal of Applied Behavior Analysis 8*, 411–420.

Koegel, R.L., O'Dell, M.C. and Koegel, L.K. (1987) 'A natural language teaching paradigm for non-verbal autistic children.' *Journal of Autism and Developmental Disorders 17*, 2, 187–220.

Lovaas, O.I. (1987) 'Behavioral treatment and normal educational and intellectual functioning in young autistic children.' *Journal of Consulting and Clinical Psychology 55*, 3–9.

McGee, G.G., Krantz, P.J. and McClannahan, L.E. (1985) 'The facilitative effects of incidental teaching on preposition use by autistic children.' *Journal of Applied Behavior Analysis 18*, 17–31.

Maurice, C. (1993) *Let Me Hear Your Voice: A Family's Triumph Over Autism.* New York: Ballantine.

The Parent Company (1997) *Reading Master Program.* Horizon Print. http://www.readingmaster.com/WebPages/index.htm (accessed 30 September 2005).

Parents As First Teachers (PAFT) (2005) *The PAFT National Centre.*
    http://www.ecd.govt.nz/paft/national.html (accessed 12 April 2005).

Skinner, B.F. (1957) *Verbal Behavior.* New York: Appleton-Century-Crofts.

Smith, T. (2001) 'Discrete trial training in the treatment of autism.' *Focus on Autism and Other
    Developmental Disabilities 16,* 2, 86–92.

Sundberg, M.L. and Partington, C.A. (1998) *Teaching Language to Children with Autism or Other
    Developmental Disabilities.* Pleasant Hill: Behavior Analysts, Inc.

CHAPTER 5

More about Colin

Setting Up an ABA-Based Pre-School Group for Children with Autism

Lynne McKerr and Stephen Gallagher

Some of you may have read about 'Colin' in the PEAT book (Keenan, Kerr and Dillenburger 2000), but for those of you who haven't, the first part of this chapter will be a brief summary of the events leading to our involvement as parents with applied behaviour analysis, and to the formation of PEAT.

Colin

Colin was born in February 1992, our fifth child and a very good and settled baby. He was alert and happy, and seemed to thrive on the attention from his siblings. Looking back I (Lynne) am not sure exactly when we began to worry about him; as with our other children he was a relatively late walker at 14 months, but very lively once on his feet. He didn't seem to be talking much – just dada and mama sounds – and gradually his activity became a problem. He never sat still, didn't watch television or play with toys, or come when his name was called; in town or shops he was a nightmare, crying and struggling to get away. Even at home, we had to keep doors closed in case he bolted outside because we lived close to the road. It finally dawned on me that we had a major problem one night when I took the older girls to Irish dancing. A small boy kept charging into the middle, calling out to his sisters, laughing and wanting to join in and when his mother told me he was 18 months I felt my heart sink. Colin was 20 months, much smaller and not vocal at all; I knew if he had been there he would have been running for the door and out into the car park, not into the middle of all the activity. The next week he had his 18-month check-up (delayed due to staff changes) and I could see the new health visitor was very concerned about his size and the fact that he failed the hearing test. She also scared the life out of me by measuring his head circumference, simply saying his head was disproportionately large; she then went on to refer him to the community medical officer, who deals with child health and development. Needless to say we were very worried and upset; none of our other children had needed any referrals and we felt out of our depth.

That was the start of almost two years of tests and appointments, with audiologists, ear, nose and throat specialists (his hearing was fine; he just wasn't listening), paediatricians, community medical officers, more health visitors, clinical and educational psychologists, speech therapists, a physiotherapist and an occupational therapist (to assess his relatively poor fine motor skills). All these visits involved dragging (often literally) a small hot tired child into busy waiting areas, often long distances from home in totally alien surroundings and keeping him occupied (or just in the room) for up to 45 minutes before he could be seen misbehaving for five or ten minutes by a professional who could not tell us why Colin behaved like this. 'Developmental delay' and 'minimal brain damage' were two early suggestions; later, 'autistic tendencies' appeared more frequently but (except for the educational psychologists' suggestions for a 'consistent' bedtime routine) no one told us how to cope with an increasingly difficult child. Our GP (i.e. family doctor) was to be a great support (thanks, Reggie), emphasizing the positive aspects of the investigations, and always stressing that whatever the outcome Colin would be a valued member of the family and wider community. However, it wasn't always easy to believe this, or cope with him. By now he slept intermittently at night, racing round the house at three and four in the morning. We had enrolled him in a small daycare centre just to spend time twice a week with other young children; when there he played in the sand or the water and ignored all the other children but he made no fuss at leaving or going in – unless I took a different route, or parked on the other side of the street, when he screamed and struggled in the car seat. At the age of just under three and a half, a consultant psychiatrist diagnosed him with Asperger's syndrome and ADHD (attention deficit/hyperactivity disorder). This was actually a relief;

there was 'something' now, so back we went to our GP thinking we would get 'something' to make this better. But it wasn't that easy; he told us he knew very little about autism (which we had begun to guess about, his colleagues as well). He was, however, very interested in 'behaviour'; he lent me a copy of *Don't Shoot the Dog* by Karen Pryor (1985). I took this home, a bit stunned, but my husband and I sat down and read it; both being science graduates, we were vaguely familiar with the work of B.F. Skinner, and the book we were asked to read – about changing *behaviour* using positive reinforcement – seemed to make sense. Colin was now due to start nursery in less than three months and still wasn't fully toilet trained. We took the book to heart, and with a packet of Maltesers (i.e. chocolate-covered candy) as reinforcers, began a campaign for full toilet training. Three weeks later, we went back to our GP and said, 'This really works – where do we go from here?' He put us in touch with a friend of his, Dr Mickey Keenan from the University of Ulster, and that is when things really began to change for the better. Mickey said from the start that he knew very little about autism, but he knew about behaviour and he would teach us. Which he did, in his own limited free time, and without charge. The changes he helped us to bring about with Colin are documented in *Parents' Education as Autism Therapists* (Keenan *et al.* 2000).

The battles with health and education professionals weren't over, of course; they nearly all actively disliked applied behaviour analysis (ABA) (though most knew very little about it) and very few of them – except our speech therapist – felt that Colin had any hope of integrating with typically developing peers in mainstream school. A year in nursery didn't bring on his speech to any great extent, nor did he engage in age-typical play with the other children there. He was assessed as having 'moderate learning difficulties'; we knew his language development and social skills were far behind, but unlike the 'experts' we knew he could learn, and learn quickly, in the right setting (the work with Mickey showed this). These gains in eye contact, compliance and time on task were ignored in his assessment and his documentation was sent to a special unit in a town more than 20 miles from home, even though we had said we wanted him to go to school with his brother and sisters. So that was another struggle, and if it hadn't been for the open and compassionate attitude of the principal of the school, he would not have had the opportunity; there was no official help with ABA training so Colin's classroom assistant joined PEAT, and gave up her Saturdays to sit and learn along with us (she has remained a very good friend, and a strong advocate for ABA). For those of you who are interested in details of the work we did with

Mickey, and Colin's ups and downs at school, I'd recommend the PEAT book. For now, I'd like to tell you about how ABA became a public issue in the North of Ireland.

Setting up PEAT

We had talked to Mickey a lot as time went on about how much ABA had helped us; our GP had put other parents in touch with us and we could see that ABA could help others. In March 1997 an article about Colin and the work with Mickey appeared in the local evening paper (*The Belfast Telegraph*) and Mickey was inundated with calls. He organized a public meeting in August at the Jordanstown campus of the University of Ulster, and then a smaller meeting in Derry; it was very difficult to get up in front of a sea of faces to talk about my son, but I really felt strongly that ABA had changed our lives, and everyone struggling to cope with children with autism should at least know enough about it to make an informed choice. From there, a small core group of parents from Belfast and Derry came together to learn about ABA. We called ourselves PEAT (Parents' Education as Autism Therapists), and every month at the Coleraine campus of the University of Ulster we had a Saturday class. Mickey trained us in the principles of ABA and we struggled with the practice, producing our results for discussion and advice. We approached the Department of Education for help with funding but got brushed off by 'autism experts' who disliked ABA; dedicated work by two skilled parents in particular (Barbara and Hilary) brought in three years' funding for an ABA consultant with administrative support and Dr Ken Kerr joined PEAT. From there it has grown, with over 100 families relying on what is now a very stretched resource; Ken has moved to Mayo, and been replaced by Dr Stephen Gallagher, who like Ken has contributed so much time and energy with such limited resources. However, every new committee still faces an uphill struggle to maintain morale and funding; it makes it so much worse to know that this is the only validated educational intervention, that it can make so much difference and yet it is not being made available through wilful lack of financial support. PEAT made such a difference to our lives and we had hoped that with proper funding, educational institutions would take over the provision of high quality ABA training and practice. Sadly, that just has not happened – yet.

Cillian

As a family, we continue to use the principles (and practices) of ABA to deal with social and educational issues for all of us; teenage children, elderly relatives and partners can all face problems that are responsive to behaviour analysis. As for 'Colin' himself, he was asked about using his pseudonym for this chapter, and wants to appear as himself. So from now on, he will be known by his own name, Cillian. He is a very happy, articulate child with a wide range of interests and has recently transferred to the same voluntary grammar school as his siblings. At 12, he has settled well in school, and his favourite subjects are history, science, home economics and Spanish. We realize that we've been very fortunate there, just as we were with his primary school. His new school is relatively small, with a very positive and caring pastoral ethos that is apparent throughout school life; our four other children attend too. The staff and pupils have got to know him well, and from the beginning, the Special Educational Needs Coordinator and his form teacher were keen to involve Dr Stephen Gallagher from PEAT in drawing up strategies for dealing with both positive and negative aspects of classroom behaviour. To their great credit, they were not afraid to say they didn't know much about autism but were prepared to try and meet Cillian's needs, and in any meetings have stressed the positive outcomes much more than the negative, which they work as a team to resolve (and we know there will continue to be issues which will cause concern, especially with his social skills). This is so very different to the reports from 'autism specialists' that always set out to measure him against the developmental landmarks of typically developing peers, which they already knew he was almost certain to 'fail'. Even when he began to confound their expectations, they refused to look on this as positive. I've forgotten how many times we heard that his good reading masked an inability to understand or draw inferences, that he counted to 100 'by parroting' (or that his increasingly good number skills were an 'islet' of ability, presumably in a sea of incomprehension) and that his strong opinions – for example on human rights or vegetarianism (which I'm sorry to say he condemns, probably because two of his sisters were vegetarians) – were due to 'rigidity' of thinking.

The openness at his school is not a common response of schools, as many PEAT parents will confirm. Most schools are unwilling to invite behavioural experts into the classroom, even if they acknowledge they are finding it difficult to cope with a child's behaviours. It still seems to be seen as the child's problem, that he or she 'can't cope' with ordinary classroom life. As parents, we can see perhaps where the school is coming from – many young children with autism do *not* have the skills necessary for fitting into the classroom environment. However, as parents we also know that within the classroom, even quite small adjustments to routine with the help of a one-to-one classroom assistant can make a lot of difference; clear guidelines, picture schedules, positive reinforcement for desired behaviour (and a positive expectation on behalf of staff) will make life much easier. This creates a positive learning attitude for everyone; once a child is given the tools to learn, then all tasks can be tailored to fit the child's developing abilities. Each skill mastered opens the way for new skills, and involvement in mainstream offers daily opportunities for modelling appropriate behaviour. Small gains become bigger gains, and with skilful help, prompts can be faded and skills generalized. Not all children with autism will make the same progress; they are all individuals but can be helped to reach their potential, which is only what we expect for *all* our children.

The STARS project

As Cillian progressed through his primary school years it was obvious that those who worked with him in school were all amazed at his academic and social development. Each year as Cillian moved class his teachers were enthusiastic about learning the techniques adopted by his family. As well as staff, the parents of other children on the autistic spectrum in the local area began to take an interest. I was working as a one-to-one assistant with another child at Cillian's school (Crossroads Primary School (PS), Kilrea) in 1999 and we often got involved in general discussions on autism; the staff could see how useful ABA was, everyone appreciated the research findings on early intervention and we could actually see that pre-school preparation with ABA did enhance the child's ability to participate in the classroom. For many of us as parents, education within the mainstream was our choice for our children where possible and we saw ABA as the best way of giving our children the appropriate skills, a way of teaching them to learn rather than short-term changes to make life manageable (thankful though we were for some of these as well).

We also knew that there was no financial support for ABA in the schools which wanted to participate, and that most parents could not afford to pay for intensive home programmes, even if PEAT had been able to provide the staff to administer them. We were also concerned about the steady increase in children who appeared to be on the autistic spectrum; our local community medical officers were interested in what was going on and they indicated their concerns about increasing numbers for possible future intake. It finally dawned on us that the only way forward was to try and raise money ourselves. Staff and parents at the school got together to form STARS – 'Striving To Achieve Real Success'. Initial attempts to attract interest from the North Eastern Education and Library Board (the funding body for education in our area) or to secure funding from the National Lottery were unsuccessful but we decided to try and make a start anyway. We knew the GPs at the health centre were supportive, and they gave us use of their large multifunction room for a weekly social skills group, which began in May 2000; it was attended initially by younger children with ASD and relations or friends. The idea was to provide structured play as a framework for establishing good social skills and dealing with problems that would arise (which we had no doubt would). This used surprisingly few resources apart from parents' and some of the teacher's time – we borrowed some games and equipment from Crossroads school and parents brought useful toys from home; everyone took turns to provide the biscuits and drinks for snack time. We had some referrals from the health visitors, and contact from local people who had heard we were starting up, who had pre-school children with 'developmental concerns'; they began to attend too. Parents using ABA were talking to other parents; the parents of pre-schoolers – some with very challenging behaviours – began to see a range of choices opening up.

By the end of June 2000 we still had no money but knew we couldn't abandon the children to the long summer holidays. The group held a sponsored (toy!) tractor ride to raise funds for a summer scheme and with just over £400 plus a later grant of £300 from Magherafelt District Council (the local government body for our area) we opened for two mornings a week in the P1 classroom of Crossroads PS, with borrowed equipment and some toys and games purchased with our funds. It was staffed mainly by parents and volunteers and we planned games and activities for pre-school and younger primary school children (up to eight years old); advice on behavioural strategies was provided by regular visits from PEAT consultants. The Summer Scheme was attended by families from as far away as Magherafelt, Armoy and Ballymoney, a radius of up to 20 miles; our contacts with the community medical services and speech therapy meant that our group became more widely known and parents from outside our own area (who had equally little access to support services) were prepared to travel considerable distances. In all, we had 18 families registered with STARS by the end of the holidays.

Although limited by financial constraints it was a great success both in terms of gains for the children and a change in outlook for many parents. For the first time many of them could see the possibility of changing often very difficult behaviours; for some it now seemed possible to think about ordinary nursery or day care for their child.

Figure 5.1: Lesley with Theresa and Debby, members of staff, at STARS

It is often the simplest things that make the most impact and lasting memories. On this occasion it was a plastic slide in the sports/dining hall. At the end of each day the children were taken to the hall to have a good run around. Among all the cars, balls, hoops and other wonderful toys was a small plastic slide. For reasons unknown to myself this became the focal point of the play sessions and it was amazing to see (thanks to plenty of social reinforcement from the staff and volunteers) children on the autistic spectrum, including Asperger's syndrome, and with ADHD queuing up with their typically developing peers to take turns on this tiny slide. There was no pushing, no jumping the line, no arguing, no fighting – just wonderful social and play skills. This simple piece of behaviour filled parents with enthusiasm and optimism.

Parents were very keen to learn more about ABA; fees from the scheme meant that – with some additional fundraising – we could continue to offer training through evening meetings at the school with PEAT consultants. Pub quizzes have been our greatest source of funding in the community, but we were also eligible for small community grants from the district councils (local government authorities), though you need to apply well in advance for these. The community medicine and speech therapy departments were also very interested in increasing awareness for parents about autism services and representatives came to evening meetings to inform parents about the steps involved in diagnosis and how best existing agencies – given the usual financial restrictions they faced – could help children with autistic spectrum disorders.

By 2002 we realized we needed to offer more; we began to put together plans for a more permanent service, which initially would concentrate on pre-schoolers with ASD alongside typically developing peers. The cost was daunting; we would always need much higher staff ratios, and continuing behavioural training both for staff and parents. Even if we raised the money for a temporary classroom, and got permission to site it within suitable grounds, staff costs were always going to be an obstacle as none of the funders we approached covered salary outlay. We decided to go ahead with the Summer Scheme again; in the course of organizing, we got together a list of names and phone numbers of local agencies (health visitors, social services and the hospital trust) and asked for support, not expecting anything substantial. Everyone we spoke to was very keen to see an improvement in services for children with autism; they wanted to know more about what we were doing and to our surprise social services (who deal with family care and support) and the Causeway Trust (the local health authority) gave us grants totalling £1500. This allowed us to run the scheme for longer sessions three times a week, and also to continue the parent training into the autumn and spring. Twenty-two families were now registered with STARS. We continued to monitor demand for the service we were offering with regular questionnaires; statistics from these proved very useful when compiling evidence of need in funding applications.

However, it was also a turning point in that we had attracted the attention of the Northern Childcare Partnership (a relatively new group which coordinates and promotes good practice in child care); a representative came out to see the 2002 Summer Scheme and seemed very keen to develop the group's potential. The result was their advice (and inclusion for our project in their portfolio) on application for premises through the 'Building Quality Childcare'

Figure 5.2: Having a laugh and a snack, while Surney, a member of staff, keeps an eye

section of the New Opportunities Fund (NOF – a section of the National Lottery) and also ongoing support from Playboard (another group which promotes access to good child care, which has been extremely useful as none of us were experienced in funding applications). The health centre had completed a new building which they were prepared to offer us for a pepper-corn rent, provided we finished it out with fixtures and flooring. On top of nominal rent was a maintenance charge for heating, lighting and general maintenance which was covered in part by our initial (one year) capital grant from the New Opportunites Fund. We heard in February 2003 that our appli-cation had gone forward, and by June we had the award confirmed. By then we had completed an application to The Children's Fund for a three-year project (with support from the Early Years Team in social services) which applied for staff costs for 16 pre-school places (for an equal number of children with ASD and without). By summer 2003, we had received news that our after-schools application to the NOF (again assisted by Playboard) had also been successful. This was all happening very fast and I have to say that it took a great deal of work both in preparing the applications and in the subsequent appointments, organization and supervising the finishing of the premises, not all of which went smoothly (at times none of it seemed to go smoothly). Probably more experienced fundraisers – or those used to organizing businesses – would have managed more efficiently, but we got there in the end. We were able to appoint a part-time administrator paid from our own funds (we're still organizing pub and fireside quizzes). If any other parents are thinking of setting up, I'd have to say not including administrative costs in our applications was a serious oversight – with three grants to manage, and paperwork from two busy projects, it is absolutely necessary. There is a lot of regulation involved in setting up – registration of the premises, vetting of staff, and health and safety legislation is a very time-consuming process and should not be underestimated in terms of starting dates. A hitch in any of the processes can mean a lengthy delay in opening the premises. You really need to keep in touch with all the agencies responsible for fire safety, health and hygiene, and staff vetting right from the start – even before you begin building if you can, as good communication will reduce most of the delays we encountered. There will always be a mass of paperwork, so you need to give agencies time to get their forms filled and signed; don't assume that anything will only take a site visit to sort out.

Following the Task Group Report in 2002 there was a lot of interest in what we were doing – in fact we were able to cite its recommendations for pre-school intervention as a part of our application procedures. In general many parents who use ABA were disappointed by the findings of the Task Group Report, a supposed in-depth study of autism provision by concerned professionals and autism organizations which minimized input from parents using behavioural interventions. It was no surprise when its overall findings supported an 'eclectic' approach, which some of us see as a dilution of definitive approaches (even on different interventions; if parents choose a school which offers TEACCH, then surely an applied TEACCH programme should be used and supported, rather than an 'eclectic' approach). However, we would fully agree with their recommendation of (appropriate) intervention as early as possible, and made this a major part of our argument for funding. The North Eastern Education and Library Board expressed some interest and their special needs officers met with the Committee; they subsequently offered to pay for an intensive training course on site (through PEAT) for the leaders and assistant leaders of both projects, which would greatly enhance the on-site training we had budgeted for in our applications.

The on-site training in ABA aimed to teach staff to understand fundamental issues concerned with applied behaviour analysis, i.e. appreciate the behavioural excesses and deficits associated with autism; understand the central importance of data-driven therapeutic decisions in an ABA programme; understand the importance of individualized educational programmes for children with autism; and understand the way in which learning principles can be incorporated into the design of effective learning environments for children with autism. Training topics included the philosophy and ethics of ABA in teaching children on the autistic spectrum, reinforcement, extinction, increasing adaptive behaviours, decreasing maladaptive behaviours, shaping and chaining new behaviours, stimulus discrimination training, precision teaching, observation and data collection, and designing and implementing a personalized curriculum.

This has given staff a basic grounding in the principles of ABA, although it does not lead to a recognized qualification. We already knew our chances of appointing trained staff would be very low; in the end, given the restraints on PEAT staffing and our limited funds we have been very happy with the way that training has worked out. It would be much better if there was an established certified course available; if a Master's course in applied behaviour analysis were to run then it would be a great advantage to our staff. This really should be a focus for all other autism groups using ABA; without stringent regulation and certified standards, we cannot be sure of the quality of training for people working with our children.

The pre-school project opened in November 2003; by June we had 33 children enrolled, 15 of whom have ASD or other special needs. We are glad to be able to offer support for children with other disabilities or with behavioural difficulties who would otherwise find it difficult to obtain a pre-school place. The after-school project opened in January and in June had 24 children enrolled, 14 of whom have ASD. Our Holiday Club offered full or part day care with the same type of structured environment for children. Disappointingly we were unable to secure enough funding for staff wages to continue the After Schools Club from the end of January 2005 but will continue to pursue this as it offers support for slightly older children, which is very difficult to access anywhere else.

We hope eventually to offer out-of-hours support and parent training as well. It has taken a lot of hard work to get things up and running; even now most of us would say we're still learning as it goes along. We hope to build on the good relationships established between ourselves and the health, social services and education professionals. We know many parents elsewhere have found their encounters with such agencies stressful and sometimes confrontational, which in the end benefits no one – especially the child whose needs are central to the discussions. Parents have enough stress without feeling they have to fight for every service their child needs; there has to be a less formal, antagonistic approach to education and support provision and, for some, the informal contacts and support through STARS have helped break down some of these barriers.

We can't say we are an 'ABA school' – we aren't able to provide an intensive one-to-one programme for every child. However, we can address many issues through individual planning with parents through Lesley, our project leader, and Stephen, the PEAT consultant, and through the observations and recommendations of our trained staff; we recognize that this is at best a 'half-way house' for ABA interventions but it does operate as a form of community outreach. Improved parenting skills, increasing confidence and much more settled family life have all been acknowledged both by parents and professionals. Parents are more informed about their choices, and can continue the interventions at home, or begin more intensive work by joining PEAT or some of the other groups which are emerging in ABA provision (although many cannot afford the high fees associated with these organizations). After more than four years' work to get this up and running, it hasn't been either easy or straightforward; without community support it would have been practically impossible. But it has been done.

Note

Anyone who wants to form a similar group is very welcome to contact STARS at Kilrea (Tel: 0044(0)28 295 42345), or come along and see us and we will help where we can.

References

Keenan, M., Kerr, K.P. and Dillenburger, K. (eds) (2000) *Parents' Education as Autism Therapists.* London: Jessica Kingsley Publishers.

Pryor, K. (1985) *Don't Shoot the Dog: The New Art of Teaching and Training.* New York: Bantam Books.

Task Group (2002) *Education for Children and Young People with Autistic Spectrum Disorders.* Report of the Task Group on Autism Northern Ireland Department of Education (April). www.DENI.gov.uk

CHAPTER 6

From a Sapling to a Forest

The Growth of the Saplings
Model of Education

Phil Smyth, Marc de Salvo
and Aisling Ardiff

The Saplings Model of Education (or Saplings) is an educational centre for 31 children who have been diagnosed as being on the autistic spectrum (see Figure 6.1). The centre delivers education to pupils through application of the principles of applied behaviour analysis (ABA). This chapter aims to set the development of Saplings in context. It begins with Jessica's story as told by her father (and Saplings chairperson) Marc de Salvo and develops into an overview of the historical development of Saplings. This chapter presents Saplings as an interesting and dynamic setting for children to learn and for staff to work, and as an organization that combines these characteristics with quality assurance technology in the realization of a model of educational excellence. Quality assurance is outlined in terms of the systems approach to organizational operation utilized within Saplings. All quality assurance systems are designed with the aim of continuing to deliver quality education to Saplings pupils, and to improving performance in all areas whenever possible. Key elements within the Saplings systems approach include the development of clear roles and responsibilities (operationally described as

Figure 6.1: Mark and Jess

behavioural objectives for staff performance) and quality control measures designed for the development of staff training and feedback. These two elements translate into practices for 1. setting performance standards, 2. monitoring performance, 3. providing supervisory and management feedback, and 4. providing staff training (LaVigna *et al.* 1994). Quality assurance, in terms of staff performance, provides the critical framework for continued Saplings pupil success. The reader of this chapter will be left with a view of Saplings as a vibrant, positive and exciting learning environment for pupils, one that also takes pride in the quality assurance measures utilized.

Jessica de Salvo's story

Jessica de Salvo was born on 4 November 1997 and was our second child. Jess walked early at around 8–9 months and appeared to develop typically in all other areas. Looking back, however, we now remember how she was not demanding during the day but that she hardly slept at all at night, either having to be carried or sleeping lying on top of my wife, Andrea. It was during a visit from a local district nurse that concerns about Jess not responding to her name were raised. At this time it was suggested that we have her hearing tested. Andrea and I clearly remember Jess waving bye to me as I went off to work. We also remember her starting 'Da Da' sounds. We had her hearing tested and it established that she did not have a hearing problem, but she did appear to have a communication problem. As we started looking closer at Jess's behaviour we noticed that she had some unusual tendencies. For example she tended to be very engrossed in some of the children's TV programmes that she watched and she rarely maintained eye contact with us.

Upon the discovery of Jess's communication problems she was assigned to an early intervention team. At their recommendation we went to see a paediatrician when Jess was approximately 15 months old. The report generated from this visit was sent directly to the early intervention team according to standard practice. The paediatrician noted that Jess presented with some autistic traits. Unaware of what the report contained we started looking at books and the World Wide Web for further information about the possible causes of Jess's communication problems. We found some sites describing autism, and began to suspect that perhaps Jess was on the autistic spectrum. When Jess was approximately 20 months old we had a formal assessment by the local childhood development team carried out at our home. (See Figure 6.2.)

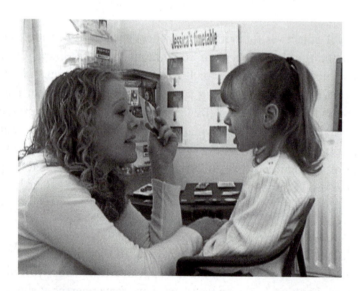

Figure 6.2: Jessica learning

During the assessment Jess displayed hand flapping and also ignored us when we tried to interact with her. We suggested to the team that she could possibly be on the autistic spectrum, but were quickly told not to label Jess; it was too early to say. The team suggested that we have her reviewed again on her third birthday and by then we should know the issues we were dealing with. Later, during our legal case against the Irish State, we were given copies of the paperwork filled out by the professionals from the childhood development team. In the remarks section of that report were the letters 'ASD', standing for autistic spectrum disorder. The report also noted that 'father was in action mode' and that 'mother was upset'. Unaware of this yet feeling dissatisfied with the outcome of the assessment, and unwilling to wait until Jess was three, we arranged a private assessment for Jess with a paediatrician who had a lot of experience in the area of autism.

Before starting the assessment the paediatrician told us he was going to ask us questions around 16 areas of Jess's development. If Jess fell into 8 out of the 16 categories on the assessment it meant she was somewhere on the autistic spectrum. As we answered the questions Jess sat in the corner of his office, not really playing with the toys in the toy box. Jess fell into 15 out of the 16 different categories on the assessment and the 16th was questionable. Every parent who has experienced this day will never forget the raw pain upon having the diagnosis of autism confirmed. The pain was strange; although we were pretty sure that Jess had autism, nothing prepared us for the shock of getting confirmation. Professionals, who have the task of informing parents of a diagnosis of autism, should not underestimate this impact. I have spoken to hundreds of parents who have related the story of how diagnosis was delivered. Almost all confirm a bald statement of 'your child has autism' without explanation of what the diagnosis entails or practical suggestions for what to do next.

At the time of Jess's diagnosis I had no idea that our local national school could refuse Jess a place because she had autism or that there were very few specialized educational places available for her. Andrea and I explored some of the 'specialized' educational placements provided by the Irish State for children with autism and were extremely dissatisfied with the implementation of the model they were based upon. Around this time an organization called ICANDO (Irish Children's Autism Network for Developmental Opportunities) was holding monthly workshops for parents of children with autism. Andrea and I attended one of the Saturday workshops on something called applied behaviour analysis (ABA), delivered by Dr Ken Kerr. Little did I know, but I had just met the future Director of Education of Saplings. I started attending, and video recording, the monthly workshops and started looking at the different models of education available for children with autism. I also started talking to parents who were running ABA home programmes. I am often asked why I came to the conclusion that intervention based upon the principles of ABA was the best possible educational intervention for Jess. To make my decision I started looking at what information was available on autism approaches. The literature around the outcomes for children with autism, who received early intervention based upon the principles of ABA, was not only impressive but research based and published in peer-reviewed scientific journals. In the end the decision was easy.

In the summer of 2000, Andrea and I took a deep breath and tried to start a home programme, using ABA, for Jess. It was not easy. We had to remortgage our home to build an extension to house Jess's classroom. Dr Ken Kerr came on board as our consultant behaviour analyst. We were very fortunate to get an experienced ABA tutor. In the year that followed, much media attention was being given to some high-profile cases taken by the parents of autistic children against the Irish State. The basis for these cases tended to centre on the Irish State's failure to provide some children with their constitutional right to education (Constitution of Ireland 1937, Article 42). Media attention tended to focus on families who were struggling, not only with autism, but also with the constant stress of trying to get services from the government.

In November 2000 I asked Dr Kerr to run a course on ABA for parents to try to equip them with some practical skills for productively interacting with their children. Dr Kerr developed the course and, in January 2001, an ABA course designed specifically for parents was run out of a community centre in Celbridge, Co. Kildare. Parents travelled from all over Ireland to attend and, although it was only an introductory course, it sparked interest in ABA. After this Dr Kerr and myself started to focus our energy on establishing an educational centre for children with autism in Kildare. Along with a group of parents we produced a document outlining a proposal for a centre called Saplings that would educate children with autism using the principles of ABA. The proposal, submitted to the Department of Education and Science (DoE&S) in June 2001, outlined the proposed centre's educational approach and how much funding we would require. After protracted communications and interactions Saplings received sanction for funding from the DoE&S in the Republic of Ireland in August 2001. And the rest, as they say, is history!

Saplings' evolution

On 1 September 2001 Saplings started training tutors. Training took the form of ten days of day-long lectures, activities and practical assessment. The course covered a variety of topics, including:

- introduction to applied behaviour analysis
- reinforcement
- prompting and fading
- shaping, chaining and task analysis
- behavioural objectives
- functional analysis and the communicative role of problem behaviour
- precision teaching
- introduction to verbal behaviour
- augmentative communication systems.

On 15 September 2001 Saplings started educating pupils. In a hurry to begin educating pupils the Board of Management of Saplings did not have sufficient time for the identification of a building or site suitable for a centre. As a result Saplings opened in the interim accommodation of the home of the parents of an enrolled pupil. Saplings (i.e. 12 pupils, 13 tutors, one supervisor, and a director of education) spent six months sharing accommodation with a family of six. A relief panel of parents, who made themselves available throughout the day, facilitated tutor breaks. The centre office was housed in a room that was to become the family bathroom. The centre, however, was functioning and educating 12 pupils diagnosed on the autistic spectrum through ABA. In the six-month period between October 2001 and April 2002 a family member of one of the pupils donated a one-acre site for a three-year period, and prefabricated buildings were designed, ordered and finally placed on site. In April 2002 the 12 pupils, 13 tutors, supervisor and director of education moved to accommodation that consisted of three classrooms, a large indoor playroom, a staff and pupil canteen, a single pupil tuition room, an office and a reception.

Since Saplings has been open its development has been both expeditious and challenging due to demand by parents for services for their children. Currently Saplings offers full-time educational placements for 31 pupils and outreach or in-home programmes for a further 15. At present Saplings employs 48 tutors, six supervisors, a director of education for the centre and a director of education for the outreach programme, a secretary and an accounts clerk. Yet, the atmosphere, character and ethos of Saplings remains as vibrant as it was the day the centre first opened. Saplings operates an open-door policy to all visitors, parents and professionals alike, and promotes a spirit of sharing and cooperation. Visitors to Saplings almost always remark on the busy and happy atmosphere that exists in the centre. Upon entering Saplings a visitor may see children walking in the corridor, some with tutors, some engaged in independent actions, but all engaged in productive activities. All children are busy doing something. There is a sense of purpose that parents and many professionals are often surprised by. The classrooms are busy, bright spaces with students having a clearly marked individual workspace if needed. Other classrooms are organized around a group or 'mainstream' structure, with pupils sharing desks and tutors. The pupils are interested in the visitors to their classrooms, but return to work with little difficulty. Again professionals often remark on students' ability to remain on task so well in such a 'distracting' environment. Tuition may be structured around a one-to-one ratio or may occur in small group or independent settings. Some children work together doing maths; some children are learning how to play; others are learning how to have conversations with each other. The learning environment is structured in a manner that meets the individual needs of each pupil as set out by the Saplings mission statement, which states that the role of Saplings is:

> to support children with a diagnosis of ASD and their family; assisting them to achieve their full potential and participate in their family and community life, through a holistic evidence-based educational model, celebrating each child's dignity, uniqueness and right to an optimal education.

Since Saplings opened, six pupils have been completely integrated into mainstream settings, another pupil has been integrated into a vocational setting, and another ten pupils are at various stages of the integration into mainstream process. In achieving this it is important to note that the atmosphere and success of Saplings is not the product of chance but rather the product of a precise and systematic approach to service and intervention delivery based directly on the principles of ABA. The reliance on the practices and philosophy of ABA complements Saplings' mission statement as noted above. ABA is characterized by a specified dedication to the improvement of people's life experiences in terms of quality of life, broadening of rewarding experiences, and social relationships and interactions. Cooper, Heron and Heward (1987) convey this objective in defining ABA as the:

> science in which procedures derived from the principles of behaviour are systematically applied to improve socially significant behaviour to a

meaningful degree and to demonstrate experimentally that the procedures employed were responsible for the improvement in behaviour.
(p.15)

It is from this definition that Saplings, and its systems and structures, derives
its status as behaviour analytic. Saplings utilizes procedures and interventions
directly derived from the principles of behaviour analysis. The principles are
applied on two levels: first to the development of appropriate programmes
and environmental arrangements for pupils to address the range of deficits
and excesses that constitute autism; second, to develop and maintain the skill
repertoire necessary to ensure pupil progress within the Saplings staff body.
At both levels Saplings demonstrates that the procedures used were responsible for behaviour change through the systematic collection of data.

The application of the principles of ABA on the two levels described
above has encouraged the development of a multi-element or systems
approach to the education of Saplings pupils. The approaches that are integrated within Saplings – including speech and language therapy, occupational
therapy, and music tuition/lessons – are all implemented through application
of the principles of ABA by generation of a clear statement of instructional
objectives, manipulation of environmental contingencies, and through appropriate data collection. This approach allows for the integration of services and
therapies into a cohesive programme of instruction, which is delivered and
monitored on a daily basis, and fosters cross-pollination of objectives between
approaches in order to create practice opportunities and to generalize skills.
As a result speech and language objectives are practised in music and occupational therapy sessions. Motor objectives generated by the occupational
therapist are practised in music and play activities. Academic objectives such
as sequencing and rhyming are practised in music sessions, as are communication and motor objectives. All objectives and associated data collection are
monitored by a supervisor who liaises with therapeutic personnel and directly
with the director of education in the monitoring, adjusting and development
of all objectives and programmes for pupils. Integration of approaches also
allows for the generation of Individualized Education Plans (IEPs) in conjunction with parents based upon multi-element assessment and
multidisciplinary input in line with best practice, resulting in the development
of a systemic model of early intervention (Twachtman-Cullen and
Twachtman-Reilly 2002).

The precise and systematic approach to service and intervention delivery
described above translates into a smooth, effective and cohesive multi-

element model that is dependent upon a comprehensive system of data-based quality assurance. Saplings' comprehensive system of quality assurance has been realized through the development of a system of data monitoring and quality assurance that contains four main elements essential for quality control in human services and education. They are 1. performance standards, 2. performance monitoring, 3. supervisory and management feedback, and 4. staff training (LaVigna *et al.* 1994), and they provide the basis for ensuring both staff development and pupil progress. Although staff training is the last element listed it is the logical first step an organization must take in the development of quality services. Training is defined as 'instruction to ensure a level of competence among staff that will enable them to perform their responsibilities' (LaVigna *et al.* 1994, p.65). Staff training within Saplings is delivered through a multifaceted modular approach. All staff complete a 21-module in-house training course designed to equip them with the basic skills necessary to effectively carry out their roles and responsibilities. Table 6.1 shows the scope and sequence of Saplings' staff training course.

Each module is broken down into a number of sub-elements which communicate what is to be learned and the medium through which it is to be learned. Additionally the sub-elements operationally define the learning outcomes for each staff member. Box 6.1 shows one of the modules contained in the Saplings staff training course.

In the module in Box 6.1, content is taught to the staff member through lecture or video presentation and also through assigned reading material. From these inputs the staff member generates written output to be reviewed by a supervisor or the director of education to ascertain if key concepts are being assimilated and understood. Also contained in the module are a number of specific activities or responses that must be engaged in and observed by either a senior tutor or a supervisor before competency in a module area is credited to a staff member. Performance on these activities is rated as 'yes' or 'no' – that is, the staff member either performed the required response or s/he did not. This represents a training model whereby specific inputs (antecedents) are provided to generate specific output (behaviour or behaviour change), rather than the often-traditional system of providing input to staff without measuring the resultant output or behaviour change. Difficulty experienced by a staff member on any of the components contained in a module provides data that is used for individualizing training content and delivery medium.

**Table 6.1 The scope and sequence of the Saplings Model
of Education training course**

Module	Module title
1	Introduction to science and Applied Behaviour Analysis
2	Selection, definition and measurement of behaviour
3	Reinforcement
4	Prompting and fading
5	Shaping, chaining and task analysis
6	Behavioural objectives and IEPs
7	Schedules of reinforcement
8	Extinction
9	Differential reinforcement
10	Functional assessment
11	Stimulus/antecedent control
12	Precision teaching
13	Stages of learning
14	Charting, data analysis and instructional decision making
15	Direct instruction
16	Skinner's analysis of verbal behaviour
17	Augmentative communication
18	Visual schedules
19	Toilet training
20	Saplings raw data sheets
21	Saplings maintenance procedure

Box 6.1 Module 6: Behavioural objectives and IEPs

Complete Day 4 of the 10-day course on Applied Behaviour Analysis

or

Watch video Number 6 in Video Training Sequence

and

Read Handout 4 from the 10-day course on Applied Behaviour Analysis

Read Chapters 3, 4 and 5 of *How Well Does Your IEP Measure Up?* by Twachtman-Cullen and Twachtman-Reilly (2002)

Write essays based upon the above

Adequately write objectives across a number of curriculum areas as detailed by Supervisor

Display appropriate use of an IEP to Supervisor by

> Listing the three main components of a behavioural objective

> Pointing to and labelling each section of an IEP

> Pointing to and labelling each content area within a section

> Pointing to and labelling each element within a behavioural objective

> Listing appropriate data collection and prompting strategies for chosen objectives

> Listing review criteria for objectives

> Listing maintenance procedure.

The outcomes that result from the Saplings staff training course are:

- the presence of certain behaviours within the staff body skill repertoire
- the performance of these behaviours at certain criterion levels.

The effectiveness of the training in achieving these outcomes is measured through the quality control elements of performance monitoring and performance standards. Within Saplings, performance monitoring occurs on a daily basis, as pupil performance is a measure of teacher performance (Lindsley 1972). The rationale behind the data collection method and the fluency framework for pupils in Saplings has been delineated elsewhere (see Kerr, Smyth and McDowell 2003 for a description of precision teaching; also Kerr, Campbell and McGrory 2002). An additional level of assessment also occurs on a rotational (five week) basis whereby the teaching and performance of staff is monitored in a more formal manner. Monitoring takes two forms. First, teaching is observed for a specified period of time and performance measured against a pre-determined set of criteria. Saplings' teaching observation assessment contains eight sections. These sections are:

1. Teaching environment set up.
2. Communication.
3. Instructional delivery during teaching.
4. Prompting and error correction.
5. Pupil performance measurement.
6. Reinforcement.
7. Data collection and analysis.
8. Direct instruction performance.

In addition to these sections the teaching observation assessment also contains a section whereby a staff member can be forwarded for inclusion in a rotational prize draw should they display exceptional application of the principles of ABA. Saplings' minimum performance standard on teaching observation assessment is 80 per cent for tutors and 85 per cent for senior tutors. Should a staff member achieve 90 per cent or above on their teaching observation assessment they will not be assessed on this section in the subsequent rotation. Table 6.2 details the reinforcement section of the teaching observation assessment.

In the second part of performance monitoring, staff members are asked 20 questions relating to the principles of ABA and the technologies of precision teaching (PT) and direct instruction. Answers to these questions are rated against a five-point scale where 5 is excellent, 4 is good, 3 is adequate, 2 is poor, and 1 is not adequate. As in the observation section of the rotational performance monitoring, performance standards are set at 80 per cent for

Table 6.2 The reinforcement section of the teaching observation assessment

	Tutor performance – mark yes or no					
Section 6: Reinforcement	Rotation					
	1	2	3	4	5	6
Reinforcement used is appropriate to the learner, i.e. token vs. tangible etc.						
Item/items chosen by student is shown to act as a reinforcer						
Reinforcer assessment has been carried out within this rotation or as indicated by Supervisor						
Varied verbal praise used appropriately throughout						
Appropriate and varied tone of voice used						
Reinforcement delivered within two seconds of learner's behaviour						
Does data tracking interfere with reinforcement delivery?						
Social praise always paired with delivery of reinforcement including token delivery where appropriate						
Differentially reinforces correct responses over prompted or incorrect responses						
Uses differential reinforcement to obtain a desired behaviour, e.g. gives more reinforcement for quick behaviour than for slow						
Intermittent reinforcement used appropriately to maintain momentum						
Creative use of reinforcement demonstrated where appropriate						

tutors and 85 per cent for senior tutors. Performance above 90 per cent allows a staff member to skip assessment on this section in the subsequent rotation. Box 6.2 contains a sample of the questions staff members may be asked during the second part of their assessment.

In situations where staff members display difficulty acquiring or performing the skills contained in the staff training course, and monitored through rotational assessment, the first response is always to return to a training situation. This training can take the form of more reading, mentoring, modelling, self-review and feedback.

The final element considered essential for quality control in the educational setting is supervisory and management feedback. Staff feedback takes a variety of forms. Upon completion of the performance monitoring assessment a supervisor will provide verbal feedback to each individual staff member in terms of their performance on both components of the assessment. Performance is then displayed on a private, individual tracking system. In situations whereby performance falls below the performance criteria set a supervisor generates an action form. In this form the areas of difficulty are outlined for the staff member, suggestions for overcoming these difficulties are included, a time frame for performance re-assessment is agreed, and supervisor and tutor sign off the plan of action.

The paragraphs above describe the systems in place for the tutor and senior tutor staff members only. Similar systems in terms of training, monitoring, standards and feedback also exist for supervisory and director level staff members. Space constraints, however, prohibit a full description of these systems within this chapter.

The future: the growth of a forest!

This chapter presents a snapshot of the development of Saplings over the last few years, the systems that development has necessitated, and the multi-element nature of the services that are provided within a behaviour analytic approach. The success Saplings has experienced in providing educational services to children with autism has been extraordinary. The success of Saplings' current and past pupils in terms of personal development, access to new and rewarding environments, and family experiences has been a constant source of reinforcement for the professionals involved. It has also sparked phenomenal interest in the Saplings Model of Education as a framework for educational service delivery for children with autism all over Ireland. The demand for Saplings' services is a reflection of the quality of service that is

Box 6.2 Sample questions asked during rotational performance monitoring

1. Define and describe a functional relation.

2. Define and describe shaping.

3. Name all parts of a good behavioural objective.

4. What is meant by free operant?

5. Name and explain the three steps in implementing PT.

6. Define and explain a task analysis.

7. Define a prompt and give examples of types of prompts.

8. Define negative reinforcement.

9. Explain the difference between a continuous and intermittent schedule of reinforcement.

10. What effect does intermittent reinforcement have on behaviour?

11. What is an establishing operation?

12. Define extinction.

13. Can you name two effects of placing behaviour on an extinction schedule?

14. Define differential reinforcement.

15. Name and describe two types of differential reinforcement.

16. What is a discriminative stimulus?

17. What is meant by the term stimulus or antecedent control?

18. What is meant by functional assessment?

19. Name three verbal operants.

20. Name and describe the measurable dimensions of behaviour.

delivered to Saplings pupils on a daily basis. While this chapter tells the story of Saplings' development to date, the story has really only begun. At present Saplings is in the process of opening two new sites, one in south Dublin and another in Kilkenny. We are in the planning stages for a fourth site at Mullingar in County Westmeath, and have recently had a request by a parent lobby group to open a centre in the Carlow area. As long as Saplings continues to place emphasis on pupil success through quality service provision utilizing evidence-based practice at all levels of the system, the demand for the development of new centres will continue. The question now is: how many Saplings make a forest?

References

Constitution of Ireland (1 July 1937) www.taoiseach.gov.ie./upload/static/256.pdf (accessed 5 July 2005).

Cooper, J.O., Heron, T.E. and Heward, W.L. (1987) *Applied Behavior Analysis*. Oklahoma, OH: Merrill Publishing Company.

Kerr, K.P., Campbell, A. and McGrory, S. (2002) 'The Saplings Model of Education: case studies in autism.' *Journal of Precision Teaching 18*, 2, 37–48.

Kerr, K.P., Smyth, P. and McDowell, C. (2003) 'Precision teaching children with autism: helping design effective programmes.' *Early Child Development and Care 173*, 4, 399–410.

LaVigna, G.W., Willis, T.J., Shaull, J.F., Abedi, M. and Sweitzer, M. (1994) *The Periodic Service Review: A Total Quality Assurance System for Human Services and Education*. Baltimore, MD: Paul H. Brookes Publishing Company.

Lindsley, O.R. (1972) 'From Skinner to precision teaching: the child knows best.' In J.B. Jordan and L.S. Robbins (eds) *Let's Try Something Else Kind of Thing* (pp.1–19). Arlington, VA: Council on Exceptional Children.

Twachtman-Cullen, D. and Twachtman-Reilly, J. (2002) *How Well Does Your IEP Measure Up? Quality Indicators for Effective Service*. Higganum, CT: Starfish.

CHAPTER 7

Lessons Learned from Starting a Community-Based ABA Programme for Kids with ASDs

Eric Messick and Shelley Wise

Percy

Autism originally introduced itself to our family in the form of a beautiful (if unusual) blond-haired, blue-eyed son, Percy, who was happy to keep to himself and play quietly. What a relief for me, his mother, to have such a placid son after my first child who required a bundle of attention. However, by the time Percy reached the age of two and a half years old it was glaringly obvious that our beautiful son was slipping away. Gone was the child who attempted to sing 'Happy Birthday' to himself at the age of two and I (Shelley) felt that if we didn't do something fast we would lose him forever.

We desperately researched and came up with strong suspicions of autism, so we pursued a diagnosis. Smack! Our first confrontation with The System. Totally desperate and completely unprepared to wait the six months that we were quoted by a local agency at the hospital, we scraped together the money to go to a private psychologist (the very same one whom we would have seen in the public health system). Much to our dismay Percy was given the diagnosis of 'global developmental delay' and we were told to wait until he was five to see how things developed. Unacceptable! Despite our every effort to hold Percy near to us, our son was so withdrawn by now that even we, his parents, felt the imaginary barriers he had constructed out of cold concrete and hard steel.

Unfortunately it also happened to be the year that our local Autistic Association of New Zealand branch (now Autism New Zealand (ANZ) Waikato) had accidentally been left out of the local phone book. After searching for some help in our local area, our minds already filled with anxiety (I didn't think to look for a National Autistic Association), we continued our quest for answers, unsupported and unaided except by the families that were going through the same desperate struggle that we were experiencing.

Left with the ensuing feeling of helplessness and the strong desire to have some control over this monster thing which had taken over our son, I was catapulted into the next 12 months determined to try anything and everything to help him. Our local pre-school special-needs agency was only able to offer support one morning a week and that support, I felt, was only reactive. I felt that a proactive approach was needed and *now*! Hearing tests, CAT scans, six intensive months doing the Doman programme (more money), heavy metal detoxification, dairy, gluten, additive and colouring-free diets, auditory integration training (lots more money), and even secretin injections. At the age of three and a half, it was during one of these therapies that Percy was finally given a diagnosis of autism by an overseas visiting child psychologist, which came as a relief and a starting point for finding him some real help.

It wasn't until we made the commitment to do applied behaviour analysis (ABA) that we began to see some real changes in Percy's behaviour. Unfortunately though, ABA was not readily available at that time in New Zealand. Any families who wanted to give it a go had to meet the expenses of flying in a consultant from Australia or elsewhere, in addition to the programme costs, and paying for therapists. We were a one-income, low-income family with three children so we begged and borrowed from our families to get the programme up and running. We unofficially used Percy's respite care hours to pay a part-time therapist and because our local special-education unit, at that time, wouldn't allow us to use his pre-school entitlement at home I acted as his therapist for the rest of the time. An unsatisfactory situation, especially when all the ABA books indicated 30–40 hours per week were required in order to be effective; but I felt we needed to do what we could because doing nothing would give us nothing in return. And so, thanks to the generosity of family, we managed to continue a part-time ABA programme for Percy at home for about 18 months.

Both the funds and my energy dried up at the same time so, luckily because of full funding from our local special-education services, Percy continued his education fully supported at our local mainstream kindergarten. It is important to note here that Percy's kindergarten help, though dedicated, was untrained and not behaviourally based. He is now at a special-needs, school which means that Percy is now in contact regularly with an occupational therapist, physiotherapist, psychologist, speech language therapist, trained teachers and teacher aides. The fact remains in New Zealand, though, that unless your child is categorized as high or very-high needs such services are difficult to access and proper ABA programmes are still only obtainable privately. It wasn't until Percy was seven and a half and I had become involved with Autism New Zealand (ANZ) Waikato, and realized the need to be part of the system so I may access services, that I returned to the hospital-based agency for his official New Zealand, state-funded diagnosis – autism and severe intellectual disability.

The techniques that I learned as his ABA therapist have put me in good stead for helping my son and I have continued to utilize these techniques as a therapist for other families and in Percy's daily life. It was through my knowledge of ABA practices and the assistance of a University of Waikato Master's student (Alena Nixon) that I was able to teach him the ABA-based Picture Exchange Communication System (PECS). Once again, this service is not readily available to all families in New Zealand. Without access to a speech language therapist on a regular basis such facilities are unreachable to the average family who are dealing with the daily stresses of the world of autism.

I continue to fight for improved service delivery, now working as service coordinator for ANZ Waikato, dealing with, on a daily basis, an increasing number of families being given a diagnosis of autism or Asperger's syndrome. It is through this group that I have come to work with Eric. As ANZ Waikato programme director, Eric now runs a variety of ABA-based programmes for children on the autism spectrum aged 2 to 13 years old. These programmes are funded by grants and donations, and although I am eternally grateful to our funders for their support, it is a constant battle to find funding to keep these services available to our families. Also, due to the lack of ABA expertise in New Zealand, we are only able to offer these programmes in our city of Hamilton although our geographical area stretches from the rural communities of Coromandel all the way down to Turangi (a very large part of the North Island of New Zealand).

In my role, I continue to come across families having to go to extreme lengths to obtain services for their family members with autism – a mother flying down to Wellington to personally convince needs assessors of her son's situation, parents of pre-schoolers at their wits' end being told that 'toddlers are hard work anyway', and an influx of adults in the community with either new diagnoses of Asperger's syndrome or being reintroduced into society having spent most of their lives in institutional settings with the aid of often poorly trained carers.

My son continues to have behavioural issues, sensory problems (he is a severe toe walker), and most likely will always require one-on-one support. However, with what I have learned through ABA I am now in control of the situation and able to cope with whatever the future may bring. I feel that ABA should be standard practice in educational settings for people with autism and that its techniques can also be utilized in helping people and carers cope with everyday living skills. My personal experiences with ABA show that it is not only effective, but also that the techniques used can hold their own in most situations and are skills that are vital for families to survive the enigma of autism.

The need for ABA programmes

Since Shelley's first confrontation with The System, the phone number of the Waikato branch of Autism New Zealand has been listed in the phone book year after year and five very basic ABA-based, group-oriented programmes have been developed for people with autism spectrum disorders (ASDs) in our community, the Waikato region. Shelley's story of Percy is certainly not a rare occurrence; people with ASDs in this country are at a distinct disadvantage due to the lack of funding for and general availability of ABA programmes. In 2001, ANZ Waikato conducted a nationwide survey to identify some of the gaps in services. The following excerpt is taken from the summary of the results:

> The most significant finding was the lack of knowledge by many professionals about autistic spectrum disorder across all sectors of Health, Welfare and Education…the survey highlights very poor referrals to support agencies and availability of financial support and respite care… An alarming number of parents stated that although they had been allocated a number of [Carer Support] days they could not use them as there is a huge difficulty in obtaining caregivers to provide the support… Evidence from parents indicates that the schools system, in particular

the mainstream High School system, is failing their sons and daughters... For those parents whose sons or daughters are in residential care, many were not happy with the level of care or the knowledge the staff had of autism... For the small group of parents who did fight for a quality of life for their child the treatment many of them received and still receive by some of the providers is appalling... As a result of the lack of public services, parents are paying for private services, however this is highly dependent on their income level so can lead to guilt for many parents who cannot afford to pay for services. (ANZ 2001, pp.i–ii)

The System was, and still is, disabling people with ASDs by not providing the help that they need.

According to a giant body of research (Cambridge Center for Behavioral Studies 2005), one type of help that people with ASD require are individually tailored ABA programmes that teach the very important life skills that are required to lead a happy and independent life. In particular, a few years of early intensive behavioural intervention can not only achieve this end, but also save communities money in the long run. In the US, Jacobson, Mulick and Green (1998) found that early intensive ABA services for children with ASDs can save taxpayers approximately US$200,000 per child to age 22 and about US$1,000,000 to age 55. The savings to the community comes from the decrease of lifelong support (such as day care or residential care) required by individuals who have been empowered through skills acquired during early intervention. In the UK, the charity Parents for the Early Intervention of Autism in Children (PEACH 1997) found that similar early intensive ABA services could save taxpayers £150,000 during the first 15 years of special education and £1,000,000 to £2,000,000 for the following 50 years of adult life, again through savings in long-term care. Yet, despite the huge benefits to individuals with an ASD and to the community, ABA programmes are still non-existent and/or not funded in many parts of the world. What, then, should be done?

We've witnessed many tears, countless people fighting for their children's and family members' rights to service, waves of miracle and pop treatments that suck money out of the pockets of desperate families, and a never-ending stream of heartbreaking stories. Four years ago, we had enough. We began a basic ABA-based programme to begin filling one of the gaps in local services and we now provide more ABA-based programmes that are the beginnings of what people with ASD in our community need. The programmes are intended to accommodate the ability range of pre-school children through to school-aged children and to fit together in a way that transitions participants from the early programmes to the later programmes. We do not intend for these programmes to substitute for more intensive ABA programmes; instead, we intend for them to be a starting point for families who are interested in ABA services and a beginning for students and future professionals who are interested in an ABA career. Also, we realize that the programmes sometimes fall short of the best practices of ABA due to resource, financial and personnel constraints. However, these same constraints are evident elsewhere in the world and are a fact of life. Despite them, we have been able to develop and expand our range of ABA-based programmes in a way that continues to approximate the best practices of ABA. In short, places in the world with absolutely no ABA need to start somewhere! What follows is an account of where we are now, how we started and where we would like to be.

Where we are now

The national body of ANZ oversees several nationwide branches that cater to the members in their region. Our branch, ANZ Waikato, is currently run by a committee consisting of mostly parents and occasional professionals and university students. Membership to the organization is free and most members are people with an ASD and their families. Members of our branch receive a monthly newsletter, have access to our field officer and service manager (Shelley) for some assistance (but not individualized programming or problem solving), and are eligible to attend the programmes and activities that we sponsor. Our ABA-based programmes include five programmes that span from ability levels of early childhood through to early teens: Little Kids' Club (Little KC), Supported Kids' Club (Supported KC), Kids' Club (KC), Rec Club, and a Holiday Programme for school-aged children.

Little KC caters to children with ASDs who are approximately aged three to five. The programme occurs weekly for one hour in the afternoon and is currently attended by two to five children. Our venue is a large church hall that is quite inexpensive to hire, but provides the basics, including storage space for our equipment and materials. The families arrive through a foyer where they are greeted by our service manager and asked to sign in. The children are immediately allowed into the hall and the parents and other family usually enter the adjacent kitchen for some coffee and a bit of respite! From the kitchen, the children can be seen either by opening and peeking through the door or by opening and peeking through a roll-up window. We've found that separating the parents (or other family) in this way sometimes increases the children's involvement because it temporarily de-creases the reinforcers (i.e. mums, dads and family members) available outside of the programme. Some parents remain with their children during the programme. This level of involvement works well for parents who are working on their own ABA skills. Other parents sit inside the hall. We ask these individuals to dissuade children from approaching them during the programme by saying something like, 'we can talk later, but right now the activity is _____', and then ignoring any subsequent approaches by avoiding eye contact and pointing to the location of the current activity. When the families have arrived and when the staff are ready, the programme begins.

It begins by the programme coordinator approaching each child in the hall and saying something like, 'one minute until Square Time'. The coordina-tor then blows a whistle and all children approach and sit in a five-metre by five-metre square demarcated by four orange marker cones and four white lines on the floor. Children who are still learning this behaviour receive physical prompts, which are faded over time, from support staff called *guides* or from their parent if a parent is serving as a guide. Guides gently coax the children to the square with the least restrictive prompt (from least to most restrictive: a word or phrase, a gesture, physical contact such as a tap in the right direction, passive blocking to disallow movement away from the square) and also provide praise, physical contact or other reinforcing consequences (such as edible items) as soon as the children enter and sit in the square. From the square, the children can see four activity cards on the wall as well as the programme coordinator (Eric) who always stands near these cards during Square Time. The cards make up an activity schedule, are arranged vertically, and are stuck to the wall with a non-permanent, reusable, putty-like adhesive. Our four activities always occur in the same order, last approximately 15 minutes each, and are called, respectively: Square Time, Sport, Art, and Square Time.

When all of the children and guides are sitting in the square, the coordina-tor becomes the focus of attention, much like a teacher, and the first Square Time begins. That is, all eyes should be on the coordinator, including the guides' eyes because the guides' behaviour may model appropriate behaviour for the children. As a means to this end, distractions should be minimized and there should be no talking in the square. The coordinator provides a high rate of praise, physical contact or other reinforcers to the children who are main-taining eye contact and sitting appropriately, while the guides provide prompts or passive blocking (gently using their body as a movable wall) to keep the children in the square. Again, prompts and blocking should be faded over time – we want the children to remain in the square because it is fun, not because they are physically manipulated to do so. Children who are always physically manipulated to do things will always need this kind of help. When the children are sitting and maintaining at least some eye contact, the coordinator calls on each child to approach and to stick their name card, presented to the child by a guide, to the wall. If necessary, the guide offers the least-restrictive prompt to get the behaviour to occur and to get the child to return to a seated position in the square. When all of the children have put their names up, the coordinator informs the children that Square Time is over, immediately removes the Square-Time activity picture from the wall (while prompting and reinforcing gazes at the activity picture), informs the children of the next activity by pointing to it and naming it, and blows the whistle. The children then move to the area of the hall where the next activity is to take place and, if necessary, prompts occur in the same manner as when the whistle blew for Square Time.

Our next activity is Sport and involves balls that are usually light, inflatable and about the size of a basketball. Children in our programme have a diverse range of sporting skills, so we tailor this activity to each child's needs. Some of the children learn kicking; others learn catching or throwing. Regardless of the specific skill taught, we tend to use discrete-trial training (DTT) for all of the children. For example, if we are teaching a child to kick, chase, and kick a ball again, we would have one guide prompt and reinforce the behaviours of kicking and chasing while another guide uses a data sheet to record corrects, incorrects, and prompts. Again, reinforcers can be anything that increases the chances that the target behaviour occurs in the future and prompts should be faded. Depending on the child and their skill, we do anywhere from 10 to 20 trials per block of trials and anywhere from one to three blocks of trials per Sport activity. Following each block of trials, we allow a break of approximately one to two minutes during which the child can run freely about the hall and play with toys and guides.

Here it is worthwhile to briefly comment on the difference between Lovaas therapy, DTT, ABA and behaviour analysis. Behaviour analysis is the science of behaviour. ABA is a broad term that describes the application of the science of behaviour to, well, behaviour of just about any kind! Lovaas therapy and DTT are specific interventions (types of therapies) and are only two of the many ways that behaviour analysis can be applied. Lovaas therapy strictly means therapy done by those trained by Lovaas or trained in his specific methods. It is often used interchangeably (and slightly confusingly) with DTT described above. Although Lovaas coined the term DTT, it is probably best to refer to programmes as DTT if they resemble the above description. Most good programmes incorporate a variety of ABA techniques, so it is generally appropriate to say that a programme is an ABA programme if it has behavioural elements such as DTT, precision teaching, PECS, etc. It would probably be silly and more confusing if there was a name for every subtly different ABA programme – please don't call our programmes Autism New Zealand Therapy!

Back to the Sport activity at Little KC. Ideally, children who have learned complementary skills may be paired so that their skills might form the basis for a cooperative-play repertoire. For example, if two children master catching and throwing, they might be paired up for part of Sport so that they may catch and throw with each other rather than with their guides. When all of the children have completed their blocks of trials, the coordinator alerts them of the soon-to-occur whistle, blows the whistle, and the children return to the square with the help of prompts as described previously. When the children return to the square and are seated with the guides, the coordinator removes the Sport activity picture in the same way as the Square-Time picture was removed, informs the children of the next activity, blows the whistle, and the guides and children move to where the next activity is to take place.

Art, the next activity, is similar to Sport in that it involves blocks of DTT for about 15 minutes. The specific skills taught, again, are tailored to each child's art-related needs. These needs have involved basic writing skills ranging from picking up a crayon and making a mark on paper to making circles or lines within boxes. Really, any skills that fall within the rubric of art would be fine. We have targeted writing skills because they are probably more important than other art-related skills. Similar to Sport, Art involves one to three blocks of trials with breaks and the activity ends when all children have completed their blocks of trials and the whistle blows.

The final Square Time begins with the removal of the Art activity picture. The coordinator then calls each child to the wall so that the child can remove their name from the wall and each child returns to the square where they remain seated, again until the other children are finished. The coordinator ends the session by removing the final Square-Time picture and blowing the whistle, after which the children walk to the foyer where their parents or caregivers await. The children hand their name cards to their respective parents or caregivers who, in turn, provide praise and other reinforcing consequences to the child. As the families and children leave, they return the name cards to the reception desk. At this time, the programme coordinator is available to discuss the session with the children's families or carers – our methods are always transparent and we always make what we are doing and why we are doing it clear. When the families or carers and children have left, the staff discuss the session and problem solve in anticipation of the next session in the following week.

Children who are more able than the children who attend Little KC or who are attending school usually attend one of the other programmes. Supported KC is the next programme in the series and works best for children who already have some direction-following skills as well as some fine and gross motor skills. Language skills are not necessary. It begins in the same way as Little KC begins. Families enter the foyer, sign in, and children enter the hall (but must report to and stay in the square) while other family members enter the kitchen area. On occasion, some family members sit along a wall in the hall and observe. We ask these individuals to dissuade children from approaching them just as we do during Little KC. The programme occurs in the same venue and runs fortnightly for an hour and a half after school and utilizes some of the Little-KC staff.

Similar to Little KC, it begins by the programme coordinator alerting the children of the whistle, then blowing the whistle to begin Square Time. Guides and children sit in the square where they can see seven activity cards on the wall as well as the programme coordinator, a sign posting four rules (participate in activities, follow directions, be nice to everybody, stay in the hall and off the stage), and another sign with a sad, neutral and happy face arranged in a horizontal row. Of the seven activities, two change with every session (Activity 1 and Activity 2) while the other five stay the same. The two changing activities can be any game or activity that fits the children, culture, available resources and budget. We tend to programme a sport-type activity and an art-type activity; there are many Internet resources and books on children's activities that might help with selecting activities. It may also be a good idea to programme activities that are likely to occur at the children's schools or homes. Simply ask a local child what is hot and what is not! The activities always occur in the following order and always correspond to the activity schedule: Square Time, Activity 1, Activity 2, Snack Time, Sit-Down Games, Square Time, and Store (see Figure 7.1).

During or prior to this first Square Time, children and their guides prepare a point sheet that is laminated and contains a place to write the child's name and

Figure 7.1: The activity schedule. Steph, programme coordinator for Kids' Club, helps a boy affix his name to the wall.

date, a mini version of the activity schedule (containing removable pictures attached with fasteners), a box next to each picture to write the name of the activity, a row of three boxes next to each picture and activity-name box for keeping track of points using stamper markers, and a place to write a point goal for the session. When all of the children and guides are sitting in the square and when the point sheets are prepared, the coordinator again becomes the focus of attention. Similar to Little KC, when the children are sitting, maintaining at least some eye contact and being quiet, the coordinator calls on each child to approach and to stick their name card (temporarily stuck to the point sheet) onto the wall under the centre neutral face. Again, the guides' behaviour should model appropriate behaviour for the children and the coordinator should offer a high rate of praise, physical contact or other reinforcers for appropriate in-square behaviour. If necessary, prompts and blocking can be used (but, again, faded over time).

The faces on the wall and the children's name cards are part of our KC behaviour management system and are only present to ease the transition from the Supported KC system to the KC system. The KC system will be described in more detail later. For five of the seven activities in Supported KC (i.e. all activities except Snack Time and Store), participants can earn up to three stamps (or tick marks, whichever works best on the laminated point sheet) per activity for a total of up to 15 stamps. If, at the end of the final Square Time, a child's earned stamps are greater than or equal to their stamp goal, the child receives five dollars' worth of *Kid Cash* which can be saved or spent at our store that opens at the end of every session. The faces and names on the wall mirror the child's current behaviour – if they are earning most stamps, their guide or the coordinator moves their name under the happy face; some stamps, under the neutral face; few stamps, under the sad face. Children's point sheets are stamped by their guides when a triple whistle is blown by the coordinator (i.e. when the coordinator blows the whistle three times in a quick succession) and only if, at the time of the triple whistle, the child's behaviour is in accordance with the posted rules. So, during each of the five stamp-eligible activities, the coordinator offers three triple whistles and the guides stamp the appropriate boxes next to the current activity if their child is following the rules. For behaviour analysts, this system is similar to a five-minute, variable-interval schedule of reinforcement meaning that roughly, following an average of every five minutes, each child can earn a stamp if they are behaving appropriately. From the child's point of view, there is no way of predicting when they will be 'checked' for appropriate behaviour, so the more time spent following the rules, the more likely the child will earn a stamp.

In addition to simply giving a stamp, the guide should immediately engage in brief conversation with the child following each triple whistle. If a stamp is earned, the guide can say things like, 'good, you are participating in the activity, following directions, being nice to everybody, and are in the hall and off the stage', can point to the rules, and then say, 'this is why you get a stamp'. If a stamp is not earned, then similar discourse may follow except the guide can point to the rules not being followed as well as the ones being followed and can offer corrective feedback such as, 'taking Jimmy's toy isn't being nice, part of being nice is asking for things, next time you should ask nicely'. Between whistles, the rules can be referred to in a similar way, especially for children who are behaving appropriately. Rules are often cited by adults when children are not following them, but a better philosophy is to spend most of the time 'catching the child being good'. A child cooperating with another child might be approached by a guide and asked, 'I just caught you doing something – what was it?' When the child describes the appropriate cooperation or is prompted to do so, the guide can say, 'great, that is being nice!'

There are occasions between triple whistles when inappropriate behaviour may occur and in these cases, an immediate consequence should be given. In such situations, we sometimes use simple correction or time-out. Simple correction means, simply, requiring the child to correct the environment to the state it was in prior to the inappropriate behaviour. For example, if a child knocks over some materials, the child may be required to put the materials back prior to returning to the activity and earning stamps. The guide would move the child's name card and might refer to the being-nice rule and inform the child that stamps can only be earned when the child is being nice again; if the stamps are working, then the child might speedily correct the situation and begin following the rules again. More severe inappropriate behaviour, such as aggression and property destruction, probably warrant time-out. A time-out means removing the child from a reinforcing environment for a brief period of time; one minute for each year of the child's age is a good rule of thumb. During this time, the child's name should be moved under the sad face and no stamps should be given. Time-out can occur either just outside of the hall or in the corner of the hall, should involve an experienced guide or the programme coordinator, and should be carefully monitored. Immediately following the time-out, the child should then restore the environment if any damage or disruption was done, as in simple correction, and should offer apologies to anyone who was affected by the behaviour. Finally, brief problem-solving discourse may help teach the child an alternative response to the inappropriate behaviour. For example, the guide might say, 'If Tom takes your toy again, what can you do?' The guide can then prompt the child, saying something like, 'tell a guide', or 'ask for it back', or something similar. There are many additional behaviour management strategies that can be incorporated into programmes like ours and we encourage prospective programme coordinators to experiment (see Figure 7.2). Generally, we find that simple strategies work the best and are adhered to more often. Also, remember to consider the individuality of each child. If a child enjoys putting objects away and you require the child to do this putting away following an episode of object throwing, you may actually be reinforcing object throwing! You'll need to be creative in situations like this or you'll need a behaviour analyst to give some input. Ideally, you'll have one working for you by now. If not, then maybe consequating object throwing with a time-out will be a start. But keep looking for that behaviour analyst; they are handy in situations like these.

Figure 7.2: Little Kids' Club activity with assistant coordinator and mum and dad volunteers

Back to the first Square Time! When all of the children have attached their name cards to the wall and after the three triple whistles occur, the coordinator informs the children that Square Time has finished, usually after approximately 15 minutes. The children, with help if need be, then remove their individual activity cards while the coordinator removes the large activity card from the wall (or calls upon a child to remove it). The coordinator then blows the whistle and directs the children to Activity 1. As described earlier, Activity 1 and Activity 2 might be a sport- and an art-related activity. Three triple whistles occur during each of these 15-minute activities and the children, coordinator and guides briefly return to the square following each activity to remove activity cards as described previously.

The five-minute Snack Time begins following Activity 2. The children sit in small groups on tablecloths laid out on the floor or at appropriately sized tables and receive some biscuits and juice when they are sitting appropriately. No triple whistles occur during Snack Time because the activity is quite brief, but, if necessary, the point system can be extended through this time. When the children have finished their snack, the coordinator prompts removal of the Snack-Time activity card, removes the corresponding card on the wall, and distributes some board games or other kinds of games for the Sit-Down Games activity. The children do not go back to the square between Snack

Time and Sit-Down Games, only to save some time. But, if necessary, a return to the square could easily occur if the routine helps the children.

During Sit-Down Games, children play in pairs or in small groups and appropriate play is prompted by the guides when necessary. The activity lasts for about 25 minutes and, as in most of the other activities, three triple whistles occur. Any games can be used, especially games that are popular in the children's homes and schools. The games should be matched to the children's skill levels and should involve waiting and turn taking when possible. Games that are less structured may be appropriate for some children, but because they do not require turn taking, they may be less effective at teaching cooperative play. However, children who are still learning to sit, wait and take turns may benefit from first playing a very simple and more active game and then changing to a more structured, turn-taking game in later sessions. Another way to accommodate children who prefer more active games is to allow a *run around* a few times during Sit-Down Games. For example, we have programmed a victory lap into some children's game playing. Immediately following a win during Tic-Tac-Toe, the child is allowed to run around the hall – a victory lap! Of course, good sportspersonship is an important part of game play. Children are encouraged to shake hands and congratulate each other following wins and losses; we take special care in congratulating the loser of games for being a good sport (by offering verbal praise, high fives, etc.) because accepting a loss is an area in which many children have difficulties (and professional athletes too!). We encourage keeping track of scores, wins and losses because competition is part of life and it is better to allow the children to experience victory and defeat in an appropriate setting than it is to expect the children to experience and cope with these situations on their own. We do, on occasion, *fudge* games. Children who are new to this kind of game play might begin playing with a guide (so that they are less distracted by others) and the guide might purposely allow the child to win so that the activity is more likely to become a reinforcer. Ideally, this fudging should eventually fade and good sportspersonship should be taught as described above; otherwise, the child may develop into a sore loser!

Sit-Down Games transitions into the final Square Time in the same way as the other activities transition. During this Square Time, the coordinator can offer short commentary on the day's session, can specifically describe how certain children followed the rules, and can provide praise and other reinforcing consequences to children who are behaving appropriately. If materials still need to be put away, some children can be called upon to assist guides in tidying up (some kids enjoy helping) while the others wait in the square. Triple whistles occur during this time and those who are helping can be congratulated for 'being nice to everybody'. We sometimes find that this kind of public praise facilitates helping from others. Publicly commenting on what other children are doing right is sometimes a better management strategy than commenting on what a single child is not doing right.

When the three triple whistles have occurred during the final Square Time, the coordinator asks the guides and children to count their stamps, and guides move the children's name cards under the appropriate faces. Name cards under the sad face belong to children who did not meet their point goal; under the middle face, they did meet their point goal but did not receive most of the available points; under the happy face, they did meet their point goal and received most or all of the available points. The coordinator then calls on children who are raising their hands and sitting appropriately. Each child who is called removes the last Square Time activity card from their point sheet, approaches the wall with their point sheet, removes their name card, puts their name card and point sheet on a desk, receives or does not receive Kid Cash, and leaves the square to visit the Store. Immediately following the Store, children rejoin their families or caregivers and go home while the staff remain for a problem-solving debrief as in Little KC.

The Store is just a table with several inexpensive toys and lollies neatly arranged upon it. Each toy and lolly contains a price tag ranging from $5 to $20 (see Figure 7.3). The price tags contain spaces for stamps so that a child can select an item and put it on lay-by. All items in our store have price tags of $5, $10, $15 or $20. If a child puts an item on lay-by, their name is written on the tag and a stamp is stamped for each $5 paid. When all the designated spaces are filled with stamps, the item is paid for.

Each time the child puts some Kid Cash towards the toy on lay-by, one of the boxes is stamped until all of the payments have been made (and all of the boxes have been stamped) and the child receives the toy. If a child selects a $15 toy, then it takes three sessions to earn the toy – quite a big task for some children! Although we encourage children to save, we do not dictate how their Kid Cash is to be spent and we never take away Kid Cash. We always have $5 items, so children who earn Kid Cash can buy something after each session. We also never bend the rules and give Kid Cash to children who did not meet their goal as this would completely undermine the system. Some difficult situations may arise at the end of sessions: two in particular. First, for children

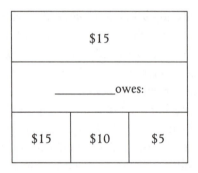

Figure 7.3: Store price tag

who did not meet their point goal, and second, for children who do not have enough Kid Cash to buy the items of their choice.

The point system works only if children come into contact with the consequences of behaving appropriately as well as inappropriately. Not getting Kid Cash is as important as getting Kid Cash when it comes to learning how to behave appropriately. If a child is disgruntled after not receiving Kid Cash, then it is probably a good sign because it suggests that Kid Cash is indeed a reinforcer. No punishment or lecture should occur for children not making their point goals; instead, any conversation should relate to what the child did right that day and what the child ought to do next time. The child should not be publicly humiliated in any way and a certain amount of empathy might be in order: 'I can see that you are sad, we'll try again next time.' Never, never give in to a tantrumming child! Instead, offer appropriate prompts and immediate consequences during the next session so that the child is more likely to behave appropriately and, consequently, is more likely to meet their point goal.

It is a fact of life that most people cannot afford everything that they want. Behaviourally speaking, reinforcers are abound, but it is not always easy or possible to get them. A way of increasing people's happiness is to teach them how to obtain these reinforcers in an appropriate and reliable fashion (and this empowerment is the aim of our programmes as well as many ABA-based programmes). Unfortunately, there is still a limit to what sorts of reinforcers individuals can obtain. If a child tantrums at the site of currently non-obtainable toys, I usually tell their parents, and the child, that I feel the same way when I press my nose against the window of the motorcycle shop and see all of the shiny, expensive motorcycles! But the world will never give me a motorcycle unless I pay for it and this kind of lesson can be taught early by not giving in to tantrums and by teaching children how to obtain reinforcers appropriately.

But aren't we bribing the children by giving them Kid Cash for behaviour that they ought to do anyway? In short, no. *We* set the rules and the conditions under which Kid Cash is given, not the children. Further, these children often do not do what they 'ought to do' without a system in place. People who work full time would stop working if their weekly pay cheque (a reinforcer for working) was no longer delivered. A lot of behaviour is maintained by consequences, sometimes very subtle consequences, and making these consequences explicit (especially in learning environments like our programmes) is not bribery, but rather a way of mimicking real life. For example, a DTT programme in which a child receives a piece of lolly following a correct letter-naming response is a mini-version of a 40-hour work week. In our programmes, the analogy is similar except the reinforcer is delivered following a one-and-a-half hour 'work week'. A good ABA programme, then, is not an artificial means of managing behaviour, but instead a systematic approximation of real life that empowers individuals by teaching new behaviours so that these new behaviours function well outside of the learning environment.

KC is the next programme in the series after Little KC and Supported KC. KC has exactly the same format as Supported KC, except the behaviour management system is less intensive. Children in this programme usually have at least some verbal skills and require less prompting, simple correction, time-out, and other consequences. Instead of using point sheets, children in this programme use behavioural contracts. Prior to or during the first Square Time, children complete their contracts (with the help of guides if need be). The contracts have spaces for the child's name, date, and the signatures of the coordinator and the child (see Figure 7.4). There are places to write two optional expected behaviours in addition to rule following. The spaces at the bottom are where the programme coordinator and child sign to make the contract 'legal'.

Each contract states that if the child follows the posted rules during the session, then they will get $5 Kid Cash (see Figure 7.5). Our Kid Cash comes in $5, $10 and $20 denominations.

It is each child's responsibility to seek out the coordinator for a signature. The coordinator can engage in a brief conversation with the child as he or she signs the contract and the conversation may include questions about what the contract states – 'what do you need to do to get Kid Cash?' – as well as questions relating to the child's history in the programme – 'remember what

I, _____, agree to do my absolute, complete best at Kids' Club today. This means that:

1. I will follow all of the Kids' Club rules all of the time.

2. _____

3. _____

If I **do** the above things (☺☺), then:

1. I will get $5 Kid Cash.

If I **do not do** the above things (☹), then:

1. I will not get $5 Kid Cash.

Sign here to agree to this contract:

_____   _____

Coordinator   Kid

Figure 7.4: A contract used at Kids' Club

happened last time when you followed all of the rules?' or 'last time you were not participating and you didn't get any Kid Cash, what should you do this time?'

Like Supported KC, triple whistles occur in this programme and similar discourse between guides and the children occur when the whistle is blown – 'are you following the rules right now?' However, the contract children do not earn stamps; instead, their name cards get moved or stay in the same place depending on their behaviour. On occasion, we do have some children who still use the point sheets in this programme and we do revert back to the point sheets for children who are not doing well with the contract system. In these cases, we use the exact same system as Supported KC, but with the intent of transitioning the point sheets to the contracts. This is why both behaviour management systems are in place in Supported KC and in KC. At the end of the last Square Time, children who have name cards under the neutral or

Figure 7.5: Kid Cash

happy face receive Kid Cash and children who have name cards under the sad face do not. The same store opens, the session ends in the same way as Supported KC, and staff remain for a debrief.

Rec Club is the next programme in the series and is currently under development, but running. Like Supported KC and KC, it takes place in the same hall, utilizes some of the same staff, and occurs fortnightly for an hour and a half. The children tend to have reasonable verbal, motor and direction-following skills but require prompting and practice when learning new games. The behaviour management system is similar to KC in that it utilizes the name cards and faces, but the children do not complete contracts and the Store is not available at the end of the session. Instead, the expectations of the children are iterated only through the posted rules, and excellent behaviour (i.e. behaviour that allows the children's name cards to be moved under the happy face) is reinforced with a chance to win a small prize during a lottery occurring at the end of every session. So the amount of structure (e.g. point sheets and contracts) is less and the amount of tangible reinforcers is less as well. In short, the children get less help to behave well.

Finally, during some school holidays we run a week-long Holiday Programme lasting for five hours daily. The Holiday Programmes that we've run have included children who attend Supported KC, KC and Rec Club, so the ability range is often quite diverse. However, we have been able to make it work regardless of this difficulty. The Holiday Programme is really a long version of KC and incorporates all of the previously discussed behaviour management strategies and types of activities. Activities last for 30 minutes instead of 15 minutes, so ten activities occur every day. We open the Store after the first five and then after the last five activities so that children who have a bad morning have a clean slate in the afternoon.

This programme is probably the most enjoyable to run because we are with the children daily and for extended periods of time, so we see behaviour change much quicker than we do during our fortnightly programmes. We can also programme more difficult and time-consuming activities such as trips to the local pool, sloppy arts and crafts, scavenger hunts and complicated obstacle courses. It is a time that families and carers can spend away from their children without the worries that accompany less-structured, less-ASD-friendly programmes (after all everyone needs a holiday!). Finally it is a time for people new to the field of ABA to see behaviour change *in vivo*.

How we started and where we would like to be

A few years ago our programmes actually started with a Holiday Programme similar to the current version described above. Our committee acquired some funding to pay a coordinator (Eric, who had a fair amount of ABA experience and relevant academic qualifications) and to purchase some very basic supplies. We literally started with nothing. On top of not having any toys or other supplies, we had no building, so we hired a hall at a very inexpensive rate and inside the hall was – nothing! We then purchased some inexpensive supplies, received a few second-hand toys from some families and local places such as the Salvation Army, and scraped together as many free and inexpensive resources as we could. We operated on the premise that often the most expensive toy's box is more fun than the toy itself and collected about 100 cardboard boxes and assembled them into a fort that we called Fort Box. It turned out to be a hit. We created point sheets (see Figure 7.6), rules and a programme structure and we advertised the programme in the newsletter indicating that each child must be accompanied by a guide, provided by the family. About a dozen children enrolled.

Day one was difficult. There were 12 children who had never attended such a programme, 12 guides with no ABA experience (and some with no autism experience at all), and a group of parents and caregivers who had been beat up by The System and did not know what to expect. When the parents and caregivers left, the day was dotted with failures and successes. Some kids hit each other, some kids ran away from the activities, some kids hit me, and others broke things and knocked over our newly acquired supplies. But some

		Goal: ......out of 15		
Arrive				
Square Time				
Snack Time				
Sit-Down Games				
Square Time				
Store				
		Kid Cash?		

Figure 7.6: A point sheet used at Kids' Club and Supported Kids' Club. There are places to write a point goal, names of activities, the child's name, and the date. The boxes on the right are where the stamps go.

of the children occasionally followed directions, most guides were implementing the point system, and some kids even participated in the activities independently. We continued to implement the behaviour management system and stuck to the routine. Unfortunately, we were not able to collect data on participation and direction following!

Anecdotally, by the end of the last day, the failures were much less and the successes were much more. Inappropriate behaviours were not the usual occurrence and participation and direction following occurred, for most of the kids, in its place. It was not the most smoothly running programme and it is difficult to gauge what might have been learned by the children, but it was a huge, difficult step in the right direction. One observation that we did record occurred at the end of the week when the families and caregivers arrived to pick up their children. Exactly three mums were in tears because they had never seen their children taking turns and behaving as appropriately as they were during the last activity of the programme: Piñata.

A piñata is a papier-mâché object, usually in the shape of an animal, and contains lollies and small toys (ours was shaped like a sun, on purpose). The piñata game is simple. Hit the piñata with a stick until the lollies and toys come out. The reason that adults are hesitant to host such a game is exactly the same reason why kids love it – it involves children destroying property by dangerously waving around a stick among other children! But it is a game nonetheless and can be taught in the same way as other games are taught. We created a large square on the floor and hung the piñata from a rope so that it was in the middle of the square. We then carefully selected three kinds of sticks of varying hardness and ensured that they were in the care of a guide as the kids positioned themselves around the square. We then simply stated the rules: 'Stay behind the line. Hit the piñata only three times. Only pick up toys and lollies when you hear the whistle.' The coordinator then modelled appropriate piñata-hitting and rule-following using the softest of the sticks, after which he passed the stick to the first child and remained very close to offer prompts if necessary. If any child's toe crossed or even touched the line, the game stopped, the rules were restated, and a pause occurred until all toes were behind the line again. The game continued in this fashion until a lolly came barrelling out of the piñata. A child quickly picked it up, after which the coordinator stopped the game, restated the rules, and required the child to put the lolly back into the square before starting the game again. All the kids had two turns with the two softest sticks and it wasn't long before the piñata met its fate. The coordinator blew the whistle and the kids made a scramble for the toys and lollies.

The point of the story is that we can either keep our kids very safe by sheltering them from experiences like the piñata. Or we can offer appropriate help to teach them how to participate in life, and piñatas are a part of life. But won't they just go off and start hitting things with sticks? Only if we do not offer them the help that they need. I don't think the mums' tears were due to their grieving for the piñata. They were proud of their children for doing the right thing, and they of all people know how hard it is for their kids to do the right thing sometimes.

The parents wanted more beyond the piñata and the Holiday Programme, so an early version of KC was born. Like the Holiday Programme, this version of KC accommodated a huge age and ability range. Another difficulty was the lack of one-on-one support. Most families could not afford such support and ANZ Waikato did not have funding either, so we needed to be innovative. We began soliciting the involvement of university students by posting advertisements that asked for volunteers for our programmes and we were successful. We provided some basic training over the course of an evening and we accepted new volunteers as they responded to the adverts. To this day, our programmes are still mostly staffed by volunteer university students with varying skill levels. We find that the university students enjoy working with the children, tend to be energetic, and are happy to get some basic training and direction for their time. So the programmes benefit not only the children and the families, but also these students. Some of these students have gone on and enrolled in autism- and ABA-related Master's degrees, others have found work within autism and ABA, and still others are currently filling the programme coordinator roles. This benefit to the community was actually a side effect of our planning, but we now realize its importance – future professionals need to start somewhere, so why not with us? (See Figure 7.7.)

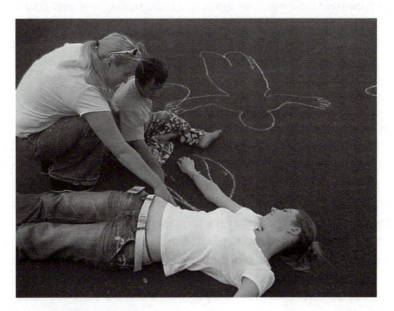

Figure 7.7: Having fun and learning outdoors

As our volunteers learned and as our programme participants increased, we were gradually able to split KC into the four weekly or fortnightly programmes described earlier. The children who were experienced in the programmes began serving as models of appropriate behaviour. New children more easily joined and new guides more easily learned the system. Our programmes attracted more funding and we acquired a large amount of toys and materials that are used by all of the programmes. We began developing a more appropriate infrastructure to support all of the programmes in a way that promotes programme continuity and integrity. We now have funding to support an infrastructure that involves a programme director (Eric) who is a

qualified and experienced behaviour analyst who oversees all of the programme coordinators. But we are not done yet!

Our next goals are to run all of these programmes as often as possible, ideally
on a daily basis, and to provide more individualized programming (as well as
data collection) for the children involved. We now have the human resources,
the materials, the venue, the infrastructure, and the demand for service, but we
do not have the funding. Volunteers can only volunteer a certain amount of
time and qualified professionals are not inexpensive. You do, indeed, get what
you pay for. In retrospect, the difficult work has been done; our task now is to
attract consistent funding. If we did attract such funding, our next goal would
be to begin providing home-based services that corroborate these programmes. Perhaps another goal would be to acquire a building that might
eventually be turned into a school. Difficult? Maybe, but then so was that first
day of our first Holiday Programme.

Final recommendations

We'd like to offer some recommendations to individuals who would like to
create programmes similar to the ones described here. If we could rewind
time, we'd stick to these recommendations ourselves! One overriding recommendation is to keep everything as simple as possible, especially when
starting from scratch. The rest of the recommendations are as follows.

First, do whatever you can to get an experienced and qualified behaviour
analyst involved as your first programme coordinator or director. With a lot of
effort and maybe some luck, things might work out with another kind of
person, but your chances will increase immensely if a behaviour analyst is
available. Depending on your location, *experienced* and *qualified* can take on
different meanings. So we recommend someone who is either a Board
Certified Behavior Analyst (see www.bacb.com for a list of Board Certified
Behavior Analysts worldwide) or someone with similar experience and qualifications. This amounts to substantial graduate-level ABA coursework, at least
a Master's degree, and one year of practising experienced while being super-
vised by a qualified behaviour analyst. An appropriate pay rate for this individual would be comparable to the pay rates of local psychologists. We do
acknowledge that such experience and qualifications are sometimes rare, but
we, again, exercise caution in implementing ABA programmes without
appropriate supervision.

Second, organize. All children should be required to register prior to the
programme, appropriate permission forms should be carefully designed and

completed, materials should be well organized and stowed in easy-to-access containers, and there should be systems in place for most aspects of the programme. For example, the arrival routine should be clear and consistent, families and carers should be informed about dates and processes via newsletters or some other means, and there should be an induction process for new children and new guides (rather than being thrown in the deep end!). Children should be asked to sit or stand in an organized fashion and guides should also follow suit to model appropriate behaviour. We consistently find that chaos breeds chaos and that order breeds order. Starting with a Holiday Programme, as we did, may be the best approach because in one week it may be possible to test and develop the subtleties of the programme.

Third, collect data on everything possible and store it electronically. We collect data on who is present and what their role is: kid, guide or visitor. Until recently, we have not collected data on children's behaviour during the programmes. Resource constraints had made this difficult for us in the past but, in fact, we probably could have done better. A very simple way of collecting data is called momentary time sampling (Cooper, Heron and Heward 1987). Briefly, it requires one observer who could probably observe approximately five children at a time, with a stopwatch or clock, and a data sheet. The data sheet should contain columns of small boxes (one column for each child) that are big enough to mark ticks and crosses and one column with times incrementing in five-minute intervals. So, for a one-and-a-half hour programme, each child's column would contain 18 boxes that represented each five-minute interval. The data collector would make an observation every five minutes (sometimes a cassette-tape with beeps every five minutes is an easy way to signal the intervals for the data collector) and would immediately mark a tick or a cross in each child's box for that interval. Ticks would be marked for children who are on task, and crosses for those who are not. At the end of the session, each child's on-task time could be calculated and plotted on a graph so that it can be compared to other sessions. Such a data collection procedure will give a better indication of the success of the programme and any graphs and other output can be shared with the staff, families and perhaps potential funders. A qualified behaviour analyst would be able to set up this kind of observation very quickly.

Fourth, take care of your staff, especially volunteers. Money is not the only way to reinforce working. Our volunteers now get petrol vouchers on occasion, but for years they stayed involved without this very small perk. Don't underestimate the power of your children's cuteness! Kids are fun to work with and many times my day has been better because of it – it is why I continue with this kind of work. Similarly, when the guides are successful and experiencing smiling children and everything else that children bring to the world, they will be more likely to remain involved. Thank-you cards, small bags of lollies, face-to-face thank-yous, and other forms of appreciation go a long way. Also remember that these people are probably learning as much from the children as the children are from them. Their experience may be written on their CVs, it may help with their career planning, and it may lead to some paid work. Many of our families have asked for our volunteers to become involved with their children outside of our programmes and, as described earlier, have begun a career in this area because of it.

Finally, remember that Rome wasn't built in a day! Programming is hard work and sometimes unrewarded. Starting anything from scratch is not an easy task and anyone embarking on a venture similar to ours should expect failure. We don't know much about Rome, but we suppose that it began with a bunch of Romans congregating in the same place. Then some columns might have been built, olives grown and a democracy formed. If you can get a small group of families together in one place, then you're off and you can begin building a programme. But you'll need to start now.

References

The Autistic Association of New Zealand, Inc. (ANZ) (2001) *The Needs and the Gaps in Services for Families and Individuals with an Autism Spectrum Disorder.* Analysis of nationwide survey conducted by the Autistic Association of New Zealand, Inc. Christchurch, New Zealand: C. Cervin (June).

Cambridge Center for Behavioral Studies (2005) *Autism and ABA.* http://www.behavior.org (accessed 16 April 2005).

Cooper, J.O., Heron, T.E. and Heward, W.L. (1987) *Applied Behavior Analysis.* New York: Macmillan Publishing Company.

Jacobson, J.W., Mulick, J.A. and Green, G. (1998) 'Cost-benefit estimates for early intensive behavioral intervention for young children with autism: general model and single state case.' *Behavioral Interventions 13,* 201–226.

Parents for the Early Intervention of Autism in Children (PEACH) (1997) *Cost Benefit Analysis for UCLA Model of Behavioural Intervention (Lovaas-styled Programme) versus Traditional Provisions (Special Schools) for Children with Autism,* Revision 1.5. United Kingdom: B. Saberi (October).

CHAPTER 8

Positive Behaviour Support

Supporting Meaningful Change for Individuals, Families and Professionals

Ken P. Kerr and Claire Lacey[1]

One thing we can be sure of in life is change. From a life-span perspective change and development occurs throughout infancy, childhood, adolescence and adulthood. Throughout our lives rich experiences, relationships and learning opportunities make us who we are. Some individuals in society, however, do not share the same rich experiences of life, the same quality of relationships, the same connection to society as the majority of the population through no fault of their own. Such individuals may be marginalized for a host of different reasons and may not be afforded the same rights and entitlements as others. Individuals with autism, learning disability and other disorders often fall into this grouping. We need to be aware of the fact that many of the people we support do not experience the same quality of life as others in the community. Awareness of quality of life and an awareness of the importance of meaningful experiences should be reflected in our practice when supporting individuals with autism and related disorders throughout

---

1   The opinions expressed herein are those of the authors and do not necessarily reflect the position or policy of Western Care Association, Co. Mayo.

their lives. In particular, provision for older children requires a focus on appropriate activities taking into account age and developmental level in the context of what is meaningful/functional for the individual. This chapter introduces a framework that guides the development of supports necessary to improve the quality of life for older children with autism who may experience behavioural difficulties. In particular, this chapter challenges parents, professionals and organizations to consider the full range of variables that can impact upon an individual's quality of life. To begin, a case scenario is presented that describes a fairly typical situation for an older child with autism who has not experienced a balanced approach to education and who has not experienced life in many meaningful ways.

Marc's story

Marc is 11 years old. He lives outside a medium size town in rural Ireland. He has three brothers and one sister ranging from 10 years old to 15 years old. Unlike his brothers and sisters Marc is not involved in activities in the community. He is educated in a local mainstream school in a separate classroom with two educators present. Over the years a number of psychologists have provided comment upon his education and provided recommendations around support required. In addition to this, several private consultants have devised a range of programmes and supports for him and his family. With regard to Marc's education, a curriculum was never specified, no meaningful Individualized Education Plan (IEP) was put in place, training in autism-specific approaches was extremely limited, and little balance in terms of the breadth and scope of tasks was apparent. Currently, Marc is doing matching, sensory play, learning to write capital letters, learning to follow two-step instruction, and learning to engage independently at school. He has been doing variations of these tasks for the last two years with little evidence of learning taking place and little evidence of change in approach or design of instruction. Marc's behaviour can be quite challenging. He would often hit out at teachers, spit, throw tables, and destroy different types of property. He would often scream in a loud voice. No formal assessment as to reasons behind any of his behaviour has ever been carried out. No formal analysis of the school approach to supporting a child with multiple needs has been conducted.

In real terms, Marc has been stuck doing the same old tasks over and over without any sense of purpose. That is, the tasks have not benefited Marc in any meaningful way. Marc has never had any inclusion targets and has had no structure around developing social skills with peers. Until recently Marc was not included in the life of the school nor in the life of the community. He has no friends outside of his family. One word describes Marc: isolated.

In reflecting upon the scenario, one may question what is important for Marc. What needs to happen for Marc to achieve a better quality of life and to become more involved in the life of his school and community? Focusing upon the minutiae of isolated academic objectives is certainly not the answer. Instead, a balanced approach to education to provide a range of experiences suitable for his age, interests and his developmental level is required. In terms of the scenario, Marc's educational objectives may have been suitable for when he was five years old; however, he is now 11 years old and many of his tasks are no longer suitable. Young children with autism typically learn a broad mix of skills with emphasis on developing academic skills, play skills and functional skills. However, as children grow older it is important to constantly re-evaluate how the skills being taught contribute to the broader goals of life. The danger of disparity between curriculum content, what is important in the child's life at that point in time, and future goals must be forefront in the minds of educators, practitioners and family members.

Like Marc, his parents' goals and dreams have changed as he has grown older. They no longer think of Marc in terms of solely needing one-to-one education. Instead, they now want to focus on Marc developing a greater social connection, playing a bigger part in family activities, and developing competencies that will help him as he moves towards adulthood. Marc is interested in sport and likes to watch his local football team play; opportunities to enjoy these activities are now considered important. In supporting Marc and his family, a framework called positive behaviour support (PBS) was employed to re-evaluate goals and objectives in an effort to improve their quality of life.

Working towards a better life

PBS emerged in the 1990s as a person-centred approach to supporting individuals with disabilities who display behavioural difficulties. PBS represents an amalgamation of conceptual, theoretical and technological perspectives derived primarily from applied behaviour analysis and person-centred planning (Holburn and Vietze 2002; Koegel, Koegel and Dunlap 1996; O'Neill *et al.* 1997). Sugai *et al.* (2000) note that:

> Positive behavioral support is not a new intervention package, nor a new theory of behavior, but an application of a behaviorally-based

systems approach to enhancing the capacity of schools, families, and communities to design effective environments that improve the fit or link between research-validated practices and the environments in which teaching and learning occurs. (p.7)

PBS uses behaviour analysis to address behavioural difficulties by focusing on meaningful lifestyle change (Risley 1996). It is important to reiterate that PBS is not a 'new intervention package, nor a new theory of behaviour'. The broad goals of this approach are to work collaboratively with key stakeholders, including parents, siblings, friends and teachers, to address the meaning/function of behavioural difficulties in context, and to effect lifestyle change thereby improving quality of life for the individual and their family (Koegel *et al.* 1996). For Marc, this means continually striving to improve his quality of life by addressing the meaning of his behaviour and developing the supports necessary such that his problem behaviour becomes 'irrelevant, inefficient, and ineffective' (O'Neill *et al.* 1997). Using this approach, Marc is supported in taking ownership and control over his life. By integrating him more in the life of his family, school and local community, he will gain respect as a person, will be treated equally by others, and will have the opportunity through structured, systematic support to gain the skills necessary to perform different social roles. To ensure Marc's participation in the community is meaningful, efforts need to focus on using these opportunities to develop Marc's ability to function more independently. Marc will ultimately have a greater sense of identity, autonomy, attainment and affiliation in his life. That is, he can enjoy a sense of control over his life and become connected in a more meaningful way to society; in short, the goal is to support Marc to ensure that he is not marginalized. By delineating the core components of PBS, readers will be provided with guidelines to tackle issues pertinent to quality of life within the established framework of behavioural practice.

Core components of PBS in practice

The following section outlines the process of achieving the goals related to a better quality of life through the use of positive behaviour support. The critical components of this process in practice include 1. developing collaborative relationships with key people, 2. adopting a person-centred planning process, and 3. developing a comprehensive support plan utilizing technology from the science of applied behaviour analysis.

The importance of developing a collaborative relationship

On accepting a referral, practitioners employing PBS advocate the development of a collaborative relationship with the focus person, their family, friends, support staff, teachers and other relevant persons (i.e. the key stakeholders) (Albin *et al.* 1996; Kincaid and Fox 2002; Lucyshyn and Albin 1993). For Marc, this means establishing a team of individuals who know different aspects of his life including his parents, teacher, special needs assistant, psychologist, and other relevant professionals. Drawing upon the multiple perspectives of those who know the person well, the team creates a picture of the person. This ultimately builds the foundations for developing a comprehensive support plan as individuals share their positive experiences of being with the person in addition to highlighting the complexities of the challenges faced. Working together in a team-based approach creates the context for honest and open discussion about concerns, goals, and ways to improve quality of life. It is important to note that no one party, professionals included, has all the answers; accordingly a multidisciplinary approach recognizing the importance of drawing upon the expertise of the family, those who know the person well, and other professionals (e.g. speech therapists, physiotherapists, dietician etc.) is advocated. By ensuring that key individuals are involved during the initial stages of planning, a greater sense of ownership and partnership is ultimately achieved (Kincaid and Fox 2002).

Person-centred planning

Person-centred planning provides the tools to create an all-inclusive portrait of the person by focusing on what the individual wants from life; in short, it's about getting to know the person and being able to arrange the resources and supports that a person requires to meet their life goals (cf. O'Brien and O'Brien 2002; Wagner 2002). A number of protocols currently exist to guide the person-centred planning process including personal outcomes (Personal Outcome Measures for Children and Youth 2000), person futures planning (Mount and Zwernik 1988), making action plans (Forest and Lusthaus 1989), essential lifestyle planning (Smull and Burke Harrison 1992), and Planning Alternative Tomorrows with Hope (PATH – Pearpoint, O'Brien and Forest 1993). Kincaid and Fox (2002) detail the shared goals of different person-centred planning approaches including a focus on community participation, developing meaningful relationships, showing preference, making choices, and on developing personal competencies. The importance of these goals to families and older children with autism is obvious. To offer support in the case scenario, the first step towards developing relationships and a greater social role requires everyone to have an understanding of what is important from Marc's perspective (see Box 8.1).

Box 8.1 Getting to know Marc

Who are the people in Marc's life?

What is Marc's life story?

Does he have friends?

Does he make choices in regard to activities?

Is he connected to other people in his community?

What does he enjoy?

What would Marc like to do in the future?

Are Marc and his family satisfied with the services they receive?

Subsequent to this discussion the team focuses on priorities for Marc, including creating more opportunities for Marc to become involved socially and to develop skills. It should be emphasized that 'arranging experiences' sets the context for skill acquisition. Knowing that Marc enjoys football, efforts could focus on arranging for him to join a supporters' club, to teach him to pay for his ticket, and providing him with opportunities to meet other supporters and players. Pitonyak (2004) highlighted the importance of person-centred planning and advised parents to consider their child's capacities and gifts, what supports their child requires, what is in need of change, and what is their vision for the future. Furthermore, he provided an interesting comment on the lives of children who need support, stating:

> Fun is a powerful antidote to problem behaviours. Count the number of things your child enjoys, the number of places she likes to go. Compare this to the number of things other children enjoy, the number of places other children go. Ask yourself, 'Is my child having fun?' (Pitonyak 2004, p.4)

While 'fun' will obviously not solve all challenges related either to autism or challenging behaviour, the central message of this quote should not be dismissed. For many children with autism and their families the question of 'fun' may not be addressed if the practitioner's focus tends to be deficit driven. Furthermore, parents of older children with autism who have experienced poor professional guidance in the choice of goals for their child may lose sight of what is important to the child. Within the framework of PBS, person-centred planning ensures that the supports are viewed from the individual's perspective and that meaningful life goals are identified. The planning process recognizes the person's strengths by identifying what he/she contributes to family, school and community. By continually listening and being responsive to the individual the process provides a framework to both celebrate the strengths of the person while also identifying barriers to leading a meaningful life. Examples of barriers include boredom, unmet needs, and attitudes towards individuals with disabilities. A lack of choice, friends, meaningful relationships, behavioural difficulties, opportunities for inclusion, financial resources, and support/expertise around skill development may also be barriers to achieving meaningful life goals. Person-centred planning in this context focuses on identifying short- and long-term goals for an individual and on building the foundations to effect lasting lifestyle change. The planning process seeks to support the individual and/or those who know the individual best by generating a living document that will be continually revised.

Developing comprehensive support plans

For some individuals, behavioural difficulties may be a barrier to inclusion in regular life settings and achievement of personal goals. That is, challenging behaviour may represent a barrier to developing a better quality of life for the individual and their family. Individuals who display severe behavioural difficulties (e.g. self-injury, aggression or property destruction) often lead restrictive lives characterized by regimented daily routines and high levels of staff support with limited opportunities to engage in meaningful activities, interactions with peers, or participation in the community (Emerson, McGill and Mansell 1994). For families, behavioural difficulties can be a considerable source of stress and often prevent the family from carrying out typical daily routines (Baker et al. 2002). For all of the barriers identified above, a support plan provides guidance and technical support to assist individuals, family and practitioners alike.

As a service delivery system, PBS uses the science of behaviour analysis in the context of person-centred planning to guide the development of supports for individuals who display behavioural difficulties (Koegel *et al.* 1996; Wacker and Berg 2002). PBS seeks to understand the broader context (i.e. at an individual and systems level) in which behavioural difficulties occur. In the context of Marc's school, this will mean examining how factors such as motivation, curriculum content and instructional strategies influence his behaviour at an individual level. It will also mean examining how factors such as existing policies (e.g. inclusion, challenging behaviour, risk assessment), staffing issues, financial resources and training at a systems level impact upon the individual.

PBS employs a number of empirically validated assessment strategies that can guide practice when supporting people with behavioural difficulties (Carr *et al.* 1994; O'Neill *et al.* 1997; Wacker, Berg and Harding 2002). These assessment strategies, derived from applied behaviour analysis, provide a practical means to assess the function of behaviour by examining the environmental, social and personal variables that influence the occurrence of problematic behaviour (McGill 1999; Michael 1993; O'Neill *et al.* 1997). This process is known as a functional assessment (see Box 8.2).

As part of the functional assessment process, information is collected via a number of indirect and direct assessment methods. Indirect assessment methods serve to obtain information about the individual, the behavioural difficulties of concern, the contexts in which behaviour occurs, and the factors that appear to set the occasion for and maintain behaviour. A combination of structured interviews, rating scales and checklists are completed with family members, teachers and other relevant persons as part of this process, e.g. Motivation Assessment Scale (MAS) (Durand and Crimmins 1988); Setting Event Checklist (Gardner *et al.* 1986); Functional Assessment Interview Form (O'Neill *et al.* 1997). These assessment tools can be used to examine the immediate contexts in which behaviour occurs (e.g. in the classroom during instruction) and other factors which may influence the occurrence of behaviour (e.g. disturbed sleep pattern, menses). A number of direct assessment methods, including scatterplots and A-B-C charts, can also be used to identify patterns of behaviour across different times and settings. Initially observations can be conducted over a number of days to examine whether there is a clear pattern or correlation between the occurrence of behaviour and particular events. For some individuals, however, it may be necessary to conduct observations over an extended time period. These recordings ultimately serve to identify the social context in which behaviour occurs, the times/activities during which behaviour is more and less likely to occur, and the events that occur prior to and following behaviour (Carr 1994; Touchette *et al.* 1985).

Box 8.2 Steps for developing a comprehensive support plan

1. Getting to know the person better and establishing supports

Focus on identifying priorities for the individual and begin assessments to identify the function of behaviour.

(a) Person-centred planning

Learn more about the person, who is part of their life, and identify what is important for the individual and family. Work towards establishing a team of people to support the individual (i.e. circle of support)

(b) Functional assessment and additional assessments

Identify the behaviours of concern, where they occur, and identify the personal, social and environmental factors that affect behaviour.

- Interviews with key individuals including parents, teachers etc., e.g. Functional Assessment Interview Format (O'Neill *et al.* 1997)

- Complete checklists and rating scales e.g. Motivation Assessment Scale (Durand and Crimmins 1988)

- Conduct direct observations e.g. Scatterplots (Touchette, MacDonald and Langer 1985); Functional Analysis Observation Form (O'Neill *et al.* 1997); A-B-C charts

- Communication and adaptive behaviour assessments e.g. Vineland Adaptive Behavior Scales (Sparrow, Balla and Cicchetti 1984)

- Medical evaluations

- Quality of life assessments (e.g. Person Centred Planning Assessments (as above); Resident Lifestyle Inventory (Kennedy *et al.* 1990); Quality of Life Questionnaire (Schalock and Keith 1993)

(c) Implement supports while assessments are being conducted

- Lifestyle change: Improving lifestyle by increasing participation in preferred activities, increasing independence and choice by working at individual and systems level (i.e. work with school and community)

- Positive approaches (i.e. reinforcing desirable behaviours)

- Crisis intervention

2. Analyse results of assessments and development of function-based support plan

Generate hypotheses about the function of the behaviour based on information taking the following into consideration: environmental arrangements, setting events, immediate antecedent and consequences, communication, adaptive skills and quality of life. Conduct a functional analysis of behaviour, if necessary.

- Lifestyle change: Continuing efforts to increasing participation and independence (i.e. support at individual and systems level to effect change)

- Antecedent manipulations (i.e. altering setting events and antecedents associated with behaviour)

- Curricular modification (i.e. adjustments to instructional strategies, instructional format, curriculum content and materials, schedule of activities, task length, difficulty etc.)

- Functional equivalence training (i.e. functional communication training)

- Increasing adaptive behaviours and daily living skills (e.g. self-care, community living, socialization)

- Positive approaches (e.g. reinforcing appropriate behaviours)

- Crisis intervention and risk assessments

3. Measuring meaningful outcomes of support plan

Evaluation of behaviour change, increase in adaptive skills, and opportunities to participate in community-based activities (see Table 8.1).

4. Building foundations for ongoing support to effect meaningful lifestyle change

(a) Building and supporting a team of people to support the individual (i.e. circle of support to include family, friends, staff, service providers)

(b) Through person-centred planning process, continually evaluate priorities for the individual and family by establishing short- and long-term goals

(c) Ongoing evaluation of effectiveness of intervention and use of functional assessment procedures, when necessary

The information gathered from both indirect and direct assessments can be used to generate hypotheses about the function of behaviour (Wacker *et al.* 2002). For example, using this information one may decipher that an individual engages in self-injury in order to communicate that they find work or activities repetitive, difficult or meaningless. Equally, an individual may display similar behaviour to communicate that they would like to spend more time engaging with the things they enjoy in life, more choice/variety as part of their daily life, and more meaningful social interactions with other people. An individual may also display such behaviour in order to obtain sensory stimulation or to attenuate the effects of pain. Other factors such as illness, sleeping difficulties or medical conditions associated with particular genetic syndromes can also influence the likelihood that an individual displays such behaviours (Kennedy and Itktonen 1993; O'Reilly, Lacey and Lancioni 2000).

For some individuals it may be necessary to conduct a more detailed assessment to understand the function of behaviour. This assessment, known as a functional analysis (Iwata *et al.* 1994), uses the information gathered from the functional assessment to examine the function(s) of behaviour. A functional analysis typically consists of a series of social situations in which antecedent and consequence events hypothesized to maintain behaviour are presented. This analysis can be conducted in home, school and clinic settings (Berg and Sasso 1993). The information gathered from the functional assessment and/or the results of functional analysis can then be used to guide the selection of function-based interventions. Knowledge of the variables controlling the emergence and maintenance of behaviour serve to guide the development of a comprehensive range of supports to address the function of behaviour across home, school and community contexts (Horner *et al.* 1996). These supports should be focused both at an individual level (e.g. functional communication training, curriculum modification, systematic instruction, development of daily living skills, crisis intervention/ reactive strategies, medical intervention) and at the systems level (e.g. opportunities for inclusion, staff training) to address the function of behaviour and effect lifestyle change strategies (cf. Donnellan *et al.* 1988; Koegel *et al.* 1996).

Within PBS, efforts focus on the achievement of socially valid and meaningful outcomes to improve an individual's quality of life (Meyer and Evans 1993). To ensure that support plans are socially valid it is important to consider how recommendations marry with values and knowledge of key individuals, beliefs in the efficacy of supports by key individuals, the appropriateness and practicality of implementing supports, and the effectiveness of the interventions on effecting change over time (Albin *et al.* 1996; Kincaid and Fox 2002; Reimers *et al.* 1992). As Albin *et al.*, (1996) state, 'support plan components that are inconsistent with people's values or that exceed current levels of knowledge, skills, and experience are not likely to be implemented with any consistency or fidelity' (p.87). While it is important to know that interventions produce decreases in behavioural difficulties, it is also important to ensure that the individual has opportunities to access integrated settings, develop new skills, develop friendships, and achieve a greater sense of enjoyment and control over their life (cf. Kennedy 2002).

To ensure that we make informed decisions about whether or not the person is actually achieving meaningful outcomes, it is of central importance to ensure that systems of evaluation are established to monitor change and guide the decision-making process. While many researchers have noted the disparity between the need to demonstrate the effectiveness of interventions and the practicalities of monitoring interventions within the constraints of regular life settings (see Meyer and Janney 1989), there are a number of user-friendly measures available to monitor meaningful outcomes. Examples of such outcomes are outlined in Table 8.1. A range of systems can be employed to monitor change in these areas including daily logs (e.g. to record frequency of behaviour, replacement behaviour, and daily activity pattern), records (e.g. communication books between home and school, medical records), check-lists, rating scales, and more informal reports. While direct measures of behaviour, communication and skill development are typically recommended at an individual level these can be complemented with more indirect measures such as noting opportunities for inclusion, staffing levels and time spent in group activities. The development of practical evaluation procedures that take into account the need for evidence-based practice and the constraints of real-life settings are required. Efforts should focus on developing a range of measures that can be used to guide the development of additional supports if necessary while providing meaningful measures to reflect lifestyle change. To further explore the impact of variables affecting quality of life, we now turn to a discussion of how families, organizations, services and society in general need to support change at an individual level.

Addressing issues at a systems level

By now the contribution of supporting an individual in a multifaceted way should be clear. Change at the level of the individual, however, should only occur whenever this change is supported by the system in general. For example, there would be no point in teaching Marc to greet fellow pupils if the school system did not promote opportunities for Marc to come into contact with others in the school. If the system, whether it be the family, school, disability service, or community at large, does not have the capacity to support an individual who experiences challenging behaviour, ultimately the support package may fail. Efforts to support individuals who display behav-ioural difficulties to achieve better quality of life must therefore look beyond the individual to the larger systems that they are a part of. PBS emphasizes the importance of addressing issues at a systems level in order to effect durable lifestyle change (see Williams 2000 for a discussion of behavioural systems analysis). For example, when working to support individuals in school

Table 8.1 Sample outcomes and evidence-based measures

Outcome	Examples	Evidence-based measure
Improvement in behaviours of primary concern (e.g. self-injury) and collateral effects	Decrease in behaviour of concern	Frequency count, measure of severity (e.g. daily recordings, incident report forms)
	Evidence of skin trauma including bruising, tearing, swelling	Evidence of trauma (e.g. present/absent or use or rating scale)
	Decrease use of medication	Number of times medication administered
	Positive affect/happiness	Evidence of enjoyment including smiling, laughing (present/absent)
Increase in replacement skill to make behaviour of concern irrelevant, ineffective, inefficient	Increase in use of alternative communication (e.g. 'I want break' card/manual sign/voice output system)	Increase in use of alternative communication (frequency)
Improvement in social relationships and more social roles in society	Participating in local after-school club, involved in integrated settings, e.g. local swimming pool	Number of groups attended Number of choices made while at group
	Development of friendships	Number and type of social interaction with peers Reduced need for one-to-one staffing when with peers
	Participating in school play	Number of steps completed independently

Outcome	Examples	Evidence-based measure
Acquisition of self-management skills to promote greater independence	Develop sight-reading repertoire	Number of correct/incorrect items on matching task and number of sight words receptively identified
	Using a picture-based activity schedule to manage free time and work time	Count of number of steps completed independently
	Increase in number of choices made	Number of choices made
	Acquisition of daily living skills	Number of steps completed independently
Greater sense of family participation	Clearly defined responsibilities/tasks within home setting (e.g. helping set table)	Number of steps completed independently
Completion of more family routines	Family outings, drive in car, going shopping etc.	Number of family routines
Improved family well-being	Reduced levels of stress, improved sleep patterns etc.	Perception of improved general health, stress level (e.g. rating scales)
Perceived improvement by parents, teachers etc.	Reports of improvements	Perception of improvements, behaviour no longer major concern (e.g. rating scales)
Inclusion in more integrated settings	Increased time spent in regular classes with same-aged peers – number of daily opportunities	Length of time spent in inclusive settings and nature of activities and interactions while present

settings it is important to examine the immediate environment including curriculum, instructional strategies, scheduling of activities, environmental arrangements, and the potential variables maintaining behavioural difficulties. At a school level, examination of policies in relation to development of

IEPs, procedures for addressing students with behavioural difficulties, and inclusion is necessary. Schools that have policies and procedures that are either disconnected or only share a loose connection to actual practice are less likely to promote or sustain desired practice. Without the school demonstrating proactive support for practice on all levels and demonstrating a capacity to listen and learn from issues on an individual level, staff may feel unsupported, which may have a detrimental effect upon support for the individual. In the case scenario, responsibility for addressing such issues would require support from two levels whereby a top-down approach is led by the Department of Education to support implementation along best practice guidelines coupled with support from practitioners on the ground to develop innovative support strategies for Marc.

As already stated, other system variables include staff attitudes and tolerance of challenging behaviour, training, resources and management within the school to support students with special needs. For Marc in the case scenario, the development of the team to consider all elements of intervention to support the individual provided the platform for future success. In Marc's school, they did not have a policy on challenging behaviour and training was not provided to ensure that staff were supported to learn about how to improve their practice. Staff therefore felt unsupported and vulnerable in terms of the approaches they adopted. Equally a lack of clear guidance from the school in terms of what should be in an IEP and who should be involved in the planning process constituted a lack of support from the system that ultimately impacted upon Marc.

For Marc and his family, life was made more complex with input provided from multiple services and systems including schools and local disability services. Difficulties in trying to coordinate all of these services can result in some services working in isolation with no shared vision for the child which leads to greater frustration for the individual and family alike. This is a barrier for the individual and family moving forward in a cohesive manner. The case scenario illustrates the need for change in terms of the school-wide approach to understanding challenging behaviour and formulation of an inclusion policy to ensure that all children are included in the life of the school. In addition a structured training process for all staff is required. Ultimately, organizations need to develop the capacity to change and to learn from the experiences of those participating in the system. These factors ultimately contribute to the success of intervention and achievement of desired outcomes.

Summary of themes

After reading this chapter we hope that parents and professionals will reflect upon the multifaceted nature of supporting individuals with autism who experience barriers to their quality of life. The case scenario highlighted what can happen when there is no shared vision for the child, when the educational goals are no longer appropriate, and when the key factors that influence quality of life for the individual and family are ignored. Failure to consider what is important for the child as he/she gets older will ultimately lead to a mismatch between the service provided and the needs of the individual. For the child this will often result in unhappiness and for the family this will often mean frustration and stress.

From a service delivery perspective, PBS seeks to develop collaborative relationships with key individuals, to identify the goals for the individual and their family through the person-centred planning process, and to address behavioural difficulties through the development of comprehensive support plans. The evidence-based nature of the support plan was also highlighted where the onus is on the support team to demonstrate the effectiveness of the supports implemented. PBS recognizes the importance of ensuring that broader systems have the capacity to support the individual and their family. In short, PBS supports people to ask what they want from life and creates the context to make it happen.

References

Albin, R.W., Lucyshyn, J.M., Horner, R.H. and Flannery, K.B. (1996) 'Contextual fit for behavioral support plans.' In L.K. Koegel, R.L. Koegel and G. Dunlap (eds) *Positive Behavior Support: Including People with Difficult Behavior in the Community* (pp.81–98). Baltimore, MD: Paul H. Brookes.

Baker, B.L., Blacher, J., Crnic, K.A. and Edelbrock, C. (2002) 'Behavior problems and parenting stress in families of three-year-old children with and without developmental delays.' *American Journal of Mental Retardation 107*, 433–444.

Berg, W. and Sasso, G. (1993) 'Transferring implementation of functional assessment procedures from the clinic to natural settings.' In J. Reichle and D. Wacker (eds) *Communication Alternatives for Challenging Behavior: Integrating Functional Assessment and Intervention Strategies* (pp.343–362). Baltimore, MD: Paul H. Brookes.

Carr, E.G. (1994) 'Emerging themes in the functional analysis of problem behavior.' *Journal of Applied Behavior Analysis 27*, 393–399.

Carr, E.G., Levin, L., McConnachie, G., Carlson, J.I., Kemp, D.C. and Smith, C.E. (1994) *Communication-Based Intervention for Problem Behavior: A User's Guide for Producing Positive Change.* Baltimore, MD: Paul H. Brookes.

Donnellan, A.M., LaVigna, G.W., Negri-Schoultz, N. and Fassbender, L. (1988) *Progress Without Punishment: Effective Approaches for Learners with Behavior Problems.* New York: Teachers College Press.

Durand, V.M. and Crimmins, D.B. (1988) 'Identifying the variables maintaining self-injurious behavior.' *Journal of Autism and Developmental Disabilities 18,* 99–117.

Emerson, E., McGill, P. and Mansell, J. (1994) *Severe Learning Disabilities and Challenging Behaviours: Designing High Quality Services.* London: Chapman and Hall.

Forest, M. and Lusthaus, E. (1989) 'Promoting educational equality for all students: circles and maps.' In S. Stainback, W. Stainback and M. Forest (eds) *Educating All Students in the Mainstream of Regular Education* (pp.43–51). Baltimore, MD: Paul H. Brookes.

Gardner, W., Cole, C., Davidson, D. and Karan, O. (1986) 'Reducing aggression in individuals with developmental disabilities: an expanded stimulus control assessment and intervention model.' *Education and Training of the Mentally Retarded 21,* 3–12.

Holburn, S. and Vietze, P. (2002) *Person-Centered Planning: Research, Practice, and Future Directions.* Baltimore, MD: Paul H. Brookes.

Horner, R.H., Vaughn, B.J., Day, H.M. and Ard, W.R. Jr. (1996) 'The relationship between setting events and problem behavior: expanding our understanding of behavioral support.' In L.K. Koegel, R.L. Koegel and G. Dunlap (eds) *Positive Behavior Support: Including People with Difficult Behavior in the Community* (pp.467–490). Baltimore, MD: Paul H. Brookes.

Iwata, B.A., Dorsey, M.F., Slifer, K.J., Bauman, K.E. and Richman, G.S. (1994) 'Toward a functional analysis of self-injury.' *Journal of Applied Behavior Analysis 27,* 209. Reprinted from *Analysis and Intervention in Developmental Disabilities 2,* 20 (1982).

Kennedy, C.H. (2002) 'Towards a socially valid understanding of problem behavior.' *Education and Treatment of Children 25,* 142–153.

Kennedy, C.H. and Itktonen, T. (1993) 'Effects of setting events on problem behavior of students with severe disabilities.' *Journal of Applied Behavior Analysis 26,* 321–327.

Kennedy, C.H., Horner, C.H., Newton, J.S. and Kanda, E. (1990) 'Measuring the activity patterns of adults with severe disabilities using the Resident Lifestyle Inventory.' *Journal of the Association for Persons with Severe Handicaps 15,* 79–85.

Kincaid, D. and Fox, L. (2002) 'Person-centered planning and positive behavior support.' In S. Holburn and P. Vietze (eds) *Person-Centered Planning: Research, Practice, and Future Directions* (pp.29–49). Baltimore, MD: Paul H. Brookes.

Koegel, L.K., Koegel, R.L. and Dunlap, G. (1996) *Positive Behavior Support: Including People with Difficult Behavior in the Community.* Baltimore, MD: Paul H. Brookes.

Lucyshyn, J.M. and Albin, R.W. (1993) 'Comprehensive support to families of children with disabilities and behavior problems: keeping it "friendly".' In G.H.S. Singer and L.E. Powers (eds) *Families, Disabilities, and Empowerment: Active Coping Skills and Strategies for Family Interventions* (pp.365–407). Baltimore, MD: Paul H. Brookes.

McGill, P. (1999) 'Establishing operations: implications for the assessment, treatment and prevention of problem behavior.' *Journal of Applied Behavior Analysis 32,* 393–418.

Meyer, L.H. and Evans, I.M. (1993) 'Meaningful outcomes in behavioral intervention: evaluating positive approaches to the remediation of challenging behaviors.' In J. Reichle and D.P. Wacker (eds) *Communicative Alternatives to Challenging Behavior: Integrating Functional Assessment and Intervention Strategies* (pp.407–428). Baltimore, MD: Paul H. Brookes.

Meyer, L.H. and Janney, R. (1989) 'User-friendly measures of meaningful outcomes: evaluating behavioural interventions.' *Journal of the Association for Persons with Severe Handicaps 14,* 263–270.

Michael, J.L. (1993) 'Establishing operations.' *The Behavior Analyst 16,* 191–206.

Mount, B. and Zwernik, K. (1988) *It's Never Too Early, It's Never Too Late: An Overview on Personal Futures Planning*. St. Paul, MN: Governor's Council on Developmental Disabilities.

O'Brien, J. and O'Brien, C.L (eds) (2002) *A Little Book About Person Centered Planning*. Toronto: Inclusion Press.

O'Neill, R.E., Horner, R.H., Albin, R.W., Sprague, J.R., Storey, K. and Newton, J.S. (1997) *Functional Assessment for Problem Behavior: A Practical Handbook* (2nd edn). Pacific Grove, CA: Brookes/Cole.

O'Reilly, M.F., Lacey, C. and Lancioni, G. (2000) 'Assessment of the influence of background noise on escape-maintained problem behavior and pain behavior in a child with William Syndrome.' *Journal of Applied Behavior Analysis 33*, 511–514.

Pearpoint, J., O'Brien, J. and Forest, M. (1993) *PATH (Planning Alternative Tomorrows with Hope): A Workbook for Planning Positive Futures*. Toronto: Inclusion Press.

Personal Outcome Measures for Children and Youth (2000) *The Council on Quality and Leadership*, Towson, MD. www.thecouncil.org/publications/92/personal-outcome-measures-for-children-and-youth (accessed 30 September 2005).

Pitonyak, D. (2004) *Notes for Parents*. www.dimagine.com (accessed 25 May 2005).

Reimers, T.M., Wacker, D.P., Cooper, L.J. and DeRaad, A.O. (1992) 'Acceptability of behavioural treatments for children: analog and naturalistic evaluations by parents.' *School Psychology Review 21*, 628–643.

Risley, T. (1996) 'Get a life: positive behavioral intervention for challenging behavior through life arrangement and life coaching.' In L.K. Koegel, R.L. Koegel and G. Dunlap (eds) *Positive Behavioral Support: Including People with Difficult Behavior in the Community* (pp.403–424). Baltimore, MD: Paul H. Brookes.

Schalock, R.L. and Keith, K.D. (1993) *Quality of Life Questionnaire Manual*. Ohio: IDS Publishing Corporation.

Smull, M. and Burke Harrison, S. (1992) *Supporting People with Severe Reputations in the Community*. Arlington, VA: NASMRPD.

Sparrow, S.S., Balla, D.A. and Cicchetti, D.V. (1984) *Vineland Adaptive Behavior Scales*. Circle Pines, MN: American Guidance Service Publishing.

Sugai, G., Horner, R.H., Dunlap, G., Hieneman, M., Lewis, T.J., Nelson, C.M., Scott, T., Liaupsin, C., Sailor, W., Turnbull, A.P., Turnbull, H.R. III, Wickham, D., Reuf, M. and Wilcox, B. (2000) *Applying Positive Behavioral Support and Functional Behavioral Assessment in Schools*. Technical Guide, OSEP Center on Positive Behavioral Interventions and Supports. http://www.pbis.org/researchLiterature.htm (accessed 25 May 2005).

Touchette, P.E., MacDonald, R.F. and Langer, S.N. (1985) 'A scatter plot for identifying stimulus control of problem behavior.' *Journal of Applied Behavior Analysis 18*, 343–351.

Wacker, D.P. and Berg, W.K. (2002) 'PBS as a service delivery system.' *Journal of Positive Behavioral Intervention 4*, 1, 25–28.

Wacker, D.P., Berg, W.K. and Harding, J.W. (2002) 'Replacing socially unacceptable behaviour with acceptable communication responses.' In J. Reichle, D.R. Beukelman and J.C. Light (eds) *Exemplary Practices for Beginning Communicators: Implications for AAC* (pp.97–121). Baltimore, MD: Paul. H. Brookes.

Wagner, G.A. (2002) 'Person-centered planning from a behavioral perspective.' In S. Holburn and P. Vietze (eds) *Person-Centered Planning: Research, Practice, and Future Directions* (pp.273–290). Baltimore, MD: Paul H. Brookes.

Williams, W.L. (2000) 'Behavioral consultation.' In J. Austin and J. Carr (eds) *Handbook of Applied Behavior Analysis* (pp.375–398). Reno, NV: Context Press.

CHAPTER 9

Mikey – Dealing with Courts, Tribunals and Politicians

Helen Byrne and Tony Byrne

We always imagined we would have lots of children and live a normal family life with all of the usual trials and tribulations that come with raising children. However, that was not to be. For reasons we do not understand we have been given a task which is more demanding than most. We live in a suburban town, in a nice detached bungalow, with a small garden…but our garden is surrounded by a six-foot wall. Two of our five children have been diagnosed with autistic spectrum disorder (ASD).

When Conor, our third child, was about 14 months old we began to notice some strange behaviours. We had watched the older two children develop normally, both bright and lively children. Conor was very different; he didn't respond to his name, he didn't develop, and he was not interested in what was going on. We became really concerned when our fourth child Dylan was born and the children came to the hospital to visit their new baby brother. There were hugs and kisses from the older two, but Conor didn't even acknowledge his mom. We knew something was wrong. Helen vaguely remembered having heard about a strange condition called autism. But when she mentioned this at first, Tony thought it was unlikely and the family doctor agreed because, he said, the condition was so rare, only one in a thousand children were affected.

But worries about Conor grew and eventually he was referred to the local child development clinic (CDC). The community paediatrician thought Conor had a hearing problem, but we knew that Conor could hear things when he wanted to – for example, he could easily follow his favourite cartoon music on TV. At two-and-a-half years old, following many visits to the CDC, we were told that Conor indeed had 'autistic tendencies'. Conor had little speech and he preferred to be on his own, walking up and down along the windowsill, naked. He screamed when anyone tried to stop him and, at night, he made strange, animal-like sounds for hours on end. We were offered 30 minutes of speech and language therapy per week for Conor, in blocks of six weeks (six weeks on and six weeks off).

The start

We first heard about applied behaviour analysis (ABA) when reading a small clipping in a local newspaper in which the mother of an autistic boy and a lecturer from the local university described how ABA had worked for him. We joined a group of parents who met once per month at the university for workshops organized by Dr Mickey Keenan. At the time Helen was struggling to come to terms with Conor's diagnosis and although she was craving knowledge on autism, this ABA stuff did not click with her. However, Tony decided to try ABA to manage Conor's behaviour and to get him to engage with us. At first, Conor would scream and yell when Tony brought him to the bedroom to work with him. But then one night Conor actually went and got his little white chair and brought it to Tony. He was beginning to re-engage and actually enjoyed the work. Conor's behaviour got better, and when he was four, he began a school for children with severe learning disability. The school had been highly recommended and we were told that it used a wide range of interventions, including ABA. In Conor's first year at school he had an excellent teacher who really helped him. We drifted away from the ABA workshops, as it was difficult to get babysitters once a month to allow us to travel the 80 miles to attend the university. Baby Dylan was now two years old and a very difficult child. Our concerns were growing about him as he too was failing to develop appropriate speech and his behaviour was quite out of control. Eventually he was diagnosed with attention deficit/hyperactivity disorder (ADHD).

Mikey

When Mikey was born, he was a beautiful baby. Helen was exhausted; five children in a small house, three boys in nappies, no one to help. Tony was working full time in a demanding job. After a while, we moved to a new and bigger house. Things became a little easier. Conor was five, Dylan was three, and Mikey had just turned one year old. Conor was attending the Special School and was in his second year. Dylan had begun to speak some few words, but his behaviour was still very difficult. Mikey was our baby.

When you have a child diagnosed with ASD you constantly question the development of your other children. We were watching Mikey every day, looking for signs of strange behaviour, hoping that he would point or speak, something that typically developing children do. One day when we were sitting in the garden, Mikey came over and said 'Didin' (his attempt at 'Dylan'). We were overjoyed. Mikey had spoken his first words. Thank God, Mikey was not autistic.

Our joy did not last. At 15 months Mikey started to avoid eye contact and stopped responding to his name. He began to behave as if he could not hear us, and he resisted being held and cuddled. He did not miss us when we left, he did not develop speech, and he did not understand what we said to him. He showed no interest in toys and was oblivious to the company of others, preferring to spend his days in meaningless and repetitive activities such as gazing at lights, hand flapping, and pacing back and forth on the floor, looking at shadows out of the corner of his eyes. Mikey did not feed or dress himself, and was not toilet trained. Every day Mikey was slipping away from us further, trapped in his own world.

Mikey was diagnosed severely autistic at two years old. We were offered bereavement counselling, respite care, half an hour speech and language therapy (SLT) per week, and we were told that when Mikey was four years old, he would be able to attend a school for children with severe learning disability.

We were devastated. How could autism come into our lives twice? What had we done to deserve this? After the first two sessions of 30-minute SLT, it was obvious to us that Mikey needed much more.

Applied behaviour analysis for Mikey

Conor was in his second year at the special needs school and seemed to regress. We decided to give ABA another go. By now, the group of parents we had met at the ABA workshops had formed the charity Parents' Education as Autism Therapists (PEAT) to provide parent training, home visits, and a small subsidy to families to help fund ABA therapists. We went to monthly workshops (now located closer to our home) and started a home programme for Mikey. Helen was Mikey's main therapist, supported by some paid therapists. The speech and language therapist did not approve and consequently we didn't see her again for nearly two years.

Initially, Mikey received up to ten hours of one-to-one teaching per week. Our first goals were to teach Mikey to keep eye contact and to sit on request. Mikey responded well to the programme (see Figure 9.1).

Figure 9.1: Mikey and Helen having fun with ABA

Education Boards

A Statement of Special Educational Needs (SEN) in the UK is a legal document that aims to identify a particular child's special educational needs and to set out how these needs should be met. Education Boards and schools must adhere to it. This is obviously an important document and all relevant professionals and the child's parents usually are asked to contribute. We knew from Conor's Statement that this was a long, drawn-out process.

In the meantime, Mikey was offered a place in a pre-school class at a school for children with severe learning disability. We were welcomed warmly and the principal said that PEAT staff would be welcomed to the school to ensure consistency between home programme and school. Mikey attended from 9 am to 1 pm and appeared to be making good progress. We established a good relationship with his teacher and there was exchange of ideas and information from both school and home. For example, we had begun using PECS (Picture Exchange Communication System) at home to give Mikey some means of communication. This was now being used and advanced in both school and home. Stephen Gallagher from the PEAT group had been to visit Mikey in his classroom and was able to exchange important information concerning Mikey's home programme. Mikey's teacher said that she found Stephen's visit beneficial and worthwhile.

When we eventually were asked for our parental opinion regarding Mikey's Statement of SEN, we stated clearly that we wanted ABA to continue in school as well as at home. We had seen it work. When Mikey began his home programme he had little or no skills. Using ABA (at that time he only had about ten hours per week), he had been taught to sit, make eye contact, point, touch, grasp, let go, reach, pull, push, shake, twist, squeeze, pinch, to come here, to give me, motor imitation, object discrimination, object function, to do jigsaws and shape sorters, play with toys appropriately, occupy his time with appropriate behaviours (i.e. decreased inappropriate stimming behaviour), to match colours, to match objects, to match shapes, to match pictures, to feed himself, to drink from a cup, to paint, and to draw. Mikey's social and communicative behaviours were improving and he was using PECS for communication.

We thought Mikey would benefit most from being taught in a Special School using an individualized ABA programme carried out by adequately trained teachers and coordinated by an ABA consultant (much the same as we were experiencing in pre-school at that time). With regard to Mikey's Individualized Education Plan (IEP), we wanted a high level of involvement from parents and ABA home programme coordinator, Dr Gallagher.

Mikey started to attend the Special School. For the first five months it seemed to work reasonably well. Then things changed dramatically. At the annual review in Conor's school, the cooperation between Mikey's school and Stephen Gallagher from PEAT was mentioned as an example of good practice. However, through the grapevine this was distorted into 'Dr Gallagher had to be brought into Mikey's school to show the teachers how to teach'. Although this was not at all a reflection of the discussion, it was the end of our good relationship with Mikey's school. We were not allowed back into the classroom and had to request a video to be able to see him being taught. When we got the video, we were most concerned. Mikey appeared to be non-responsive to the teacher and very unhappy in the classroom. Clearly, he was not responding to the educational approach adopted by the school and we wondered why ABA was not used when it was working so well at home.

When we eventually received Mikey's final Statement of SEN, it did not include ABA. We decided to appeal, hoping that a tribunal would decide in favour of Mikey benefiting from ABA. There have been many high-profile tribunal cases in the UK, Ireland and across the world – for example, in New Zealand, where parents had to fight for ABA for their children through the courts. Some cases were more successful than others, but all of the cases were long drawn-out processes that placed extra stress on families already coping with the fact that at least one of their children was diagnosed with ASD. There is no one to guide parents through the process. This is why we thought it would be useful to write about our experiences. Of course each case is different, but at the time it would have helped us to read about someone else's case and what they did, so we hope that the following paragraphs will help others who find themselves in a similar position.

Tribunals

First, we withdrew Mikey from school, remortgaged our home, and increased his ABA home-based programme to around 35 hours per week. Everything is relative. While we thought Mikey had made progress with ten hours of ABA per week, that was nothing compared to the progress we observed now. Mikey was taught initially using PECS and, within eight months (the time taken to get to the SEN tribunal hearing), Mikey had begun to verbalize his requests. He could look into our eyes and call us 'mama' and 'daddy'. He knew the names of his brothers and sister. He could ask for the things he wanted, follow simple commands, he knew his shapes, colours and body parts. He was beginning to show an interest in his surroundings and wanting to play with his brothers and sister. He was beginning to realize that he was part of our family.

To ensure independent assessment and expert representation, we employed an independent educational psychologist, an independent social worker, and a specialist solicitor (all had to be flown in from England and paid for at our family's expense). As if we did not have enough to cope with!

The Education Board decided to contest our appeal and sent us their detailed reaction, which was very extensive. We summarize the main points here, to show what parents may have to contend with if they decide to 'fight' the opinion of Education Boards. In brief, the Education Board attributed Mikey's progress to his attendance at the Special School rather than his home-based ABA programme; they argued that research was not unified about ABA and that it could create false hopes for parents; they even referred to a potential placebo effect; and they argued that their own method was just as effective; they said that Stephen Gallagher's visits had unsettled the other children in the classroom; and, finally, they stated that a decision about the most appropriate methodology should be left to professionally qualified teachers.

We thought that this was very patronizing and it disturbed us greatly. Nevertheless, we decided to retort. We outlined that we had read the literature as well and our choice of ABA was solely based on the progress our son was making. Mikey had made more progress in eight weeks of ABA home-based programme than he had made in the preceding two years. We wrote that employing ABA ourselves was not a decision that was taken lightly as it involved hard work and considerable expense, that there is an abundance of research evidence showing effectiveness of ABA, and that we were not on a crusade for one method over another. In fact, we clarified that ABA is not a treatment method for children with ASD but an applied science and that our future expectations for Mikey had been raised solely due to his remarkable progress using ABA. With regard to Stephen's presence in the classroom unsettling the children, we even had a note from one of the teachers saying how beneficial Stephen's advice and ideas had been and how much she had learned.

When the SEN tribunal eventually heard our appeal, the hearing lasted for eight hours. Summing up had to be carried out in writing, as they had run out of time. We waited five weeks for the decision, only to find that our appeal had been dismissed. The tribunal found that although Mikey had made considerable progress there was no evidence to suggest that he could not have made such progress under the eclectic approach advocated by the Education Board. Mikey had spent nearly six months in a Special School using an eclectic approach with no evidence of considerable progress, yet this was not even mentioned. It had taken eight months (of stress) and cost us £6000 to bring our appeal to tribunal. The Education Board had spent £9000 of public money to fight us, altogether enough for nearly one year of ABA for Mikey!

Politicians

We were devastated by the tribunal decision and didn't know where to turn, so we went to the press. The following day Mikey was front-page news. There was a beautiful photograph of him and beside it, in giant letters, 'Give Mikey life he deserves'. A lot of media attention followed, including TV and radio interviews. The Education Board repeatedly declined to comment.

We even met with the Minister for Education. She was surprised and promised to investigate. Mikey's ABA programme cost around £20,000 per year. In England the average amount paid out for educational provision for an ASD child can range from £20,000 to £120,000. Unfortunately, two weeks after our meeting with the Education Minister, there was a cabinet reshuffle and someone else got her job. We were back to square one, fundraising, sponsored walks, coffee mornings, pub quizzes, collection boxes in shops, a fashion show, a sponsored cycle, a sponsored marathon, Mikey's therapist even recording her own CD to raise funds, including one song specially written for Mikey.

It was decision time. Should we appeal in the High Court? With no legal aid, no legal background, how would we be able to identify the crucial 'point of law', the basis of an appeal? If we lost, we would be liable for our own costs and those of the Education Board, easily running into tens if not hundreds of thousands of pounds sterling. Fortunately, a local, well-respected solicitor offered to take our case, free of charge. He conferred with a Queen's Counsel (QC) and together they advised that it was unlikely that we would win a High Court appeal on a point of law. They thought we would just be sent back to tribunal for a second hearing. Very perplexing!

It was coming up to one year since our original tribunal hearing and the Education Board requested a review of Mikey's Statement of SEN. We agreed to attend and decided to bring Mikey's data files – over 1000 pages of detailed and meticulous ABA data, showing Mikey's step-by-step progress. We asked for a new assessment of Mikey's needs, which was carried out by the Board's own educational psychologist. She concluded that Mikey no longer fell within the category of severely learning disabled. He had made significant gains in performance skills and IQ, and moderate gains in verbal skills (where previously Mikey had little or no functional speech, he now had over 800 words). He was placed within the moderate learning disability range. To save any further delay, we asked the Board to issue the final Statement of SEN.

A compromise of sorts

Once we had received the final Statement of SEN, we again submitted an appeal to the SEN tribunal. By now, Mikey had been on a home-based intensive ABA programme for two years and we felt he was ready to be integrated into a school environment. Both Conor and Dylan now attended our local mainstream primary school. This school was opening a new ASD-specific unit and we wanted Mikey to join. The Board agreed in principle. We had numerous meetings and correspondence (not all of which were very helpful). The Board still did not offer ABA; instead they proposed a 'combined skills', as opposed to 'eclectic', approach (we did not really see the difference). But the atmosphere was very different. We were met with smiles and greetings, and they seemed to be open to compromise. So were we. We suggested that if the Board responded positively to the following arrangements by the date on which we had to submit our response, we would withdraw the appeal:

1. Mikey was to be accompanied by his ABA therapist in the transition period to the Unit.

2. The Unit teacher was to be given introductory training by a behaviour analyst (Dr Gallagher from PEAT had developed an excellent introductory training course for professionals).

3. The level of speech and language input was to be quantified.

The positive response from the Board arrived quickly and we were able to inform the tribunal that a hearing would no longer be required.

What we have achieved for Mikey is not wholly satisfactory. However, if we had proceeded, relationships between the Board, the school and ourselves would have been beyond repair, and there would be no hope for home–school cooperation. Mikey has started school now, accompanied by his ABA therapist, and he has settled in well. Another ABA therapist works with him in the afternoons at home (we fund that ourselves). Time, and behaviour analytic data, will tell the rest of the story. Conor is in mainstream school now and doing really well. His was a battle too, and we probably will have to fight for the needs and rights of our children until we die. It is diabolical that parents of children with disabilities should have to do this in the 21st century, in a so-called developed country. We are heavily involved in the PEAT Charity trying to help our kids and other families living with ASD. Tony is Chairperson of PEAT and he is also on the Committee of Irish Autism Action, an umbrella group that represents voluntary groups from all over Ireland. (See Figure 9.2.)

Figure 9.2: Helen and Tony with Mikey

We have written this account of our experience so that other parents will know and be prepared for what may lie ahead. We hope that this is not the case and that the statutory bodies change their attitudes towards families of children with ASD and towards ABA. These are our children – let's not forget that.

CHAPTER 10

A Sibling's Perspective

Jonny (17)

When you live with something you become used to it because it is a part of your everyday life. People by their very nature adapt to the environment they are faced with. What you are given in life is not up to you, but what is up to you is what you take from it, what you learn.

Living with two autistic brothers has taught me that I (Jonny) am very lucky in what I have been given, because I have touched upon what it must feel like to have nothing.

In today's society you always hear people complaining about how little they have, but I'm not talking about the kind of 'nothing' that is not to have the latest edition of electrical device in home entertainment or high-speed Internet connection or 50 pounds less a week than the guy who works alongside you in the factory. I'm talking about having nothing, not a thing: I'm talking about the loss of one's humanity.

Conor was born when I was ten years old. He started off just like any other baby, round, chubby, cute, and demanding. I was excited about this new, glowing, screaming, belching bundle of beginning that had entered my life, bringing with him potent baby odours of dry milk formula, spew, malting scalp, and continuous bottom belching. He had entered the world wailing for attention and gurgling for love and I couldn't wait to take up his demands, give what I was required to give. How little would be required of me. Little did I know that soon Conor would lose his will to yell when he needed his family.

It was like he didn't know whether we were there or not; it was like he didn't care.

I think Conor was about two years old when he began to slip away from us. At first I thought his disconnected and wild behaviours were just part of the growing process and that soon he would reach back to us. However, his behaviours became more and more erratic and strange. He spent his days living like a cave man; refusing to wear clothes, preferring to fire his toys down the stairs or pile and roll them while grunting and howling, rather than play with them constructively. But by far Conor's favourite activity was to pace from one side of the windowsill to the other, patrolling back and forth, stopping only to batter the panes and yell like a monkey in the zoo. Now I find it hilarious looking back on the 'old' Conor, but at the time I remember feeling a great deal of shame towards that howling grunting little monster that had invaded my life. Each day walking from school I felt terribly anxious as to what I could be faced with when I arrived home. What dastardly antics had Conor come up with, what chaos had ensued and, most importantly (for a 12-year-old boy), what precious items of mine had been caught in the cross fire? It wasn't long before I acquired a 'trained eye'; a visual perception as to what would attract the toddling menace. Anything that was brightly coloured, shiny or intricate in design had to be placed out of reach of his grubby little paws. Under the prevailing threat of Conor's tyranny everything in our house had to be armoured. A stair guard was erected to prevent him from sending our valuables rolling; anything glass, ceramic or of a delicate nature was forced to move to higher ground; doors had to remain locked at all times and a six-foot-tall fence was erected surrounding our garden and sealing Conor in.

Mum tried her best to bring Conor on as many outings as possible: all of which ended in chaos. Trips to the park, town or beach were particularly treacherous. Wide-open spaces had a 'wild' effect on Conor. It was like he got a buzz out of running away from us; a change would come over his face as he charged into the distance, his eyes lit up with sheer pleasure and his mouth wide, grunting, and howling like an escaped convict. Yes, Conor unlike any other child I had ever seen wanted to escape his family and what's more he revelled in it. At first thought it would seem that he did it for attention but this wasn't the case because even when we didn't chase after him he still ran. I believe he simply didn't respond and that he would have ran and ran whether we gave him any attention or not.

Conor was more interested in destroying my things and the house I lived in rather than playing and building a relationship with me. I often attempted to relate to the estranged little boy who lived alongside me but never really lived with me.

There were ways that I could make contact with Conor but they were never on a personal level. You could tickle him and he would laugh, you could throw him up in the air and he would scream but you could never look him in the eye. To Conor people were like objects. Sometimes these objects made him feel good but most of the time they were obstacles in his way.

He often overcame the obstacles in his way.

In our house silence was a bad thing, silence meant that something underhand was happening, the chaos had been taken somewhere else. When an eerie silence drifted into our house everyone became apprehensive. Had Conor escaped?

Many a time he did. I often wondered what would happen if we had to report him missing to the police – 'What was he last seen wearing?' the police officer would say, and my mum would reply (probably with a red face), 'Well…er…nothing.'

Fortunately we never had to face that event as Conor would usually be found wandering the nearby cul-de-sac or ranting through a neighbour's house, foraging for boiled eggs and ham. Another thing that was strange about Conor was his diet. He lived only on ham and boiled eggs. I often remember how he used to squat naked in the garden sucking on an egg or gobbling ham like a Neanderthal.

And so life went on like this for some time, with Conor spending his days in a monotony of meaningless behaviour, clueless to what was going on within the perimeter of our garden fence, let alone outside it. I began to notice how thin and pale Mum was becoming. Her plight was a lot worse than the rest of the family. Forced to submit every inch of her energy into caring for Conor, she spent all of her time cooped up in the house. On top of this Dylan had been born a year after Conor. He was a little fiery-haired menace, who was later diagnosed with ADHD. Mum sought outside help, and social services stepped in. They took Conor on outings just to give Mum a break for a while. Everyone who worked with Conor would leave scarred. He never could abide having people hold his hand, so he held on with his teeth instead. To further lighten the load for Mum, Conor also began to attend a Special School.

Throughout the turmoil Mum and Dad had begun to read up on autism. Their persistence was incredible and their knowledge mounted up. It wasn't long before they discovered a way of treating autism called ABA. It's not a miracle cure but a long drawn-out process of therapy serving to remove the wall of autism brick by brick rather than simply topple it over. Things were beginning to look up, the turmoil was settling and Mum had another baby on the way.

Mikey came silently into our chaotic lives. He was a quiet baby, very well behaved. At first we were glad of his sanctity, his untouched innocence. Someone fresh ready to begin, all kinds of expectations we had. However, Mikey remained untouched for much longer than expected. While Conor and Dylan battled and yelled and Mum went about her usual duties as peace-keeper, Mikey sat silent. While everyone played in the garden in the sun Mikey sat in the shade hooded by his pram cover. When we rolled and laughed on the carpet, Mikey remained subdued, preferring to roll his eyes over the carpet patterns. The only things that made him laugh were shadows that skimmed past his eyes, and what made him cry we couldn't see. He spent his days in a meaningless dome, cut off from everything around him. Gazing at lights, flapping his hands back and forth, and looking at shadows out of the corner of his eyes.

No one wanted to admit it this time; he was overlooked due to the turmoil caused by Conor and Dylan; he was just a quiet baby. We had become so used to noise and unruly behaviour that we had forgotten serenity and, when we saw it, we saw it as a fault. No matter how much we tried to make sense of it and explain why, we all knew another had been taken. The dark cloud of autism had overshadowed another little cute bundle of joy.

Mikey was more lost than Conor. At least Conor had the ability to lash out and give us a little taster of his chaotic mind but Mikey could not. He was totally beyond all contact. He hated being touched and would withdraw the second you reached over to him. It was like he neglected us being there and wanted to be alone. Before people recognized autism as a disability some believed that it was due to negligence on the part of the parent but it seems to be more like negligence on the part of the child. As a sibling of the little chap it was hard to watch Mikey push us off – I can only imagine the horror that my parents must have felt.

Meanwhile Conor had come on immensely thanks to ABA coupled with Mum and Dad's persistence. He grew and grew over those next few years and his personality no longer lay dormant beneath the frost of autism but began to blossom.

Mikey began to attend a Special School in the hope that he too would come on. However, it soon became clear that he wasn't. ABA had released

Conor so it was only natural that Mum and Dad introduced Mikey to therapy. ABA gives so much back to children with autism (I should know; I've seen it work). The only problem is what it takes from the rest of the family: money! Throughout their efforts to save their children from autism Mum and Dad have spent thousands. Then again, what price can you put on a child's life? In any case, we all ploughed on, raising money where we could; we did sponsored cycles, fun runs, held fashion shows, and just plain begged, anything to help Mikey.

With Mikey the process of ABA has been much longer and more drawn out. ABA redirects children with autism, teaches them appropriate behaviour. When Conor began ABA his behaviours were wild and unpredictable; he needed to be shown how to relate to the world in another way. However, when Mikey began ABA he wasn't capable of behaving in any way either appropriate or inappropriate, meaning a lot more work had to be done with him. (See Figure 10.1.)

Figure 10.1: Brothers Jonny and Mikey

If you think of ABA as building a house, Conor was like an old building that needed renovation whereas Mikey would be the equivalent to an empty building site.

The work continued with Mikey and still is today. Our house is always filled with a buzz of noise and activity, with therapists coming in and out and Mum and Dad creating and discussing new ways to help Mikey's programme. I'm glad that we found ABA, because if we didn't, I am sure Mikey would have lapsed further away from us. Instead he now relates to the whole family and prances up to us with all sorts of little demands. The once alienated and estranged little boy who couldn't bear being touched now comes and tugs on my hand when he wants to play. He still has a long way to go, but the fact that he recognizes me as a part of his life is a milestone in itself.

As for Conor, he has gone from strength to strength; the little boy who was more like a wild animal than a human being is now more or less completely normal. His personality has come bursting out and he now enjoys us all, nearly as much as we enjoy him.

My Brother Mikey

by Meghan (11)

Mikey is my six year old brother,

He's very different from any other,

He's normal as far as the eye can see,

But his behaviour is very peculiar to me,

As a baby nothing seemed wrong,

But he didn't stay perfect for long,

Every time you walked near him he started to cry,

He wouldn't even look you in the eye,

Up and down the radiator he would pace and pace,

While he flapped his hands in front of his face,

He didn't find amusement with his toys,

He wasn't like other little boys,

You could stand in front of him and look him in the eye,

But his stare would simply pass you by,

He didn't play with others for hours on end,

He only chose himself to be his friend.

Mum and Dad said autism has to go now!

They would have to teach Mikey and show him how,

Then they found the perfect way,

They would teach Mikey with ABA,

But ABA teaching doesn't grow on a tree,

It costs lots and lots of money,

And after all poor Mum and Dad's done,

The Board* simply will not fund!

With ABA Mikey can run, climb, hop, sing, and dance,

If only the Board would give it a chance!

* Education Board

Figure 10.2: Meghan

CHAPTER 11

ABA is not 'A Therapy for Autism'

Mecca Chiesa

Growing up in Scotland in the 1960s, one of our playgrounds was the old cemetery at the top of the hill. We played typical childhood games: tag, hide and seek, various made-up war games, skipping where it was possible, and ball games until the custodian chased us out. In quieter moments we ambled about reading headstones and wondering how it was that lots of families seemed to have lost so many children in the space of just a few years. Large numbers of gravestones recorded the burial of child after child of the same family from two or three years old to teenagers of 16 or 17. There could be as many as eight or nine young deaths recorded on one gravestone. This was puzzling because no one in my immediate milieu was either dying or losing brothers or sisters at this alarming rate. I asked my mother, born 1924, who explained that when she was growing up it was entirely common for families to be large in number and for lots of children to die before adulthood. In my mother's generation tuberculosis, rheumatic fever, polio, diphtheria, scarlet fever, and other illnesses I had never heard of were an everyday worry for parents, children, and whole communities. In this small industrialized country they disappeared in the time span of only one generation.

When I began postgraduate studies in 1986, I and my postgraduate friends thought ourselves at the cutting edge of technology in that we shared one small black box with a keyboard and a tiny screen on which appeared our texts in hard-to-read green script. We typed, edited, wrote and re-wrote, rather daringly shifting paragraphs around and marvelling that we could make and correct errors without retyping entire pages. Today, I sit in front of another small black box with a keyboard. It's called a laptop, and with it I accomplish tasks we only fantasized about in the mid-1980s. I input data, draw different styles of graphs, do complicated calculations in less than a second, and discover patterns in the data within the hour. Less than 20 years ago, the same operations took painstaking days to complete. Plugging a cable into a phone socket opens up the world. Messages arrive from Auckland, San Diego and Iceland. Recent pictures from the Hubble spacecraft appear at the click of a button. I listen again to favourite radio shows, surf the world's libraries and bookstores, and read the latest scientific papers in the comfort of my own living room.

These are only two out of countless examples of startling changes brought about by the interplay between science and technology in recent decades. The debilitating, disabling and often fatal diseases common in my mother's generation were all but eradicated by the time I was born by advances in scientific understanding and the development and delivery of technologies based on those advances. The laptop giving me access to the rest of the world today also shows what can be achieved by this human activity called science and its technological applications. In less than 20 years the technology has progressed from mere word-processing capacity to rapid access to a world of information and computing power undreamt of in the 1980s. Scientific activity and the development of technologies based on science continue to make life longer, safer, more comfortable, and more interesting.

Because science and technology have these effects, we willingly embrace them in most areas of modern life. But we find ourselves in a curious position in the early 21st century when we propose applying science to the problem known as autism. In this book and other places, parents of autistic children describe the difficulties encountered in trying to access science-based treatment for autism or funding for such treatment. When parents turn to specialists for advice, they are met with seemingly endless disagreements over what might be the best intervention for their child. These specialists are no doubt well-meaning and concerned to provide the best (as they understand it) information and guidance to vulnerable parents, but such is the confusion and conflict between them that parents are often at a loss to know how to make a decision regarding treatment for their child.

A great deal of the confusion is due to what philosophers call a category error (or category mistake) – essentially a misunderstanding of what constitutes ABA and how it relates to other procedures promoted as interventions for autism. The point of this chapter is to explain what is meant by a category error and to show how the category error in question is unhelpful when it comes to deciding on the best care and education for autistic children.

What is a category error?

A modified version of one of Ryle's (1949) examples illustrates what is meant by a category error. Imagine American visitors to Oxford sign up for a walking tour that includes the famous Oxford University. A guide shows them the science library, biology department, computing services, playing fields, physics lab, refectory, and senior common room. After the tour, the visitors grumble, 'We saw the biology department, the computing services, playing fields, physics lab, and so on, but where was the university? We didn't see the university!' The visitors made a category error (see Figure 11.1 on p.229) in assuming that the term *university* belongs to the same category as the other terms, a category that might be described as 'a building or bounded area where a specific activity (scientific, sporting, scholarly, recreational) occurs'. In fact, the term *university* refers to the way in which all those activities are organized. The *university* is not one building or bounded area. It is the sum of all the places seen.

Why does it matter?

When presenting these kinds of issues to students there is always one who asks 'isn't this just an exercise in semantics?', as though the meaning of words is irrelevant for practical purposes. The pejorative *just* seriously underestimates the importance of words and of getting them right. The crucial point, not often appreciated, is that words, and the way words are embedded (in categories for example), make things happen. They are events that occur in the world that bring about actions and reactions. At the dinner table the words 'pass the salt' make something happen. Getting into a taxi in London, the words 'take me to King's Cross station' make something happen, something different to what would happen if the words 'take me to Buckingham Palace' occurred. In the doctor's office the words 'I've had a bad cough for about three months now' make something happen, something different to what would happen if the words 'I've been having a terrible time sleeping lately' occurred.

Research in the psychology of memory demonstrates something more remarkable than these fairly simple illustrations of the causal power of words. Research in eyewitness testimony and what is known as recovered memory syndrome demonstrates that people can be *made* (caused) to remember things that never happened, and to see things they never saw, by the words used in talking to them about an event or the way in which words are embedded in questions about an event (see, for example, Loftus and Loftus 1980; Loftus and Palmer 1974; Loftus and Zanni 1975; Roediger, McDermott and Goff 1997). Words are powerful causes, and they need careful consideration.

Using Ryle's (1949) example, it is worth considering how the American visitors might respond to their tour of Oxford. Likely they would feel disappointed or disgruntled at having missed out on seeing the famous Oxford University. They might return from their trip and tell friends and family not to bother taking the Oxford walking tour because it doesn't cover the university. They might complain to the tour guide and leave Oxford with negative feelings about the tour guide. These possible reactions are worth speculating on because they would be generated (caused) quite simply by the category error. If the error didn't occur, those emotional reactions wouldn't occur. If the visitors correctly categorized the university (see Figure 11.2) as the organization of particular kinds of scientific, sporting, scholarly and recreational activities, they would more likely return from the tour satisfied they had indeed seen the famous Oxford University, have positive feelings about the tour guide, and recommend the tour to friends and family when they return home. The way words are embedded in categories also needs careful consideration.

In Figure 11.2 *university* is correctly categorized as the organization of particular kinds of scientific, sporting, scholarly and recreational activities.

ABA and applied science

ABA is the acronym for applied behaviour analysis, the application of principles discovered by the science of behaviour analysis. For decades, behaviour analysts have engaged in the same practices as other natural scientists in attempting to discover causal connections in their subject matter. Sciences, regardless of their subject matter, have basic assumptions and practices in common. First, they share the assumption that nothing in the universe is 'uncaused'. All events are brought about by other events that happened before them. Behaviour is no different in this regard from the subject matter of other sciences; something makes it happen, and the scientific task is to discover what kinds of prior events bring it about. Second, all sciences share the

Science library	Biology department	Computing sciences
Maths department	Physics lab	Playing fields
University	Refectory	Philosophy department
Psychology lab	Law library	Senior common room

Figure 11.1: Example of a category error

The University		
Science library	Biology department	Computing sciences
Maths department	Physics lab	Playing fields
Business school	Refectory	Philosophy department
Psychology lab	Law library	Senior common room

Figure 11.2: Example of correct categorization

assumption that events in the universe are related in some kind of lawful or regular manner, and a principal function of science is the discovery of those laws or regularities.

While all natural sciences, including behaviour analysis, share these assumptions, different sciences are named according to their subject matter. The *Shorter Oxford English Dictionary* (1985) defines the major sciences in the following ways. Physics: 'the science, or sciences, treating of the properties of matter and energy, or of the action of different forms of energy on matter in general (excluding chemistry and biology)' (p.1576). Biology: 'the science of physical life, dealing with organized beings or animals and plants, their morphology, physiology, origin, and distribution' (p.194). Chemistry: 'that branch of science which deals with the several elementary substances, or forms of matter, of which all bodies are composed, the laws that regulate the combination of these elements in the formation of compound bodies, and the phenomena that accompany their exposure to diverse physical conditions' (p.321). A dictionary definition of behaviour analysis might read: 'A science whose subject matter is relations between behaviour and other events that influence its occurrence, concerned with lawful relations between the beha-viour of organisms and historical and current events in the context in which it occurs, including internal context.'

Some clarification of the subject matter is needed, however, because of the various cultural interpretations of what counts as 'behaviour'. Like the subject matter of other sciences, behaviour is a naturally occurring phenomenon and is defined quite simply as *anything an organism does*. What counts as behaviour for the purpose of scientific study is anything that can be expressed in the form of a verb. Dressing, shouting, doing maths, dropping litter, drinking, eating, reading, laughing, crying, driving, throwing a ball, are all examples of behaviour (anything an organism does) which are unlikely to cause confusion. Some other acts included in the definition are not ordinarily considered to be in the same domain: thinking, talking, writing, remembering, and planning are examples. Thinking is more usually referred to in its noun form, as thoughts, and studied as though it belonged to a category of events other than behaviour. Talking is typically considered to be in a domain of events called language rather than the broader domain of events called behaviour. Writing may also be considered in a similar way. Remembering tends to be referred to in its noun form as memory, and planning is usually associated with some-thing called intentions. Referred to in verb form, however, they fall within the definition of the subject matter of *anything an organism does* and are thus open to scientific analysis to the same extent as other acts. Like the subject matter of other sciences, they can be analysed for their operation as dependent variables (effects) brought about by other, prior events, or they can be analysed for their operation as independent variables (causes) bringing about other events at a later time. The acts of thinking, talking, remembering, and planning can bring about subsequent events in the repertoire of the actor and other people.

As well as sharing the basic assumptions of causation and regularity with other sciences, behaviour analysis shares a set of practices that have proved useful, indeed powerful, in the attempt to discover relations in the subject matter. Scientists, whatever their subject matter, engage in systematic, deliber-ate, and carefully designed recording of events. They typically record events more than once, since a single recording is not likely to reveal regularities that may exist between and among events. Wherever possible, scientists go further than recording observations and actually manipulate events in the world. This is known as experimentation. An experiment is the practice of controlling conditions, isolating and simplifying the subject matter, manipulating inde-pendent variables (causes) systematically and recording any changes that follow (effects). Finally, wherever possible, scientists repeat experiments to see if the same patterns or regularities occur. One demonstration is not as convincing as two or three demonstrations, and the practice of repeating experiments is important in confirming whether or not a perceived regularity is a real regularity.

In addition to these underlying assumptions and systematic procedures, sciences require clearly defined theoretical terms to discuss and explain relations within the subject matter. Some scientific language involves creating new words for naming previously unknown objects or processes (this is often done by putting two Greek or Latin roots together), while other cases rely on everyday words but define those words precisely for the purpose of analysis and discussion. To a lay-person, *grass* is green stuff that grows in parks and gardens and needs regular cutting and watering during summer months. To a botanist, *grass* is a broad term for considerably more types of plants with common characteristics, and botanists would specify types of grass for the purpose of scientific discussion. To a lay-person, a *schedule* is a kind of to-do list to be kept track of in a diary or on a calendar. In the technical vocabulary of behaviour analysis *schedule* refers to the timing of reinforcement and, like grass to the botanist, refers to something more than its everyday meaning. Precision of language is as important in behaviour analysis as in any other science.

Behaviour analysts have spent more than six decades developing procedures for measuring behaviour systematically and repeatedly and for answering questions about the causes of behaviour through experimentation (e.g. Chiesa 1994; Sidman 1960; Skinner 1938). In common with other sciences, as the discipline has grown, behaviour analysts specialize. Some behaviour analysts work in tightly controlled experimental settings with simple organisms such as pigeons, rats, flies, mice, bees, chickens, and so on, exploring causal relations in the same manner as basic researchers in other major sciences. A basic researcher in genetics uses simple organisms such as fruit flies in an attempt to discover principles of the understanding of genes and chromosomes. Humans are unlike fruit flies in many respects, as they are unlike mice or chickens in many respects. But the understanding of genes and chromosomes, like the understanding of behavioural principles, has been considerably advanced by this basic research approach. Highly controlled, basic experimental research is a fundamental feature of the major sciences. As scientists in other fields become specialists in neurobiology, cell biology, plastics manufacture, materials vibration, solar power development, and so on, some behaviour analysts specialize in particular areas such as eating disorders, education (mainstream and remedial), learning disabilities, performance management, obesity, depression, and so on. As other kinds of scientists disseminate, question and review findings in their specific technical vocabulary at conferences and in professional journals, behaviour analysts have a thriving professional community with a distinct vocabulary for sharing and challenging findings. In all sciences, the discovery, testing and dissemination of general principles allows for the development of new and powerful technologies.

In common with other sciences, the discovery of behavioural principles has led to technologies that considerably improve the human condition in a wide variety of settings. Figure 11.3 illustrates relations between behaviour analysis and other scientific disciplines as they are applied to practical matters. For all of the sciences mentioned, the list of applications is a mere sketch. And, in practice, there are many areas of overlap between different sciences that are not illustrated here. Note that autism is *one* among many possible applications of behaviour analysis as fluid dynamics is *one* among many possible applications of physics.

It would be difficult to deny that the practice of science and the innumerable technologies it has given rise to has considerably improved life in modern times. As science and technology develop, they do of course raise new problems for society to consider. But it would be hard to deny that all of our lives have been made considerably longer, healthier, and more comfortable by science and its applications.

The category error: ABA and 'therapies for autism'

The category error involved in referring to ABA as 'a therapy for autism' is illustrated in Figure 11.4. With the exception of one term (VBA), terms in Figure 11.4 are taken from websites for the National Autistic Society (NAS), the main UK-based charity concerned with autism, and the Autism Society of America (ASA), its equivalent in the US. Both the NAS and ASA use *therapies* and *approaches* interchangeably, as well as terms such as *interventions* and *treatments*. There are no discernible differences in meaning, so the terms *therapy* and *therapies* will continue to be used here. The term VBA (standing for verbal behaviour analysis) has been included because it is currently marketed as a specific type of behavioural intervention.

Science	Areas of Application
Physics	Civil engineering, mechanical engineering, electrical engineering, computing, sound engineering, aerodynamics, fluid dynamics, sensing technology, optics, communications technology, liquid metals technology, semiconductors, x-ray imaging, etc.
Biology	Immunology, histology, oncology, dermatology, neurology, rheumatology, infection control, surgery, vaccination, etc.
Chemistry	Paints, solvents, materials development, petro-chemicals, interventions in air purity/pollution, etc.
Bio-chemistry	Chemical interventions for illness and disease
Behaviour analysis	Parenting, health-care compliance, older populations, autism, obsessive-compulsive behaviour, panic, phobias, anorexia, obesity, marital relationships, attention deficit/hyperactivity, clinical behaviour therapy (including cognitive behaviour therapy), self-management, business and industry, sports, education (from pre-school to university), social anxiety, performance anxiety, etc.

Figure 11.3: The major sciences and some examples of areas in which they are applied

Figure 11.4 shows terms described as approaches, therapies, interventions, treatments for autism, extracted from NAS and ASA websites (except VBA).

It must be noted that more than one category error is in play in Figure 11.4. Presenting PECS, Lovaas, VBA and ABA in this manner implies they are all different examples of the category 'therapies for autism'. In reality, PECS, Lovaas and VBA *are* applied behaviour analysis. PECS stands for 'Picture Exchange Communication System', a set of procedures based on Skinner's (1957) suggestion that communication may be usefully analysed from a functional rather than structural perspective (Bondy 2001). Lovaas therapy draws on a wide range of principles and procedures of behaviour analysis (see Lovaas 1993), and VBA draws on behavioural procedures developed and experimentally tested from the 1960s onwards and usually referred to as 'incidental teaching' (see Fenske, Krantz and McClannahan 2001 for elaboration).

Therapies for autism		
Auditory integration therapy	Facilitated communication	PECS
Floor Time	Social Stories^{TM}	Sensory integration
TEACCH	SPELL	Lovaas
Son-Rise	VBA	Picture symbols
ABA	Music therapy	

Figure 11.4: Category error of listing ABA among 'therapies for autism'

To treat them as though they were something other than applications of behaviour analysis is like asking dinner guests to choose between apples, bananas, pears, grapes, and fruit for dessert. The question implies that from a category called *dessert*, one can choose apples, bananas, pears, grapes, *or* fruit – when, in fact, apples, bananas, pears and grapes are examples of the category *fruit*. The choice is not between those various items and fruit. The choice is between different kinds of fruit.

Putting that category error aside for the moment, the point here is to ask what kinds of events flow from the major category error of putting ABA alongside those other terms as though there were legitimate comparisons to be made between them. As the error of mistaking the university for 'a building or bounded area where a specific activity occurs' led to negative reactions in the scenario depicted earlier, the error of representing ABA as a therapy for autism in the manner illustrated above also brings about reactions. And these are worth considering, particularly in relation to how they affect decision making and provision of services for autistic children.

Applied science versus…?

The relationship between ABA and other procedures promoted, advertised, and indeed sold for large amounts of money as possibly therapeutic for autism is illustrated in Figure 11.5 (About Health and Fitness 2005). The question mark above the right-hand column indicates first that terms included there cannot claim to be examples of applied science, and second that it is not obvious how to categorize them. They were not derived from six or seven decades of controlled, systematic, experimental research disseminated to a scientific community that could replicate or question findings. They are not based on known scientific principles that gave rise to them as technologies in the way that principles of biology and chemistry give rise to medical interventions. They have not been subjected to the same rigorous measurement and testing as the various procedures employed by behaviour analysts. And they are carried out without the kinds of systematic recording and measurement procedures (data collection) that might give some clue to their usefulness or otherwise in bringing about meaningful and long-lasting changes for autistic children, their families, their schools and the wider community. In other words, they rarely, if ever, provide outcome measures. In light of this, it is hard to know how to categorize them.

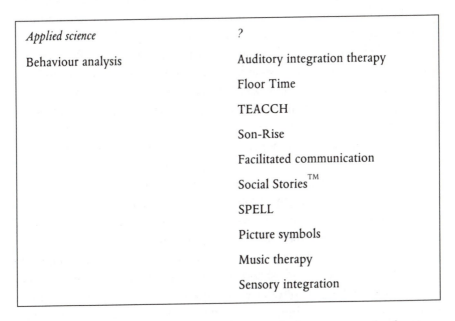

Applied science	?
Behaviour analysis	Auditory integration therapy
	Floor Time
	TEACCH
	Son-Rise
	Facilitated communication
	Social Stories[TM]
	SPELL
	Picture symbols
	Music therapy
	Sensory integration

Figure 11.5: Relationship between ABA as applied science and other terms promoted as therapies for autism

What does the category error give rise to?

Given the causal power of words, it is reasonable to assume that the category error causes reactions that would not occur if it was not in play. One consequence of the category error is that it confuses all sorts of interested and well-meaning parties about the choices available for improving the lives of autistic children and their families. Parents of newly diagnosed children, distressed and often desperate, are counselled to choose between a variety of 'therapies for autism', with ABA presented as though it were one among several possibilities. Indeed, the NAS and ASA specify that the information they provide on the various approaches named in Figure 11.4 does not carry their recommendation or endorsement. Readers (assumed to be parents) are counselled to seek further advice. But no guidance is given on what kinds of criteria might be used for selecting one procedure over another. When ABA is properly categorized, as in Figure 11.5, the choice faced by parents and service providers changes to a choice between applied science and…something else. The new choice is like having a chest infection diagnosed by a doctor and hearing the doctor say 'you can choose to take these antibiotics, scientifically developed and rigorously tested, or you can take some of this white powder that my friend at the golf club says might be quite good'. In practice, where a reliable medication is available, doctors don't offer a choice between applied science and something else. And we, consumers, would not expect them to. We would be puzzled if our medical practitioners suggested we choose between medicine and something else as though *choice* was a legitimate notion in this context. Yet this is what is happening in the professional realms of autism diagnosis and treatment as a result of the category error (Ives and Munro 2002).

A second consequence of the category error is that it misleads parents and professionals into believing that professional training can be accomplished on the same time scale in applied behaviour analysis as in other procedures promoted as 'therapies for autism'. Exposing the category error again changes the choice to be made, this time in terms of training and selecting competent professionals. No one would claim that a person could be trained as an expert in chemistry, biology or physics in the space of a one-day symposium, a two-day workshop or a three-week training course. But these are the time scales on which training is often provided in other procedures. Competent application of any science requires extended and rigorous education in the broad science followed by lengthy practical training under the supervision of experienced professionals.

Positive and negative dangers of ignoring science

Physical, chemical, biological and behavioural principles operate regardless of our feelings about them or our training with them. Because I am not a physicist doesn't mean I am not affected by gravity. When I drop an egg and it smashes on the kitchen floor, there's hardly any point in railing against gravity. Gravity will bring that egg to the floor if I let it go, and I should be more careful. Chemical reactions and interactions occur in my body, my car, the aeroplane I fly in, and the refrigerator that hums in the corner of my kitchen regardless of the fact that I know very little about chemistry. I don't need to be a chemist for these things to occur. They happen independently of my training. And precisely because I am not trained in these areas of science and technology I consult an appropriately trained expert when the need arises. To do otherwise would be dangerous.

When something clatters in my car and it begins to corner badly, I consult a mechanic. To not do this, or to attempt to deal with it myself, would be to put me and my family in harm's way. If my refrigerator leaks chemicals on the floor, the safe thing to do is to call in a refrigeration engineer. Untrained in the science and technology of chemistry and refrigeration, who knows what might come to pass if I either ignored the problem or tinkered with it myself? If I confess I know almost nothing about electricity, junction boxes, voltage and wiring cables, you would consider me utterly insane if I proposed to rewire my new house rather than employ a properly trained electrician to do it. And if my husband seems tired and complains of chest pains, my obligation is to persuade him to visit the doctor immediately. Something is happening that is beyond his or my expertise and it would be dangerous to let it pass or to think we could deal with it ourselves. We may not *like* the fact that physical, chemical or biological forces are at play in these ways, or that positive and expert action has to be taken, but most ordinary, untrained people would not dream of ignoring these problems or attempting to deal with them personally.

Ignoring the operation of scientific principles or dabbling with them in ignorance creates two kinds of dangers, positive and negative. In the case of behavioural principles and autistic children, positive dangers involve causing something to happen that is detrimental to the physical and social well-being of the child. This occurs when physically harmful or socially inappropriate behaviour is strengthened by well-meaning but inadequately trained carers. Negative dangers involve failing to make something happen that is to the physical, academic or social benefit of the child. This occurs where carers have no training in how to develop behavioural repertoires that will allow a child to function independently and participate in the kinds of desirable activities available to other children and adults in the social milieu. Unfortunately, I have seen many examples of both.

I once watched a teacher deliver an instruction at least a dozen times to a five-year-old autistic boy, to absolutely no effect. She was trying to get him to leave the room he was in and go to another room by loudly instructing 'Charlie, to the blue room' and holding up a square of paper with a symbol on it. The child continued to crawl under the table, throw a toy tractor across the room, run strips of paper through his fingers, climb on and off a table, roll on his back, run from one side of the room to the other aimlessly and frantically. Catching sight of one of her colleagues passing in the corridor, the teacher asked for the box of 'sweet reinforcers'. Her colleague returned with a box and the teacher, within sight of the child, took out a sweet which she held up while instructing 'Charlie, to the blue room'. Charlie rushed at her and jumped up, grabbing at the sweet. He kicked her, bit her hand, grabbed hold of her arm and swung on it, grabbed her leg and clung to it as she limped across the corridor into the blue room where she gave him the sweet. The teacher explained to me apologetically 'we use the sweet reinforcers as a last resort'. She was conscientiously doing what she had been taught to do, and no doubt had the best interests of the child at heart. Someone somewhere in the world had taught this teacher that such a thing exists as 'sweet reinforcers' (a disastrous mismatch of concepts) and that tangible reinforcers should be used as a last rather than first resort. What she failed to appreciate, given her inadequate training, was that her actions strengthened a cluster of aggressive behaviours that could well bring about negative consequences for the boy at a later date. I am confident this teacher would have been distressed if she had realized what she had done. And I wondered how the boy's parents would react if they knew that the people into whose care they gave their son every day were causing and reinforcing aggressive behaviour.

On another occasion I was working in a special needs classroom with a seven-year-old autistic boy. I was intrigued by the child's (call him Simon) response to an initial stimulus of 'come to the table'. He went to the top of the room, switched on an electric fan, jumped from one foot to the other on tiptoe, flapped his arms wildly above shoulder level, and shouted loudly in staccato bursts. I asked a teacher if she had seen this before. She told me a speech therapist had recently spent time with Simon using 'an options approach, getting inside his behaviour and using his interest in the fan to communicate with him' (as close to a direct quote as I can manage). Clearly, the speech therapist had been doing what some 'expert' had taught her was appropriate when a child engaged for long periods with some object. She was taught to interpret this as an 'expression of interest' and 'work with it'. Unfortunately, what transpired was that the speech therapist's actions reinforced this bizarre and entirely inappropriate cluster of behaviours and it took me almost 15 minutes to establish more socially appropriate responses. I have no doubt the speech therapist thought she was doing something useful. The sad truth is that what she had been taught was simply made-up nonsense, scientifically and conceptually unsound and detrimental in terms of Simon's need to learn to engage with his social and academic world like other children. The speech therapist's behaviour *caused* Simon's bizarre response, and again I wondered how his parents would react if they knew this. In terms of positive dangers, children are at risk of developing socially inappropriate, bizarre, aggressive and self-injurious behaviour as they interact with teachers and carers inadequately trained in scientific principles.

In terms of negative dangers, autistic children are at risk of failing to develop the kinds of skills that allow them to function independently in the social world and of having to be cared for throughout childhood and adulthood. They are at risk of never learning to speak, read or write, communicate needs and desires, or engage socially with parents, siblings, peers, teachers, and the wider community. All of those skills are possible when treatment is in the hands of trained scientists. I have seen more children than I care to think about consigned to wandering aimlessly around or sitting vacantly in the corner of special needs classrooms because their carers have no training in the scientific principles that can make useful and socially important behaviour happen.

Like other scientific principles, behavioural principles operate universally and without regard to the training or knowledge base of the teacher, speech therapist, educational psychologist or parent. Stimulus control and reinforcement occur whether we know about it or not. Socially appropriate behaviour can be strengthened or weakened, as can inappropriate behaviour such as aggression, self-injury, biting, screaming, food refusal, perseveration and rituals. To disregard these facts is to put autistic children in danger.

Conclusion

Experts and advisers mistakenly represent ABA as one among several 'therapies for autism' in the manner illustrated in Figure 11.4. Clarifying ABA to be an applied science opens up new choices for parents and education providers.

The choice is no longer between different 'therapies for autism', but between scientifically-derived technology and procedures that do not emerge a scientific tradition, have not been subject to experimental testing, and may therefore lead to the kinds of positive and negative dangers described above. In addition, it highlights the need for the same kind of extended and rigorous training in behaviour analysis that we require for experts in other sciences. Autistic children, their families, education professionals and providers need applied behaviour analysis to the same extent that they need applied physics, chemistry and biology – because it brings about benefits to the same extent as those other sciences.

References

About Health and Fitness (2005) *Treatments and Therapies for Autism Spectrum Disorders.* http://autism.about.com/od/treatments/a/snakeoil.htm (accessed 4 October 2005).

Bondy, A. (2001) 'PECS: potential benefits and risks.' *The Behavior Analyst Today 2,* 2, 127–132.

Chiesa, M. (1994) *Radical Behaviourism: The Philosophy and the Science.* Boston: Authors Cooperative.

Fenske, E.C., Krantz, P.J. and McClannahan, L.E. (2001) 'Incidental teaching: a not-discrete-trial procedure.' In C. Maurice, G. Green and R.M. Foxx (eds) *Making a Difference: Behavioral Intervention for Autism* (pp.75–82). Austin, TX: Pro-Ed.

Ives, M. and Munro, N. (2002) *Caring for a Child with Autism: A Practical Guide for Parents.* London: Jessica Kingsley Publishers.

Loftus, E.F. and Loftus, G.R. (1980) 'On the permanence of stored information in the human brain.' *American Psychologist 35,* 5, 409–420.

Loftus, E.F. and Palmer, J.C. (1974) 'Reconstruction of automobile destruction: an example of the interaction between language and memory.' *Journal of Verbal Learning and Verbal Behavior 13,* 585–589.

Loftus, E.F. and Zanni, G. (1975) 'Eyewitness testimony: the influence of the wording of a question.' *Bulletin of the Psychonomic Society 5,* 86–88.

Lovaas, O.I. (1993) 'The development of a treatment research project for developmentally disabled and autistic children.' *Journal of Applied Behavior Analysis 26,* 4, 617–630.

Roediger, H.L., McDermott, K.B. and Goff, L.M. (1997) 'Recovery of true and false memories: paradoxical effects of repeated testing.' In M. Conway (ed) *Recovered Memories and False Memories* (pp.119–149). Oxford: Oxford University Press.

Ryle, G. (1949) *The Concept of Mind.* Harmondsworth: Penguin.

Shorter Oxford English Dictionary (1985) New York: Oxford University Press.

Sidman, M. (1960) *Tactics of Scientific Research.* New York: Basic Books.

Skinner, B.F. (1938) *The Behavior of Organisms.* New York: Appleton-Century-Crofts.

Skinner, B.F. (1957) *Verbal Behavior.* Englewood Cliffs, NJ: Prentice Hall.

CHAPTER 12

What Do Parents Think of ABA?[1]

Karola Dillenburger and Mickey Keenan

There is overwhelming evidence that applied behaviour analysis (ABA) provides the most effective form of intervention for children with autistic spectrum disorder (ASD) (see 'Resources for Parents' at the end of this book). There is less evidence, however, about how parents perceive and evaluate ABA programmes. In this chapter, parents of the PEAT group who are involved in ABA programmes with their children were asked what they think of ABA and how they rate its effectiveness.

Background

In common with many of the other natural sciences behaviour analysis has a conceptual, an experimental and an applied strand (Baer 1997; Chiesa 1994). In this chapter we concentrate on the applied strand of behaviour analysis, i.e. applied behaviour analysis (ABA). ABA is defined as the use of knowledge gained within the science of behaviour analysis for the improvement of behaviours that are socially important (Baer, Wolf and Risley 1968). It is used in many areas such as community development, social work, nursing, industry, education and medicine. For over 30 years ABA has been employed successfully

---

1   This chapter is based on Dillenburger *et al.* (2004). Reprinted with permission of Taylor and Francis Ltd (www.tandf.co.uk).

with children with ASD (Matson *et al.* 1996) and has been found to be more effective than so-called eclectic approaches (Howard *et al.* 2005).

While the exact neurological differences between children with ASD and their typically developing peers remain unclear, the diagnosis generally relies on observations of differences in behaviour. Children are diagnosed with ASD if they engage in specific behavioural excesses (e.g. 'stimming', temper tantrums, stereotypic, emotionless play) and particular behavioural deficits (e.g. lack of language, social interaction, social initiation and interactive play) (cf. DSM-IV 1994). In behaviour analysis the term 'behaviour' has a wide definition. Anything a person does is regarded as behaviour; this includes publicly observable behaviours as well as 'private' behaviours, such as feeling and thinking (Reese 1978). This holistic perspective on being a person means that the term ASD is viewed as a summary label for publicly observable behaviour patterns as well as private responses (Holth 2001).

ABA for children with ASD

The best-known applications of behaviour analytic knowledge for children with ASD are discrete-trial training methods. However, ABA involves a wide range of other strategies, including Picture Exchange Communication System (PECS), precision teaching, shaping and chaining of new behaviours, and planning for generalization and maintenance to name but a few. It is not the aim of this chapter to describe in detail what is involved in a comprehensive ABA programme. Interested readers are referred to other chapters in this book and other available literature (e.g. Keenan, Kerr and Dillenburger 2000; Maurice 1993; 1999; Maurice, Green and Luce 1996).

Extensive research over 30 years shows that early intensive behavioural intervention can lead to significant gains in cognitive, social, emotional and motor functioning that can be generalized to other situations and maintained in the long term (McEachin, Smith and Lovaas 1993). A review of over 500 studies shows that ABA consistently offers positive outcomes in terms of educating children with ASD and enhancing life skills (Matson *et al.* 1996). Even in cases of less intensive parent-managed behavioural intervention it was found that children were able to live in less restrictive environments than if they had not received behavioural interventions (Bibby *et al.* 2002). The level of ABA training and expertise of professionals varies considerably and ranges from having some experience in the 1970s (Jordan 2001) to rigorous internationally recognized qualifications, such as those offered by the Behavior Analyst Certification Board today.

ABA treatment and parent education

The quality of ABA training is a crucial factor in the determination of treatment outcome. Exact data relating to quality of training is generally unavailable (Bibby *et al.* 2002) with the exception of one study which found that parent-employed therapists who had received short-term training were less effective than college-trained therapists (Smith, Buch and Gamby 2000). More research has concentrated on the quality of parent training in general (Callias 1994; O'Reilly and Dillenburger 1997).

The approach to ABA training for parents differs between programmes (Richman 2001). Some training programmes teach parents the use of distinctive treatment procedures (Boyd and Corley 2001) while others start by educating parents about general behavioural principles (Keenan 2001; Keenan and Dillenburger 2000). The former approach has been criticized as a 'cookbook approach to practice' (Bronson and Thyer 2001), likened to giving 'recipes' for treatment, a 'one size fits all' approach. The latter approach offers detailed knowledge of the broad spectrum of behavioural principles so that parents are empowered to adapt interventions to the individual, ever-changing needs of their own child (Webster-Stratton and Herbert 1994). In the PEAT group, the latter approach is used; in other words, parents are educated in general principles of ABA to enable them to design individually tailored treatment programmes for their children.

Parent training in ABA

Education in general principles of ABA begins by giving the parents a basic understanding of the philosophy of the science on which ABA is based (Chiesa 1994; Keenan and Dillenburger 2000). Behaviour analysis encourages the scientist to go to the root of traditional assumptions and beliefs by exposing the futility of mind/body dualism inherent in much of contemporary psychology. This philosophy of science informs parents so they can recognize the tautology inherent in the term 'autism' and avoid category mistakes (Holth 2001). From this basis parents are then taught some of the basic principles of behaviour and how these are applied to children with autism.

To date there exists only one parental satisfaction survey of early intensive behavioural intervention for young children with autism in a community setting in California (Boyd and Corley 2001). In Boyd and Corley's study tutors and supervisors were trained in autism and discrete-trial training; in other words, they were trained in one specific one-to-one treatment procedure rather than in the full range of applications of ABA. Weekly review meetings then were held with parents, tutors and supervisors. Boyd and Corley reviewed 22 cases (average length of treatment about two years; average age of children between three and four years). Two children were in home programmes, the remainder in schools. Boyd and Corley found that although all children had made progress, they did not achieve full 'recovery'. Parents were generally satisfied or very satisfied with the implementation of their child's programme and outcome.

What we did was different in a number of ways. First, parent training did not concentrate on one particular method of intervention. Instead parents were educated in general if basic principles of ABA that enabled them to tailor individual training programmes according to the changing needs of their own children using the full range of strategies developed within ABA. Second, PEAT includes older children. Third, all children were on home programmes with parents as their main therapists; and fourth, the effect of treatment duration was assessed.

PEAT parents

When we did this evaluation, 50 families were actively engaged in home-based ABA programmes through PEAT in Northern Ireland. All of these families were asked to take part and 22 families did. The length of time they had been involved in ABA training was used to differentiate between two groups of families. The long-term group (LTG; 12 families) had been involved in ABA programmes for an average of just under three years; the short-term group (STG; 10 families) had been involved in ABA programmes for an average of six months. Although the age range of children in both groups was virtually the same (3–13 years) more of the older children were in the LTG than in the STG. This was due to the fact that at the start of treatment the children in the LTG were older (average seven years old) than those in the STG (about four years) and, of course, the length of time they had been involved in ABA differed.

Parents in the LTG were slightly older (in their early to mid 40s) than those in the STG (in their late 30s). The groups were equivalent with regard to employment status (most families had at least one parent in employment) and with regard to socio-economic status (most parents were in professional or skilled occupations). The reasons why parents were not employed were similar between the two groups and were mainly related to caring for a child with autism. With regard to gender the two groups were equivalent. About 60 per cent were mothers and 30 per cent were fathers. Most of the children were boys; only one or two of the children were girls per group. All families were two-parent families except for one father-led one-parent family. All families had between one and four other children.

Training for PEAT parents

PEAT Director of Training Dr Stephen Gallagher offered an introductory course in ABA that ran one evening per fortnight in a local university for an 18-week period for parents of children with ASD. The topics covered included the philosophy of applied behaviour analysis, reinforcement, extinction, increasing adaptive behaviours and decreasing maladaptive behaviours, shaping and chaining new behaviours, stimulus discrimination training, observation and data collection, designing and implementing an intervention, and a session dedicated to revision. Parents read assigned chapters from a textbook (Grant and Evans 1994) in preparation for each session and were given a multiple-choice questionnaire at the end of each session. The parents used what they had learned in the course at home with their children as frequently as possible throughout the day. An ABA professional visited each family on a weekly basis for approximately two hours to supervise and adjust individualized programmes together with the parents.

Questions and answers

A specially designed ABA evaluation questionnaire was circulated to the families. The questions related to the validity of ABA, including significance of goals of the intervention, appropriateness of the intervention strategies, and importance of the outcomes (Kazdin 1977; Wolf 1978).

Significance of goals of the intervention

Parents felt that the goals of ABA intervention were significant and virtually all parents reported that ABA had made a difference in terms of independence, quality of life, skills development, skills maintenance, and interaction in their children's lives. The areas where parents thought the greatest difference was made were in relation to general quality of life, skills development and skills maintenance and interaction. There were only small differences in perception between LTG and STG parents.

Effectiveness of the intervention strategies

Overall, parents stated that ABA was effective in relation to promoting their children's self-help skills, social skills, dealing with problem behaviour, obsessional behaviour, improving gross motor skills as well as fine motor skills, communication, and concentration. These improvements were particularly apparent for the LTG, although significant improvements were reported by STG as well.

Importance of the outcomes in relation to family life

In response to the question 'What impact has ABA had on your family life?' parents in both LTG and STG considered that ABA had a positive effect on family life, although one parent drew attention to the amount of work and finance necessary for an intensive ABA programme (see Table 12.1).

Importance of the outcomes in relation to parents

In response to the question 'What impact has ABA had on you/how you feel about yourself?' all parents felt that ABA had positively impacted on them and how they feel about themselves (see Table 12.2).

Importance of the outcomes in relation to child

In response to the question 'What impact has ABA had on the life of your child?' all parents responded that ABA had had a very positive impact on their child's life (see Table 12.3).

Finally

In this chapter we talked about an examination of parents' perceptions of the outcome of home-based ABA programmes. We found that parents considered ABA to have high validity in facilitating development of their children. In particular they expressed that ABA outcomes were important and had made a substantial difference for the family as a whole and raised the general level of parents' confidence and empowerment. In the context of other similar programme evaluations the findings reported here are noteworthy for a number of reasons.

**Table 12.1 Examples of parents' statements regarding
the impact of ABA on family life**

Categories	Examples from LTG parents	Examples from STG parents
Before ABA treatment	Autism equals disruption, loss of a bedroom, wife having to leave work, cannot book holidays…	
General effect on family life	Made it easier. Immense impact. We are now approaching normal family life. We have a level of reasoning. More manageable.	Time with other children has been reduced although they understand this. Entirely positive. Great impact. Life is a bit calmer.
Effect on family cohesion	We have a level of reasoning. Entirely positive. Brought the family tighter to help child. Great impact, more normal family life.	ABA has improved family life immensely. We have a direction now. Gives us hope. Brought the family together to help child.
Work load	Made it more manageable.	A lot of time and energy used up on implementing ABA programmes.
Structure	More structured than before. It has helped give a focus. Able to deal with difficult situation.	It has put a strain on it to organize sessions.
Finance		Financially very stressful.
Freedom	Made us able to go on more outings.	It has raised expectations of relations.

Table 12.2 Examples of parents' statements regarding the impact of ABA on themselves

Categories	Examples from LTG parents	Examples from STG parents
General impact	Entirely positive. I now feel like a normal person.	ABA works and that impresses me. I feel it is brilliant.
Communication	A good impact through improved communications.	
Confidence	Made me more confident and relaxed. I feel capable of helping my son. It has made me feel confident. Confident as a mother. I feel as if I have done something constructive in helping my child. A sense of control over situations.	Given me confidence to help my child. Gives me a sense of control in my child's life. Feel more focused. I feel more in control. Determination to change things.
Coping	More able to cope with situations at home. It has helped me in everyday situations and can cope better. Enables me to cope with life and not lost as I felt when my son was first diagnosed. Gives me a greater understanding of my son and how to work properly with his needs.	Encouragement of X. I am more hopeful. I feel I am actually doing something to help my child. Given me hope for the future. Has given me the hope that I can improve my daughter's life without being dependent on professionals and their opinion.
Worry/stress	Made me worry less and enjoy my child more. Given hope and reduced stress levels. Given me some hope.	It makes me realize what can be achieved but I sometimes feel inadequate to the task. It has to some extent increased stress but as we become more familiar with the concepts stress levels are decreasing slowly!

Categories	Examples from LTG parents	Examples from STG parents
Self-esteem/ empowerment	Initially one feels rather inadequate in terms of what we had been doing to help X with his autism. However, undertaking ABA has been a definite step forward and constantly increases self-esteem. Makes me feel more empowered.	It gives me skills. It has given me the ability to help him.

Prior to the introduction of ABA, only one other treatment approach (Treatment and Education of Autistic and related Communications Handicapped Children – TEACCH; Schopler *et al.* 1981) had been available in Northern Ireland. Sines' (2001) evaluation of TEACCH had shown that parents were generally satisfied with the service they received for their child, although they were not convinced of the effectiveness of TEACCH in achieving the goals that they were expecting. Data presented here show that when offered an alternative, parents reported very substantial levels of satisfaction with the significance of goals of ABA intervention, the appropriateness of ABA intervention strategies, and social importance of ABA outcomes for the child, the parents, and the family as a whole. This is important because these answers came about despite the fact that ABA training was carried out 'on a shoe string', without any support from public agencies charged with caring for children with autism.

When compared with Boyd and Corley's (2001) parental evaluation of ABA programmes in California, findings reported here confirm a high level of parental satisfaction with ABA. The subtle downward shift in terms of parental satisfaction of treatment outcome noted by Boyd and Corley was not detected in this study. As mentioned earlier, PEAT's parent education does not concentrate on one particular method of intervention (e.g. one-to-one discrete-trial training); instead parents are educated in general principles of ABA and then get involved in the development of individually tailored treatment plans that encompassed the full range of methods developed within ABA. It is possible that this difference accounts for the high levels of satisfaction.

Indeed, through this kind of education in ABA it is likely that, in general, parental interactions with the child change and that this change affects the

**Table 12.3 Examples of parents' statements regarding
the impact of ABA on life of child**

Categories	Examples from LTG parents	Examples from STG parents
General demeanour	Has controlled his outbursts and made him a happy child. Improved tasks and difficult issues. Completely back in control and can deal with problem behaviours.	Calming influence, responds well to commands. There has been a very big change in X.
Communication /speech	He is less frustrated and easier to manage.	It has improved his communication hugely. He is more settled, more spontaneous, speech much better. The improvements have been dramatic. Her language and awareness have exceeded all expectations.
Academic skills	I don't believe my child would be at mainstream primary school and coping academically without ABA.	Exceptional results. He has had nothing else. Better concentration and vast improvements in writing, reading and many other areas. He is starting to write/read and is doing things I would never dream he could do.
Independence	Improved. He has learned to be more independent and acquired some basic skills. She has learned skills she did not have!	He is now toilet trained. Taught my son that we expect him to participate/ cooperate/interact/ communicate.
Relationships	Not only has it helped my child but also the whole family quality of life has improved dramatically.	ABA has certainly helped modify X's behaviours and has had a positive impact on family life in general. Large impact. Lots of family life changes. Excellent positive effect.

child on a 24-hours-a-day/7-days-a-week basis. If this is the case it has impli-cations for an analysis of treatment intensity. Is it possible that educating parents in ABA achieves increased levels of treatment intensity? Future studies should include direct assessment of parental programme implementation as well as a component analysis of parent education to shed more light on this tentative conclusion.

Previous research showed that the age of the child at the onset of treatment is an important factor in treatment success (Fenske et al. 1985). Results reported here confirm Eikeseth, Jahr and Eldevik's (1997) findings that while there may be an optimum age for starting behaviour analytic treatment, late treatment onset still makes important impacts on child behaviour and therefore has high levels of validity from a parental point of view.

Length of treatment is also usually viewed as a decisive factor with long-term treatment achieving better results than short-term treatment (Smith 1999). Results reported here, however, show that parents educated in ABA in the short term can achieve significant changes in their own child's behaviour. The present study was based on the premise that there was no time limit on ABA intervention. Instead, work with the child goes on as long as it takes to achieve the desired outcomes.

As far as we know, this was the first examination of parents' perceptions of the outcome of home-based ABA programmes. Usually more rigorous objec-tive scientific research methodologies are harnessed to measure the effect of ABA on various indices associated with a child's development (Keenan 2003). Despite the wealth of quantitative research reported in the literature (e.g. Anderson et al. 1987; Smith 1996, 1999; Weiss 1999), it is argued by some that the jury is still out on whether ABA is as effective as it is purported to be (Ives and Munro 2002; Jordan, Jones and Murray 1998; Task Force Report 2001). Although we did not include evaluative, continuous data on behaviour changes in the child, parents are satisfied with the outcomes achieved through very basic ABA training and perceive ABA to be valid in terms of significance of behavioural goals, appropriate in relation to intervention strategies, and important as regards outcomes for the quality of life for the children, their own confidence and feeling of empowerment, and the impact on family life as a whole.

References

Anderson, S.R., Avery, D.L., DiPietro, E.K., Edwards, G.L. and Christian, W.P. (1987) 'Intensive home-based early intervention with autistic children.' *Education and Treatment of Children 10*, 352–366.

Baer, D.M. (1997) 'Foreword.' In K. Dillenburger, M. O'Reilly and M. Keenan (eds) *Advances in Behaviour Analysis* (pp.vii–x). Dublin: University College Dublin Press.

Baer, D.M., Wolf, M.M. and Risley, T.R. (1968) 'Some current dimensions of applied behavior analysis.' *Journal of Applied Behavior Analysis 1*, 91–97.

Bibby, P., Eikeseth, S., Martin, N.T., Mudford, O.C. and Reeves, D. (2002) 'Progress and outcomes for children with autism receiving parent-managed intensive interventions.' *Research in Developmental Disabilities 23*, 81–104.

Boyd, R.D. and Corley, M.J. (2001) 'Outcome survey of early intensive behavioral intervention for young children with autism in a community setting.' *Autism 5*, 430–441.

Bronson, D.E. and Thyer, B.A. (2001) 'Behavioral social work: where has it been and where is it going?' *The Behavior Analyst Today 3*, 192–195.

Callias, M. (1994) 'Parent training.' In M. Rutter, E. Taylor and L. Hersov (eds) *Child and Adolescent Psychiatry: Modern Approaches* (pp.918–935). Oxford: Blackwell.

Chiesa, M. (1994) *Radical Behaviorism: The Philosophy and the Science.* Boston: Authors Cooperative, Inc.

Dillenburger, K., Keenan, M., Gallagher, S. and McElhinney, M. (2004) 'Applied Behaviour Analysis for children with autism: parental programme evaluation.' *Journal of Intellectual and Developmental Disabilities 29*, 113–124.

DSM-IV (1994) *Diagnostic and Statistical Manual of Mental Disorders* (4th edn). Washington, DC: American Psychiatric Association.

Eikeseth, J., Jahr, E. and Eldevik, S. (1997) *Intensive and Long Term Behavioural Treatment for Four to Seven-Year-Old Children with Autism: A One-Year Follow-Up.* Paper presented at PEACH Early Intervention Conference, 12 September.

Fenske, E.C., Zalenski, S., Krantz, P.J. and McClannahan, L.E. (1985) 'Age at intervention and treatment outcome for autistic children in a comprehensive intervention program.' *Analysis and Intervention in Developmental Disabilities 5*, 49–58.

Grant, L. and Evans, A. (1994) *Principles of Behavior Analysis.* New York: HarperCollins College Publishers.

Holth, P. (2001) 'The persistence of category mistakes in psychology.' *Behavior and Philosophy 29*, 203–219.

Howard, J.S., Sparkman, C.R., Cohen, H.G., Green, G. and Stanislaw, H. (2005) 'A comparison of intensive behavior analytic and eclectic treatments for young children with autism.' *Research in Developmental Disabilities 26*, 359–383.

Ives, M. and Munro, N. (2002) *Caring for a Child with Autism: A Practical Guide for Parents.* London: Jessica Kingsley Publishers.

Jordan, R. (2001) 'Book review of Keenan *et al.* (2000).' *Journal of Child Psychology and Psychiatry 42*, 421–423.

Jordan, R., Jones, G. and Murray, D. (1998) *Educational Interventions for Children with Autism: A Literature Review of Recent and Current Research.* Final Report to the DfEE. Birmingham, England: University of Birmingham, School of Education.

Kazdin, A.E. (1977) 'Assessing the clinical or applied importance of behavior change through social validation.' *Behavior Modification 1*, 427–451.

Keenan, M. (2001) 'Power to the parents.' *Cambridge Center for Behavioral Studies.* www.behavior.org/ (accessed 20 November 2001).

Keenan, M. (2003) 'Autism in Northern Ireland: the tragedy and the shame.' *British Psychological Society.* Annual conference, Award for Promoting Equality of Opportunity Lecture (13–16 March).

Keenan, M. and Dillenburger, K. (2000) *Behaviour Analysis: A Primer* [computer software]. New York: Insight Media.

Keenan, M., Kerr, K.P. and Dillenburger, K. (2000) *Parents' Education as Autism Therapists: Applied Behaviour Analysis in Context.* London: Jessica Kingsley Publishers.

Matson, J.L., Benavidez, D.A., Compton, L.S., Paclawskyj, T. and Baglio, C. (1996) 'Behavioral treatment of autistic persons: a review of research from 1980 to the present.' *Research in Developmental Disabilities 17,* 433–465.

Maurice, C. (1993) *Let Me Hear Your Voice: A Family's Triumph Over Autism.* London: Hale.

Maurice, C. (1999) *ABA and Us: One Parent's Reflections on Partnership and Persuasion.* Address to the Cambridge Center for Behavioral Studies (CCBS) Annual Board Meeting, Palm Beach, Florida (5 November).

Maurice, C., Green, G. and Luce, S.C. (eds) (1996) *Behavioral Intervention for Young Children with Autism: A Manual for Parents and Professionals.* Austin, TX: Pro-Ed.

McEachin, S.J., Smith, T. and Lovaas, I.O. (1993) 'Long-term outcome for children with autism who receive early intensive behavioral treatment.' *American Journal of Mental Retardation 97,* 4, 359–372.

O'Reilly, D. and Dillenburger, K. (1997) 'Compliance training as an intervention strategy for anti-social behaviour: a pilot study.' In K. Dillenburger, M. O'Reilly and M. Keenan (eds) *Advances in Behaviour Analysis* (pp.135–156). Dublin: University College Dublin Press.

Richman, S. (2001) *Raising a Child with Autism: A Guide to Applied Behavior Analysis for Parents.* London: Jessica Kingsley Publishers.

Reese, E.P. with Howard, J. and Reese, T.W. (1978) *Human Operant Behavior: Analysis and Application* (2nd edn). Iowa: W.M.C. Brown Company Publishers.

Schopler, E., Mesibov, G.B., DeVillis, R. and Short, A. (1981) 'Treatment for autistic children and their families.' In P. Mittler (ed) *Frontiers of Knowledge in Mental Retardation. Vol. 1: Special Educational and Behavioral Aspects* (pp.293–301). Baltimore: University Park Press.

Sines, D. (2001) *Evaluation Study of the Northern Ireland TEACCH Project.* Jordanstown, NI: University of Ulster.

Smith, T. (1996) 'Are other treatments effective?' In C. Maurice, G. Green and S.C. Luce (eds) *Behavioral Intervention for Young Children with Autism: A Manual for Parents and Professionals* (pp.45–49). Austin, TX: Pro-Ed.

Smith, T. (1999) 'Outcome of early intervention for children with autism.' *Clinical Psychology: Science and Practice 6,* 33–49.

Smith, T., Buch, G.A. and Gamby, T.E. (2000) 'Parent-directed intensive early intervention for children with pervasive developmental disorder.' *Research in Developmental Disabilities 21,* 297–309.

Task Force Report (2001) *Educational Provision and Support for Persons with Autistic Spectrum Disorders: The Report of the Task Force on Autism.* http://www.education.ie/education/servlet/blobservlet/sped_autism.pdf (accessed 30 November 2001).

Webster-Stratton, C. and Herbert, M. (1994) *Troubled Families – Problem Children.* Chichester: John Wiley and Sons.

Weiss, M.J. (1999) 'Differential rates of skill acquisition and outcomes of early intensive behavioural intervention for autism.' *Behavioral Interventions 14*, 3–22.

Wolf, M.M. (1978) 'Social validity: the case for subjective measurement or how applied behavior analysis is finding its heart.' *Journal of Applied Behavior Analysis 11*, 203–214.

Resources for Parents

Compiled by Eric V. Larsson

Intensive early intervention using behaviour therapy is no longer experimental

Many fad-like interventions have been attempted to treat people who suffer from autism, but most have had little or no tangible results. Therefore it is not surprising that insurance companies and government agencies are hesitant to extend benefits to young children who suffer from autism. However, in 1987, after 25 years of investigation comprising over 400 research studies conducted at university centres throughout the world by many researchers in the field of autism, the UCLA Young Autism Project, under the direction of O. Ivar Lovaas, PhD, was able to publish a long-term outcome study showing that 47 per cent of the children treated were able to fully recover from autism. By all published accounts, these results were unprecedented. Subsequent research by independent laboratories around the world is continuing to replicate these profound results and empower families to effectively treat their children.

The difficulties of conducting such research are daunting. In order to be effective, the behaviour therapy programme must be intensive and must be delivered in early childhood. In effect, a family which chooses this therapy must organize their household into a 24-hour therapeutic environment for three or more years in order to remediate all of the symptoms of autism. To do so, they require 55 hours per week of extensive, specialized consultation and direct home-based treatment for 50 weeks per year. Such long-term research has been difficult to conduct and poorly funded.

To be able to access such expensive specialized treatment, many families have litigated with their governments, schools and insurance companies for funding, and many have succeeded. However, these expensive actions have polarized the payors and the advocates. One argument against funding has been that the treatment is still experimental. And, indeed, up until the late 1990s there was little consensus over interpretations of this large body of research.

But as a result of the findings, and the extreme expense required, over the past five years, state and federal agencies and independent review panels have investigated and found that the findings, in their total sum, have been bona fide. In 1999, task forces of the New York State Department of Health and the Maine Administrators of Services for Children with Disabilities each stringently applied scientific standards of proof to the programme and found that it alone, *of all possible treatments* for children with autism, had been proven effective. Also in 1999, US Surgeon General David Satcher promoted the results of the programme in his report on mental health. (The National Institutes of Mental Health have funded research on this programme for over 30 years.) Professional associations such as the American Academy of Child and Adolescent Psychiatry, the American Academy of Neurology, and the American Academy of Pediatrics also followed suit in their development of practice standards. These independent professional review panels are reporting that the intensive early intervention is highly effective in meeting the needs of the children. Each of these agencies have no vested interest in these services, and the panel members have largely been experts in the field who themselves are not treatment providers. Actual statements from these published reports are quoted below. Where the meaning of the quotes seems ambiguous, the reader is directed to the original source, where it will be found that the citations provided are largely to seminal papers from the field of Applied Behaviour Analysis, the most commonly cited paper being Lovaas, 1987.

Independent reviews of intensive early intervention using behaviour therapy

Policy Statement of the American Academy of Pediatrics: *The Pediatrician's Role in the Diagnosis and Management of Autistic Spectrum Disorder in Children*. The AAP regularly issues policy statements to guide and define the child health care system. This policy statement is accompanied by a lengthy technical report. In both papers, the AAP clearly defines accepted treatments as behavioural interventions, and draws heavily on the ABA literature to support their findings. For example, in the introduction to the treatment section, the AAP makes two central statements, as follows:

> Currently accepted strategies are to improve the overall functional status of the child by enrolling the child in an appropriate and intensive early intervention program that promotes development of communication, social, adaptive, behavioral, and academic skills; decrease maladaptive and repetitive behaviors through use of behavioral and sometimes pharmacologic strategies.
>
> Early diagnosis resulting in early, appropriate, and consistent intervention has also been shown to be associated with improved long-term outcomes.

Then, among many other specific behavioural recommendations, the AAP makes such statements as:

> Behavioral training, including communication development, has been shown to be effective in reducing problem behaviors and improving adaptation. (p.1223)

American Academy of Pediatrics (2001) 'Policy Statement: The Pediatrician's Role in the Diagnosis and Management of Autistic Spectrum Disorder in Children (RE060018).' *Pediatrics 107*, 1221–1226.

In the more detailed technical report, the AAP states:

> There is a growing body of evidence that intensive early intervention services for children in whom autism is diagnosed before 5 years of age may lead to better overall outcomes.

The most heavily emphasized treatment strategy in the technical report is 'behavioral management,' about which the AAP states:

> One of the mainstays of the management of ASD in children at any age is the implementation of behavioral training and management protocols at home and at school. Behavioral management must go hand-in-hand with structured teaching of skills to prevent undesirable behavior from developing. Behavioral training, including teaching appropriate communication behaviors, has been shown to be effective in decreasing behavior problems and improving adaptation.

> Committee on Children with Disabilities (2001) 'Technical Report: The Pediatrician's Role in the Diagnosis and Management of Autistic Spectrum Disorder in Children.' *Pediatrics 107*, e85, pp.8–10.

The US Department of Education commissioned the National Research Council to provide input into the controversy circling around the press for school funding for behaviour therapy and early intervention. In turn, the National Research Council engaged the services of a large number of respected researchers in the field of autism. The resulting report, Educating Children with Autism, clearly focused on ABA-based interventions. For example, the chapter on 'comprehensive programs' identifies ten 'well-known model approaches,' all of which are ABA-based. A sample of the many statements, upon which it can be fairly said that the primary focus of the book is on ABA-based treatment, are offered here:

> Early research on the benefits of applied behavior analysis by Lovaas and his colleagues (1973) showed that children with autism who returned to a home prepared to support their learning maintained their treatment gains better than children who went to institutional settings that failed to carry over the treatment methods. (p.35)

> Outcomes of discrete trial approaches have included improvements in IQ scores, which are correlated with language skills, and improvements in communication domains of broader measures... There is now a large body of empirical support for more contemporary behavioral approaches using naturalistic teaching methods that demonstrate efficacy for teaching not only speech and language, but also communication. (p.53)

> Behavioral interventions use the powerful tools of operant learning to treat symptoms of autism spectrum disorders. (p.68)

> Some advantages of the behavioral research on teaching social skills have been the measurement of generalization and maintenance, attention to antecedents and consequences, and use of systematic strategies to teach complex skills by breaking them down into smaller, teachable parts. Some drawbacks of traditional behavioral approaches are the complex data systems that often accompany them and that may impede their use in more typical settings, as well as the lack of training in their use that most staff members on early childhood teams receive. (p.72)

The conclusions and recommendations of the report revolve around how to set up easily accessible funding and training for more teachers. While the report clearly endorses school department funding for intensive early intervention with behaviour therapy, it also suggests that health care based funding, such as the US Medicaid program would also be appropriate:

> A state fund for intensive intervention, or more systematic use of Medicaid waivers or other patterns of funding currently in place in some states, should be considered. (p.224)

> National Research Council (2001) *Educating Children with Autism*. Committee on Educational Interventions for Children with Autism, Division of Behavioral and Social Sciences and Education, Washington, DC: National Academy Press.

While the above reports focused on ABA methods, two earlier state committees endeavoured to compare all of the potential treatments, both behavioural and nonbehavioural for scientific merit. Both clearly found that only the ABA-based intensive early interventions have sufficient research behind them to be endorsed. Sample statements follow from the report by the Maine Administrators of Services for Children with Disabilities:

> Over 30 years of rigorous research and peer review of applied behavior analysis' effectiveness for individuals with autism demonstrate ABA has been objectively substantiated as effective based upon the scope and quality of science... Early interventionists should leverage early autism diagnosis with the proven efficacy of intensive ABA for optimal outcome and long-term cost benefit. (p.29)
>
> The importance of early, intensive intervention for children with autism cannot be overstated... Furthermore, early, intensive, effective intervention offers the hope of significant cost/benefit. (p.6)

> Maine Administrators of Services for Children with Disabilities (2000) *Report of the MADSEC Autism Task Force*. Manchester, ME: MADSEC.

The New York State Department of Health published a three volume report in 1999 based upon its extensive analysis of the available treatments. It also found that only ABA-based treatments had sufficient scientific support to merit endorsement. The three volumes include 'The Technical Report,' which contains the most complete information, including all the evidence tables from the articles reviewed, a full report of the research process, and the full text of all the recommendations. 'The Report of the Recommendations' gives the background information, the full text of all the recommendations and a summary of the supporting evidence. 'The Quick Reference Guide' gives a summary of background information and a summary of the major recommendations, and is also written in a less technical manner. Some statements from the Quick Reference Guide follow:

> Based upon strong scientific evidence, it is recommended that principles of applied behavior analysis and behavior intervention strategies be included as

an important element of any intervention program for young children with autism... Based upon the panel consensus opinion, it is recommended that all professional and paraprofessionals who function as therapists in an intensive behavioral intervention program receive regular supervision from a qualified professional with specific expertise in applied behavioral approaches... Based upon strong scientific evidence, it is important to include parents as active participants in the intervention team to the extent of their interests, resources, and abilities... Based upon strong scientific evidence, it is recommended that training of parents in behavioral methods for interacting with their child be extensive and ongoing and include regular consultation with a qualified professional.

New York State Department of Health Early Intervention Program (1999) *Clinical Practice Guideline Report of the Recommendations for Autism/Pervasive Developmental Disorders.* Albany, NY: New York State Department of Health.

The US Surgeon General published an extensive report in 1999 on mental health in general. In the section on autism, the Surgeon General reported:

Thirty years of research demonstrated the efficacy of applied behavioral methods in reducing inappropriate behavior and in increasing communication, learning, and appropriate social behavior... A well-designed study of a psychosocial intervention was carried out by Lovaas and colleagues. Nineteen children with autism were treated intensively with behavior therapy for 2 years and compared with two control groups. Followup of the experimental group in first grade, in late childhood, and in adolescence found that nearly half the experimental group but almost none of the children in the matched control group were able to participate in regular schooling. (p.164)

Satcher, D. (1999) *Mental Health: A Report of the Surgeon General.* Bethesda, MD: US Public Health Service.

A large number of major professional organizations formed a practice parameters consensus panel on the diagnosis of autism because:

The press for early identification comes from evidence gathered over the past 10 years that intensive early intervention in optimal educational settings results in improved outcomes in most young children with autism, including speech in 75% or more and significant increases in rates of developmental progress and intellectual performance. (p.440)

The Practice Parameters Consensus Panel comprised of the following professional organizations and agencies:

American Academy of Neurology
American Academy of Family Physicians
American Occupational Therapy Association
American Psychological Association
American Speech-Language Hearing Association

Society for Developmental and Behavioral Pediatrics
Autism Society of America
National Alliance for Autism Research
National Institute of Child Health and Human Development
National Institute of Mental Health.

While the focus of this report was on diagnosis, the panel made a number of significant statements about the need for early and intensive treatment. For example:

> However, these kinds of outcomes have been documented only for children who receive 2 years or more of intensive intervention services during the preschool years. (p.440)
>
> Autism must be recognized as a medical disorder, and managed care policy must cease to deny appropriate medical or other therapeutic care under the rubric of 'developmental delay' or 'mental health condition'... Existing governmental agencies that provide services to individuals with developmental disabilities must also change their eligibility criteria to include all individuals on the autistic spectrum, whether or not the relatively narrow criteria for Autistic Disorder are met, who nonetheless must also receive the same adequate assessments, appropriate diagnoses, and treatment options as do those with the formal diagnosis of Autistic Disorder. (p.472)

Filipek, P.A., Accardo, P.J., Ashwal, S., Baranek, G.T., Cook, E.H. Jr, Dawson, G. *et al.* (1999) 'The screening and diagnosis of autistic spectrum disorders.' *Journal of Autism and Developmental Disorders, 29*, 439-484.

The American Academy of Child and Adolescent Psychiatry committee also clearly depended upon the ABA literature for its major findings, in its 1999 report on practice parameters for autism:

> At the present time the best available evidence suggests the importance of appropriate and intensive educational interventions to foster acquisition of basic social, communicative, and cognitive skills related to ultimate outcome... Early and sustained intervention appears to be particularly important, regardless of the philosophy of the program, so long as a high degree of structure is provided. Such programs have typically incorporated behavior modification procedures and applied behavior analysis... These methods build upon a large body of research on the application of learning principles to the education of children with autism and related conditions. (p.475)
>
> It is clear that behavioral interventions can significantly facilitate acquisition of language, social, and other skills and that behavioral improvement is helpful in reducing levels of parental stress. (p.476)
>
> Considerable time (and money) is required for implementation of such programs, and older and more intellectually handicapped individuals are apparently less likely to respond. (p.515)

Volkmar, F., Cook, E.H., Pomeroy, J., Realmuto, G. and Tanguay, P. (1999) 'Practice parameters for the assessment and treatment of children, adolescents, and adults with autism and other pervasive developmental disorders.' *Journal of the American Academy of Child and Adolescent Psychiatry 38* (Supplement), 32s–54s.

In an extensive report on the facts of litigation by parents for health-care funding in British Columbia, the Supreme Court made the following conclusions. In a subsequent ruling, the Court found that it was more appropriate for the executive to set policy than to have it imposed upon them by the courts, but its conclusions on the facts remain:

> What children experience in their early years will shape the rest of their lives. We now know from research in a variety of sectors, that children's early brain development has a profound effect on their ability to learn and on their behaviour, coping skills and health later in life... Research also indicates that intensive early behavioural intervention with children with autism can make a significant difference in their ability to learn and keep pace with their peers. With the intervention many children with autism will make considerable gains by grade one... These words embody the philosophy underlying the Ontario Government's "Intensive Early Intervention Program For Children With Autism" commenced in 1999, and numerous programmes undertaken in other provinces, the United States and several countries... The Crown discriminates against the petitioners contrary to s. 15(1) by failing to accommodate their disadvantaged position by providing effective treatment for autism. It is beyond debate that the appropriate treatment is ABA or early intensive behavioural intervention.

> Auton *et al*. v. AGBC (2000) British Columbia Supreme Court 1142.

Resulting state action

As a result of these independent reviews, many states have already initiated formal funding for this treatment. The states of Maine, Massachusetts, Vermont, Connecticut, New York, Pennsylvania, Maryland, North Carolina, and Wisconsin, as well as the provinces of Ontario, Manitoba, and Alberta, have formal state-wide funds for the programme, most of which use Medicaid funds. In California, the Regional Centers administer Medicaid funds, and several regions have formal Medicaid funding streams for the programme. In Minnesota, a state law was passed providing for Medicaid funding of the programme, which came into effect on 1 January 2003 (Minnesota Statutes 2001, section 256B.0625, Subd. 5a: Intensive Early Intervention Behaviour Therapy Services for Children with Autism Spectrum Disorders).

Summary

One of the most thorough and well regarded independent reviews is the report commissioned by the National Research Council. Commenting on the specific question of whether this treatment is experimental, the Council reported: 'However, there is substantial research supporting the effectiveness of many specific therapeutic techniques and of comprehensive programs in contrast to less intense, nonspecific interventions.' It is important to keep in mind that this form of treatment is the only extensively researched and validated form of treatment of autism, and it is ironic that those who would be required to fund the research use the fact that researchers have been in the forefront of the development of such treatment, to imply that the treatment continues to be experimental. Intensive early intervention using behaviour therapy is the only proven form of treatment for young children who suffer from autism.

Bibliography

Independent reports on the effectiveness of intensive early intervention and behaviour therapy

American Academy of Pediatrics (2001) 'Policy Statement: The Pediatrician's Role in the Diagnosis and Management of Autistic Spectrum Disorder in Children (RE060018).' *Pediatrics 107*, 1221–1226. http://www.aap.org/policy/re060018.html

Auton *et al.* v. AGBC (2000) British Columbia Supreme Court 1142. Decision can be read at: http://www.featbc.org/legal_issues/

Committee on Children with Disabilities (2001) 'Technical Report: The Pediatrician's Role in the Diagnosis and Management of Autistic Spectrum Disorder in Children.' *Pediatrics 107*, e85. http://www.pediatrics.org/cgi/content/full/107/5/e85

Filipek, P.A. *et al.* (1999) 'The screening and diagnosis of autistic spectrum disorders.' *Journal of Autism and Developmental Disorders 29*, 439–484.

Maine Administrators of Services for Children with Disabilities (2000) *Report of the MADSEC Autism Task Force, Revised Edition.* Kennebec Center, RR 2 Box 1856, Manchester, ME 04351, http://www.madsec.org/docs/atf.htm

National Research Council (2001) *Educating Children with Autism.* Committee on Educational Interventions for Children with Autism, Division of Behavioral and Social Sciences and Education, Washington, DC: National Academy Press. http://books.nap.edu/books/0309072697/html/index.html

New York State Department of Health Early Intervention Program (1999) *Clinical Practice Guideline: The Guideline Technical Report, Autism/Pervasive Developmental Disorders, Assessment and Intervention for Young Children.* Publication #4217. Health Education Services, PO Box 7126, Albany, NY 12224.

New York State Department of Health Early Intervention Program (1999) *Clinical Practice Guideline: Report of the Recommendations, Autism/Pervasive Developmental Disorders, Assessment and Intervention for Young Children.* Publication #4215. Health Education Services, PO Box 7126, Albany, NY 12224. http://www.health.state.ny.us/nysdoh/eip/menu.htm

Rimland, B. (1994) 'Recovery from autism is possible.' *Autism Research Review International 8*, 3.

Satcher, D. (1999) *Mental Health: A Report of the Surgeon General.* Bethesda, MD: US Public Health Service. Available at: http://www.surgeongeneral.gov/library/mentalhealth/chapter3/sec6.html#autism

Simeonsson, R.J., Olley, J.G. and Rosenthal, S.L. (1987) 'Early intervention for children with autism.' In M.J. Guralnick and F.C. Bennett (eds) *The Effectiveness of Early Intervention for At-Risk and Handicapped Children.* Orlando, FL: Academic Press.

Volkmar, F., Cook, E.H., Pomeroy, J., Realmuto, G. and Tanguay, P. (1999) 'Practice parameters for the assessment and treatment of children, adolescents, and adults with autism and other pervasive developmental disorders.' *Journal of the American Academy of Child and Adolescent Psychiatry 38* (Suppl), 32S–54S.

Data-based research in support of intensive early intervention

LONG-TERM OUTCOME EVALUATIONS OF THE UCLA YOUNG AUTISM PROJECT

Baer, D.M. (1993) 'Quasi-random assignment can be as convincing as random assignment.' *American Journal on Mental Retardation 97*, 377–379.

Foxx, R.M. (1993) 'Sapid effects awaiting independent replication.' *American Journal on Mental Retardation 97*, 375–376.

Kazdin, A. (1993) 'Replication and extension of behavioral treatment of autistic disorder.' *American Journal on Mental Retardation 97*, 382–383.

Lovaas, O.I. (1980) 'Behavioral teaching with young autistic children.' In B. Wilcox and A. Thompson (eds) *Critical Issues in Educating Autistic Children and Youth* (pp.220–233). Washington, DC: US Department of Education, Office of Special Education.

Lovaas, O.I. (1987) 'Behavioral treatment and normal educational and intellectual functioning in young autistic children.' *Journal of Consulting and Clinical Psychology 55*, 3–9.

Lovaas, O.I., Koegel, R., Simmons, J.Q. and Long, J.S. (1973) 'Some generalization and follow-up measures on autistic children in behavior therapy.' *Journal of Applied Behavior Analysis 6*, 131–166.

Lovaas, O.I., Smith, T. and McEachin, J.J. (1989) 'Clarifying comments on the Young Autism Study.' *Journal of Consulting and Clinical Psychology 57*, 165–167.

McEachin, J.J., Smith, T. and Lovaas, O.I. (1993) 'Long-term outcome for children with autism who received early intensive behavioral treatment.' *American Journal on Mental Retardation 97*, 359–372.

Mesibov, G.B. (1993) 'Treatment outcome is encouraging.' *American Journal on Mental Retardation 97*, 379–380.

Mundy, P. (1993) 'Normal versus high-functioning status in children with autism.' *American Journal on Mental Retardation 97*, 381–382.

Schopler, E., Short, A. and Mesibov, G. (1989) 'Relation of behavioral treatment to "normal functioning": comment on Lovaas.' *Journal of Consulting and Clinical Psychology 57*, 162–164.

Replications of long-term outcome evaluations

Anderson, S.R., Avery, D.L., DiPietro, E.K., Edwards, G.L. and Christian, W.P. (1987) 'Intensive home-based early intervention with autistic children.' *Education and Treatment of Children 10*, 352–366.

Bibby, P., Eikeseth, S., Martin, N.T., Mudford, O.C. and Reeves, D. (2001) 'Progress and outcomes for children with autism receiving parent-managed intensive interventions.' *Research in Developmental Disabilities 22*, 425–447.

Birnbrauer, J.S. and Leach, D.J. (1993) 'The Murdoch early intervention program after 2 years.' *Behaviour Change 10*, 63–74.

Boyd, R.D. and Corley, M.J. (2001) 'Outcome survey of early intensive behavioral intervention for young children with autism in a community setting.' *Autism 5*, 430–441.

Dunlap, G., Robbins, F.R., Dollman, C. and Plienis, A.J. (1988) *Early Intervention for Young Children with Autism: A Regional Training Approach.* Huntington, WV: Marshall University.

Eikeseth, S. (1999) 'Intensive School-based Behavioral Treatment for Four to Seven Year Old Children with Autism: A One Year Follow-up.' Paper presented at the first internet conference on autism: http://www.autism99.org/flash/papers_front.htm

Eikeseth, S., Smith, T., Jahr, E. and Eldevik, S. (2002) 'Intensive behavioral treatment at school for 4- to 7-year-old children with autism – a 1-year comparison controlled study.' *Behavior Modification 26*, 46–68.

Fenske, E.C., Zalenski, S., Krantz, P.J. and McClannahan, L.E. (1985) 'Age at intervention and treatment outcome for autistic children in a comprehensive intervention program.' *Analysis and Intervention in Developmental Disabilities 5*, 49–58.

Green, G., Brennan, L.C. and Fein, D. (2002) 'Intensive behavioral treatment for a toddler at high risk for autism.' *Behavior Modification 26*, 69–102.

Harris, S.L. (1986) 'Parents as teachers: a four to seven year follow up of parents of children with autism.' *Child and Family Behavior Therapy 8*, 39–47.

Harris, S.L. and Handleman, J.S. (2000) 'Age and IQ at intake as predictors of placement for young children with autism: a four- to six-year follow-up.' *Journal of Autism and Developmental Disorders 30*, 137–142.

Harris, S., Handleman, J., Gordon, R., Kristoff, B. and Fuentes, F. (1991) 'Changes in cognitive and language functioning of preschool children with autism.' *Journal of Autism and Developmental Disorders 21*, 281–290.

Mudford, O.C., Martin, N.T., Eikeseth, S. and Bibby, P. (2001) 'Parent-managed behavioral treatment for preschool children with autism: some characteristics of UK programs.' *Research in Developmental Disabilities 22*, 173–182.

Perry, R., Cohen, I. and DeCarlo, R. (1995) 'Case study: deterioration, autism, and recovery in two siblings.' *Journal of the American Academy of Child and Adolescent Psychiatry 34*, 232–237.

Sheinkopf, S. and Siegel, B. (1998) 'Home-based behavioral treatment for young autistic children.' *Journal of Autism and Developmental Disorders 23*, 15–23.

Smith, T., Buch, G.A. and Gamby, T.E. (2000) 'Parent-directed, intensive early intervention for children with pervasive developmental disorder.' *Research in Developmental Disabilities 21*, 297–309.

Smith, T., Eikeseth, S., Klevstrand, M. and Lovaas, O.I. (1997) 'Intensive behavioral treatment for preschoolers with severe mental retardation and pervasive developmental disorder.' *American Journal of Mental Retardation 102*, 238–249.

Smith, T., Groen, A.D. and Wynn, J.W. (2000) 'Randomized trial of intensive early intervention for children with pervasive developmental disorder.' *American Journal on Mental Retardation 105*, 269–285.

Strain, P.S., Hoyson, M.H. and Jamieson, B.J. (1985) 'Normally developing preschoolers as intervention agents for autistic-like children: effects on class deportment and social interactions.' *Journal of the Division for Early Childhood 9*, 105–115.

Weiss, M.J. (1999) 'Differential rates of skill acquisition and outcomes of early intensive behavioral intervention for autism.' *Behavioral Interventions 14*, 3–22.

Helpful readings about behaviour therapy and autism

American Academy of Pediatrics (2001) 'Policy Statement: The Pediatrician's Role in the Diagnosis and Management of Autistic Spectrum Disorder in Children (RE060018).' *Pediatrics 107*, 1221–1226. http://www.aap.org/policy/re060018.html

Aram, D.M., Ekelman, B.L. and Nation, J.E. (1984) 'Preschoolers with language disorders: 10 years later.' *Journal of Speech and Hearing Research 27*, 232–244.

Baer, D.M. (1991) 'Tacting "to a fault".' *Journal of Applied Behavior Analysis 24*, 429–431.

Baker, B.L. and Feinfield, K.A. (2003) 'Early intervention.' *Current Opinion in Psychiatry 16*, 503–509.

Becker, W.C. (1971) *Parents are Teachers*. Champaign, IL: Research Press.

Berger, K. (1967) 'The most common words used in conversation.' *Journal of Communication Disorders* 1, 201–214.

Bryson, S. and Smith, I. (1998) 'Epidemiology of autism: prevalence, associated characteristics, and implications for research and service delivery.' *Mental Retardation and Developmental Disabilities Research Reviews 4*, 97–103.

Carr, E.G., Levin, L., McConnachie, G., Carlson, J.I., Kemp, D.C. and Smith, C.E. (1994) *Communication Based Intervention for Problem Behavior: A User's Guide for Producing Positive Change.* Baltimore, MD: Paul H. Brookes.

Catania, A.C. (1984) *Learning*. Englewood Cliffs, NJ: Prentice-Hall.

Chakrabarit, S. and Fonbonne, E. (2001) 'Pervasive developmental disorders in preschool children.' *Journal of the American Medical Association 24*, 3093–3099.

Chance, P. (1998) *First Course in Applied Behavior Analysis*. Pacific Grove, CA: Brooks/Cole.

Committee on Children with Disabilities (2001) 'Technical Report: The Pediatrician's Role in the Diagnosis and Management of Autistic Spectrum Disorder in Children.' *Pediatrics 107*, e85. http://www.pediatrics.org/cgi/content/full/107/5/e85

Cooper, J.O., Heron, T.E. and Heward, W.L. (1990) *Applied Behavior Analysis*. Englewood Cliffs, NJ: Prentice-Hall.

Dyer, K. and Larsson, E.V. (1997) 'Developing functional communication skills: alternatives to aberrant behavior.' In E. Cipani and N.N. Singh (eds) *Practical Approaches to the Treatment of Severe Behavior Problems*. Sycamore, IL: Sycamore.

Eikeseth, S. (2001) 'Recent critiques of the UCLA young autism project.' *Behavioral Interventions 16*, 249–264.

Eikeseth, S. and Lovaas, O.I. (1992) 'The autistic label and its potentially detrimental effect on the child's treatment.' *Journal of Behavior Therapy and Experimental Psychiatry 23*, 151–157.

Filipek, P.A. *et al.* (1999) 'The screening and diagnosis of autistic spectrum disorders.' *Journal of Autism and Developmental Disorders 29*, 439–484.

Fowler, S.A. (1982) 'Transition from preschool to kindergarten for children with special needs.' In K.E. Allen and E.M. Goetz (eds) *Early Childhood Education: Special Problems, Special Solutions*. Rockville, MD: Aspen.

Freeman, B.J. (1997) 'Guidelines for evaluating intervention programs for children with autism.' *Journal of Autism and Developmental Disorders 27*, 641–651.

Freeman, B.J., Rahbar, B., Ritvo, E.R., Bice, T.L., Yokota, A. and Ritvo, R. (1991) 'The stability of cognitive and behavioral parameters in autism: a 12-year prospective study.' *Journal of the American Academy of Child and Adolescent Psychiatry 30*, 479–482.

Freeman, S. (2003) *Science for Sale in the Autism Wars*. Lynden, WA: SKF Books USA.

Gillberg, C. and Coleman, M. (2000) *The Biology of the Autistic Syndromes* (3rd edn). London, England: MacKeith Press.

Goldstein, H. (1993) 'Structuring environmental input to facilitate generalized language learning by children with mental retardation.' In A.P. Kaiser and D.B. Gray (eds) *Enhancing Children's Communication: Research Foundations for Intervention. Communication and Language Intervention Series*, Vol. 2 (pp.317–334). Baltimore, MD: Paul H. Brookes Publishing.

Guess, D., Sailor, W. and Baer, D.M. (1976) *Functional Speech and Language Training for the Severely Handicapped*. Lawrence, KS: H & H Enterprises.

Hamilton, L.M. (2000) *Facing Autism: Giving Parents Reasons for Hope and Guidance for Help*. Colorado Springs, CO: WaterBrook Press.

Harris, S.L. and Handleman, J.S. (1994) *Preschool Education Programs for Children with Autism.* Austin, TX: Pro-Ed.

Harris, S.L. and Weiss, M.J. (1998) *Right From the Start: Behavioral Interventions for Young Children with Autism.* Bethesda, MD: Woodbine House.

Horner, R.H., Dunlap, G. and Koegel, R.L. (eds) (1988) *Generalization and Maintenance: Life-style Changes in Applied Settings.* Baltimore, MD: Brookes.

Howlin, P. and Moore, A. (1997) 'Diagnosis in autism: a survey of over 1200 patients in the UK.' *Autism 1*, 135–162.

Jacobson, J.W. (2000) 'Early intensive behavioral intervention: emergence of a consumer-driven service model.' *The Behavior Analyst 23*, 149–171.

Jacobson, J.W., Mulick, J.A. and Green, G. (1998) 'Cost-benefit estimates for early intensive behavioral intervention for young children with autism: general model and single state case.' *Behavioral Interventions 13*, 201–226.

Johnson, E. and Hastings, R.P. (2002) 'Facilitating factors and barriers to the implementation of intensive home-based behavioural intervention for young children with autism.' *Child Care Health and Development 28*, 123–129.

Kanner, L. (1943) 'Autistic disturbances of affective contact.' *Nervous Child 2*, 181–197.

Kazdin, A.E. (2001) *Behavior Modification in Applied Settings* (6th edn). Belmont, CA: Wadsworth.

Keenan, M., Kerr, K.J. and Dillenburger, K. (Eds) (2000) *Parents' Education as Autism Therapists. Applied Behaviour Analysis in Context.* London: Jessica Kingsley Publishers

Keenan, M., Henderson, M., Kerr, K.P. and Dillenburger, K. (Eds.) (2005) *Applied Behaviour Analysis and Autism: Building a Future Together.* London: Jessica Kingsley Publishers

Koegel, L., Koegel, R. and Dunlap, G. (eds) (1996) *Positive Behavioral Change.* Baltimore, MD: Paul H. Brookes.

Koegel, R.L. and Koegel, L.K. (1995) *Teaching Children with Autism: Strategies for Initiating Positive Interactions and Improving Learning Opportunities.* Baltimore, MD: Paul H. Brookes.

Koegel, R.L., Rincover, A. and Egel, A.L. (1982) *Educating and Understanding Autistic Children.* San Diego, CA: College-Hill Press.

Koegel, R.L., Schreibman, L., Good, A., Cerniglia, L., Murphy, C. and Koegel, L. (1989) *How to Teach Pivotal Behaviors to Children with Autism: A Training Manual.* Santa Barbara: University of California.

Kozloff, M.A. (1973) *Reaching the Autistic Child: A Parent-Training Program.* Champaign, IL: Research Press.

Krantz, P.J., MacDuff, G.S., Wadstrom, O. and McClannahan, L.E. (1991) 'Using video with developmentally disabled learners.' In P.W. Dowrick (ed) *Practical Guide to Using Video in the Behavioral Sciences.* New York: John Wiley and Sons.

Kymissis, E. and Poulson, C.L. (1990) 'The history of imitation in learning theory: the language acquisition process.' *Journal of the Experimental Analysis of Behavior 54*, 113–127.

Larsson, E.V., Luce, S.C., Anderson, S.R. and Christian, W.P. (1992) 'Autism.' In M.D. Levine, W.B. Carey and A.C. Crocker (eds) *Developmental-Behavioral Pediatrics.* Philadelphia: W.B. Saunders.

Lord, C. and Schopler, E. (1989) 'The role of age at assessment, developmental level, and test in the stability of intelligence scores in young autistic children.' *Journal of Autism and Developmental Disorders 19*, 483–499.

Lord, C., Rutter, M. and LeCouteur, A. (1994) 'Autism Diagnostic Interview – Revised: a revised version of a diagnostic interview for caregivers of individuals with possible pervasive developmental disorders.' *Journal of Autism and Developmental Disorders 24*, 659–685.

Lovaas, O.I. (1977) *The Autistic Child: Language Development Through Behavior Modification.* New York: Irvington.

Lovaas, O.I. (1993) 'The development of a treatment-research project for developmentally disabled and autistic children.' *Journal of Applied Behavior Analysis 26,* 617–630.

Lovaas, O.I. (2002) *Teaching Individuals with Developmental Delays: Basic Intervention Techniques.* Austin, TX: Pro-Ed.

Lovaas, O.I. and Buch, G. (1996) 'Intensive behavioral intervention with young children with autism.' *Behavioral Approaches to the Treatment of Severe Behavior Disorders in Children* (pp.61–86). New York: Brooks Cole Publishers.

Lovaas, O.I. and Newsome, C.D. (1976) 'Behavior modification with psychotic children.' In H. Leitenberg (ed) *Handbook of Behavior Modification and Behavior Therapy.* Englewood Cliffs, NJ: Prentice Hall.

Lovaas, O.I. and Smith, T. (1988) 'Intensive behavioral treatment for young autistic children.' In B.B. Lahey and A.E. Kazdin (eds) *Advances in Clinical Child Psychology* (Vol. 11, pp.285–324). New York: Plenum.

Lovaas, O.I. and Smith, T. (1989) 'A comprehensive behavioral theory of autistic children: paradigm for research and treatment.' *Journal of Behavior Therapy and Experimental Psychiatry 20,* 17–29.

Lovaas, O.I., Ackerman, A., Alexander, D., Firestone, P., Perkins, M., Young, D.B., Carr, E.G. and Newsom, C. (1981) *Teaching Developmentally Disabled Children: The Me Book.* Baltimore, MD: University Park Press.

Lovaas, O.I., Koegel, R.L. and Schreibman, L. (1979) 'Stimulus overselectivity in autism: a review of research.' *Psychological Bulletin 86,* 1236–1254.

Luce, S.C., Christian, W.P., Anderson, S.R., Troy, P.J. and Larsson, E.V. (1991) 'Development of a continuum of services for children and adults with autism and other severe behavior disorders.' *Research in Developmental Disabilities 13,* 9–25.

Maine Administrators of Services for Children with Disabilities (2000) *Report of the MADSEC Autism Task Force, Revised Edition.* Kennebec Center, RR 2 Box 1856, Manchester, ME 04351, http://www.madsec.org/madsec/ATFReport.doc

Malott, R.W., Whaley, D.L. and Malott, M.E. (1993) *Elementary Principles of Behavior* (2nd edn). Englewood Cliffs, NJ: Prentice Hall.

Maltby, J. (2000) 'The cost of autism: more than meets the eye.' *Advocate,* November–December, 12–16.

Martin, G. and Pear, J. (1992) *Behavior Modification: What It Is and How To Do It* (4th edn). Englewood Cliffs, NJ: Prentice Hall.

Mash, E.J. and Barkley, R.A. (1998) *Treatment of Childhood Disorders* (2nd edn) (pp.416–467). New York: Guilford Press.

Mason, S.A. and Iwata, B.A. (1990) 'Artifactual effects of sensory-integrative therapy on self-injurious behavior.' *Journal of Applied Behavior Analysis 23,* 361–370.

Maurice, C. (1993) *Let Me Hear Your Voice: A Family's Triumph Over Autism.* New York: Knopf.

Maurice, C. (2001) 'Recovery.' *Leadership Perspectives in Developmental Disability: an online journal for consumers, professionals, family, and friends.* Volume 2, Issue 4. Internet resource found at: http://www.mnip-net.org/ddlead.nsf/d0124d90f77b83c9852569a7005c7c68/a24fac36d7c1 e41b052566b050071836f!OpenDocument

Maurice, C., Green, G. and Fox, R.M. (2001) *Making a Difference: Behavioral Intervention for Autism.* Austin, TX: Pro-Ed.

Maurice, C., Green, G. and Luce, S.C. (1996) *Behavioral Intervention for Young Children with Autism: A Manual for Parents and Professionals.* Austin, TX: Pro-Ed.

McEachin, J., Leaf, R., Boehm, M. and Harsh, J.D. (1999) *A Work in Progress: Behavior Management Strategies and a Curriculum for Intensive Behavioral Treatment of Autism.* New York: Different Roads to Learning.

Michael, J. (1984) 'Verbal behavior.' *Journal of the Experimental Analysis of Behavior 17,* 23–34.

Michael, J.L. (1993) *Concepts and Principles of Behavior Analysis.* Kalamazoo, MI: SABA.

Miller, L.K. (1980) *Principles of Everyday Behavior Analysis* (2nd edn). Pacific Grove, CA: Brooks/Cole Publishing Company.

Miltenberger, R.G. (2001) *Behavior Modification: Principles and Procedures* (2nd edn). Belmont, CA: Wadsworth.

Mudford, O.C., Cross, B.A., Breen, S., Cullen, C., Reeves, D., Gould, J. and Douglas, J. (2000) 'Auditory integration training for children with autism: no behavioral benefits detected.' *American Journal of Mental Retardation 105,* 118–129.

National Research Council (2001) *Educating Children with Autism.* Committee on Educational Interventions for Children with Autism, Division of Behavioral and Social Sciences and Education, Washington, DC: National Academy Press. http://books.nap.edu/books/0309072697/html/index.html

New York State Department of Health Early Intervention Program (1999) *Clinical Practice Guideline: The Guideline Technical Report, Autism/Pervasive Developmental Disorders, Assessment and Intervention for Young Children.* Publication #4217. Health Education Services, PO Box 7126, Albany, NY 12224.

New York State Department of Health Early Intervention Program (1999) *Clinical Practice Guideline: Report of the Recommendations, Autism/Pervasive Developmental Disorders, Assessment and Intervention for Young Children.* Publication #4215. Health Education Services, PO Box 7126, Albany, NY 12224. http://www.health.state.ny.us/nysdoh/eip/menu.htm

Newsom, C. (1998) 'Autistic disorder.' In E.J. Mash and R.A. Barkley (eds) *Treatment of Childhood Disorders* (2nd edn) (pp.416–467). New York: Guilford Press.

Patterson, G.R. (1975) *Families: Applications of Social Learning to Family Life.* Champaign, IL: Research Press.

Peterson, G.B., Larsson, E.V. and Riedesel, K.L. (2003) 'A conceptual toolkit for intensive early behavioral intervention teachers.' *Journal of Behavioral Education 12,* 131–146.

Rapin, I. (1991) 'Autistic children: diagnosis and clinical features.' *Supplement to Pediatrics 87,* 751–760.

Rimland, B. (1994) 'Recovery from autism is possible.' *Autism Research Review International 8,* 3.

Rogers, S.J. (1998) 'Neuropsychology of autism in young children and its implications for early intervention.' *Mental Retardation and Developmental Disabilities Research Reviews 4,* 104–112.

Rogers, S.J. (1998) 'Empirically supported comprehensive treatments for young children with autism.' *Journal of Clinical Child Psychology 27,* 167–178.

Sailor, W., Anderson, J.L., Halvorsen, A.T., Doering, K., Filler, J. and Goetz, L. (1989) *The Comprehensive Local School: Regular Education for All Students with Disabilities.* Baltimore, MD: Brookes.

Sallows, G.O. and Graupner, T.D. (2005) 'Intensive Behavioral Treatment for Children With Autism: Four-Year Outcome and Predictors.' *American Journal of Mental Retardation, 110,* 6, 417–438.

Satcher, D. (1999) *Mental Health: A Report of the Surgeon General.* US Public Health Service. Bethesda, MD. Available at:
http://www.surgeongeneral.gov/library/mentalhealth/chapter3/sec6.html#autism

Schreibman, L. (1988) *Autism.* Beverly Hills, CA: Sage.

Siegal, B. *et al.* (1988) 'How children with autism are diagnosed: difficulties in identification of children with multiple developmental delays.' *Developmental and Behavioral Pediatrics 9*, 199–204.

Simeonsson, R.J., Olley, J.G. and Rosenthal, S.L. (1987) 'Early intervention for children with autism.' In M.J. Guralnick and F.C. Bennett (eds) *The Effectiveness of Early Intervention for At-Risk and Handicapped Children.* Orlando, FL: Academic Press.

Skinner, B.F. (1957) *Verbal Behavior.* New York: Appleton-Century-Crofts.

Smith, T. (1993) 'Autism.' In T.R. Giles (ed) *Handbook of Effective Psychotherapy.* New York: Plenum.

Smith, T., Klevstrand, M. and Lovaas, O.I. (1995) 'Behavioral treatment of Rett's Disorder: ineffectiveness in three cases.' *American Journal on Mental Retardation 100*, 317–322.

Stokes, T. and Baer, D. (1977) 'An implicit technology of generalization.' *Journal of Applied Behavior Analysis 10*, 349–367.

Sulzer-Azaroff, B. and Mayer, G.R. (1991) *Behavior Analysis for Lasting Change.* New York: Holz, Rinehart and Winston.

Sulzer-Azaroff, B. and Reese, E.P. (1982) *Applying Behavior Analysis: A Program for Developing Staff Competencies.* New York: Holtz, Rinehart and Winston.

Van Houten, R. and Axelrod, S. (eds) (1993) *Behavior Analysis and Treatment.* New York: Plenum Press.

Venter, A., Lord, C. and Schopler, E. (1992) 'A follow-up study of high-functioning autistic children.' *Journal of Child Psychology and Psychiatry and Allied Disciplines 33*, 3, 489–507.

Volkmar, F., Cook, E.H., Pomeroy, J., Realmuto, G. and Tanguay, P. (1999) 'Practice parameters for the assessment and treatment of children, adolescents, and adults with autism and other pervasive developmental disorders.' *Journal of the American Academy of Child and Adolescent Psychiatry 38* (Suppl), 32S–54S.

Warren, S.F. and Rogers-Warren, A.K. (eds) (1985) *Teaching Functional Language.* Austin, TX: Pro-Ed.

Watthen-Lovaas, N. and Lovaas, E.E. (1999) *The Reading and Writing Program: An Alternative Form of Communication.* Austin, TX: Pro-Ed.

Wetherby, B. and Striefel, S. (1978) 'Application of miniature linguistic system of matrix training procedures.' In R.L. Schiefelbusch (ed) *Language Intervention Strategies.* Baltimore, MD: University Park Press.

Yell, M.L. and Drasgow, E. (2000) 'Litigating a free appropriate public education: the Lovaas hearings and cases.' *The Journal of Special Education 33*, 205–214.

The applied behaviour analysis of autism

The beginning, in the 1960s

Baer, D.M. and Sherman, J.A. (1964) 'Reinforcement control of generalized imitation in young children.' *Journal of Experimental Child Psychology 1*, 37–49.

Baer, D.M., Peterson, R.F. and Sherman, J.A. (1967) 'The development of imitation by reinforcing behavioral similarity to a model.' *Journal of the Experimental Analysis of Behavior 10*, 405–416.

Buell, J., Stoddard, P., Harris, F.R. and Baer, D.M. (1968) 'Collateral social development accompanying reinforcement of outdoor play in a preschool child.' *Journal of Applied Behavior Analysis 2*, 167–173.

Cook, C. and Adams, H.F. (1966) 'Modification of verbal behavior in speech deficient children.' *Behaviour Research and Therapy 4*, 265–271.

Cowan, P.A., Hoddinott, B.T. and Wright, B.A. (1965) 'Compliance and resistance in the conditioning of autistic children: an exploratory study.' *Child Development 36*, 913–923.

Davison, G.C. (1964) 'A social learning therapy programme with an autistic child.' *Behavior Research and Therapy 2*, 149–159.

Ferster, C.B. (1961) 'Positive reinforcement and behavioral deficits of autistic children.' *Child Development 32*, 437–456.

Ferster, C.B. and DeMyer, M.K. (1961) 'The development of performances in autistic children in an automatically controlled environment.' *Journal of Chronic Diseases 13*, 312–345.

Fineman, K.R. (1968) 'Visual-color reinforcement in establishment of speech by an autistic child.' *Perceptual and Motor Skills 26*, 761–762.

Foss, D. (1968) 'Learning and discovery in the acquisition of structured material: effects of number of items and their sequence.' *Journal of Experimental Psychology 77*, 341–344.

Guess, D. (1969) 'A functional analysis of receptive language and productive speech: acquisition of the plural morpheme.' *Journal of Applied Behavior Analysis 2*, 55–64.

Guess, D., Rutherford, G., Smith, J.O. and Ensminger, E. (1968) 'Utilization of sub-professional personnel in teaching language skills to mentally retarded children: an interim report.' *Mental Retardation 8*, 17–22.

Guess, D., Sailor, W., Rutherford, G. and Baer, D.M. (1968) 'An experimental analysis of linguistic development: the productive use of the plural morpheme.' *Journal of Applied Behavior Analysis 1*, 292–307.

Hall, R.V. and Broden, M. (1967) 'Behavior changes in brain-injured children through social reinforcement.' *Journal of Experimental Child Psychology 5*, 463–479.

Hart, B.M., Reynolds, N.J., Baer, D.M., Brawley, F.R. and Harris, F.R. (1968) 'Effect of contingent and non-contingent social reinforcement on the cooperative play of a preschool child.' *Journal of Applied Behavior Analysis 1*, 73–76.

Hewitt, F.M. (1965) 'Teaching speech to an autistic child through operant conditioning.' *American Journal of Orthopsychiatry 35*, 927–936.

Hintgen, J.N. and Coulter, S.K. (1967) 'Auditory control of operant behavior in mute autistic children.' *Perceptual and Motor Skills 25*, 561–565.

Hollis, J.H. (1965) 'The effects of social and nonsocial stimuli on the behavior of profoundly retarded children: Part I.' *American Journal of Mental Deficiency 71*, 984–986.

Kerr, N., Meyerson, L. and Michael, J. (1965) 'A procedure for shaping vocalizations in a mute child.' In L.P. Ullman and L. Krasner (eds) *Case Studies in Behavior Modification.* New York: Holt, Rinehart, and Winston.

Lovaas, O.I. (1961) 'Interaction between verbal and non-verbal behavior.' *Child Development 32*, 325–336.

Lovaas, O.I. (1964) 'Cue properties of words: the control of operant responding by rate and content of verbal operants.' *Child Development 35*, 245–256.

Lovaas, O.I. (1968) 'Some studies on the treatment of childhood schizophrenia.' *Research in Psychotherapy 3*, 103–121.

Lovaas, O.I. (1968) 'A program for the establishment of speech in psychotic children.' In H.N. Sloane and B.D. MacAulay (eds) *Operant Procedures in Remedial Speech and Language Training.* Boston: Houghton, Mifflin.

Lovaas, O.I. and Simmons, J.Q. (1969) 'Manipulation of self-destruction in three retarded children.' *Journal of Applied Behavior Analysis 2*, 143–157.

Lovaas, O.I., Berberich, J.P., Perloff, B.F. and Schaeffer, B. (1966) 'Acquisition of imitative speech in schizophrenic children.' *Science 151*, 705–707.

Lovaas, O.I., Freitag, G., Gold, V.J. and Kassorla, I.C. (1965) 'Experimental studies in childhood schizophrenia: analysis of self-destructive behavior.' *Journal of Experimental Child Psychology 2*, 67–84.

Lovaas, O.I., Freitag, G., Kinder, M.I., Rubenstein, B.D., Schaeffer, B. and Simmons, J.W. (1966) 'Establishment of social reinforcers in two schizophrenic children on the basis of food.' *Journal of Experimental Child Psychology 4*, 109–125.

Lovaas, O.I., Freitas, L., Nelson, K. and Whalen, C. (1967) 'The establishment of imitation and its use for the development of complex behavior in schizophrenic children.' *Behavior Research and Therapy 5*, 171–181.

Martin, G.L., England, G., Kaprowy, E., Kilgour, K. and Pilek, V. (1968) 'Operant conditioning of kindergarten-class behavior in autistic children.' *Behavior Research and Therapy 6*, 281–294.

McReynolds, L.V. (1969) 'Application of time out from positive reinforcement for increasing the efficiency of speech training.' *Journal of Applied Behavior Analysis 2*, 199–205.

Metz, J.R. (1965) 'Conditioning generalized imitation in autistic children.' *Journal of Experimental Child Psychology 2*, 389–399.

O'Connor, R.D. (1969) 'Modification of social withdrawal through symbolic modeling.' *Journal of Applied Behavior Analysis 2*, 15–22.

Ottinger, D.R., Sweeney, N. and Loew, L.H. (1965) 'Visual discrimination learning in schizophrenic and normal children.' *Journal of Clinical Psychology 21*, 251–253.

Rabb, E. and Hewitt, F.M. (1967) 'Development of appropriate classroom behaviors in a severely disturbed group of institutionalized children with a behavior modification model.' *American Journal of Orthopsychiatry 37*, 313–314.

Risley, T.R. and Wolf, M.M. (1966) 'Experimental manipulation of autistic behaviors and generalization into the home.' In R. Ulrich, T. Stachnik and J. Mabry (eds) *Control of Human Behavior*. Glenview, IL: Scott, Foresman.

Risley, T.R. and Wolf, M.M. (1967) 'Establishing functional speech in echolalic children.' *Behavior Research and Therapy 5*, 73–88.

Risley, T.R. and Wolf, M.M. (1968) 'Establishing functional speech in echolalic children.' In H.N. Sloane and B.D. MacAulay (eds) *Operant Procedures in Remedial Speech and Language Training*. Boston: Houghton, Mifflin.

Salzinger, K., Feldman, R., Cowan, J. and Salzinger, S. (1965) 'Operant conditioning of verbal behavior of two young speech deficient boys.' In L. Krasner and L. Ullman (eds) *Research in Behavior Modification*. New York: Holt, Rinehart, and Winston.

Schell, R.E., Stark, J. and Giddan, J. (1967) 'Development of language behavior in an autistic child.' *Journal of Speech and Hearing Disorders 32*, 51–64.

Sherman, J. (1964) 'Modification of nonverbal behavior through reinforcement of related behavior.' *Child Development 35*, 717–723.

Sloane, H.N., Johnston, M.K. and Harris, F.R. (1968) 'Remedial procedures for teaching verbal behavior in speech deficient or defective young children.' In H.N. Sloane and B.D. MacAulay (eds) *Operant Procedures in Remedial Speech and Language Training*. Boston: Houghton, Mifflin.

Stark, J., Giddan, J.J. and Meisel, J. (1968) 'Increasing verbal behavior in an autistic child.' *Journal of Speech and Hearing Disorders 3*, 42–48.

Wolf, M.M., Risley, T.R., Johnston, M., Harris, F. and Allen, E. (1967) 'Application of operant conditioning procedures to the behavior problems of an autistic child: a follow-up and extension.' *Behavior Research and Therapy 5*, 103–111.

Wolf, M.M., Risley, T.R. and Mees, H. (1964) 'Application of operant conditioning procedures to the behavior problems of an autistic child.' *Behavior Research and Therapy 1*, 305–312.

Zimmerman, E.H., Zimmerman, J. and Russel, C.D. (1969) 'Differential effects of token reinforcement on instruction-following behavior in retarded students instructed as a group.' *Journal of Applied Behavior Analysis 2*, 101–112.

In the 1970s

Baer, D.M. and Guess, D. (1971) 'Receptive training of adjective inflections in mental retardates.' *Journal of Applied Behavior Analysis 4*, 129–139.

Baer, D.M. and Guess, D. (1973) 'Teaching productive noun suffixes to severely retarded children.' *American Journal of Mental Deficiency 77*, 5, 498–505:

Baer, A.M., Rowbury, T. and Baer, D.M. (1973) 'The development of instructional control over classroom activities of deviant preschool children.' *Journal of Applied Behavior Analysis 6*, 289–298.

Barton, E.J. and Ascione, F.R. (1979) 'Sharing in preschool children: facilitation, stimulus generalization, response generalization, and maintenance.' *Journal of Applied Behavior Analysis 12*, 417–430.

Burgess, R.L., Burgess, J.M. and Esveldt, K.C. (1970) 'An analysis of generalized imitation.' *Journal of Applied Behavior Analysis 3*, 39–46.

Carnine, D.W. (1976) 'Effects of two therapist-presentation rates on off-task behavior, answering correctly, and participation.' *Journal of Applied Behavior Analysis 9*, 199–206.

Carnine, D.W. and Fink, W.T. (1978) 'Increasing the rate of presentation and use of signals in elementary classroom therapists.' *Journal of Applied Behavior Analysis 11*, 35–46.

Carrier, J.K. (1974) 'Non-speech noun usage training with severely and profoundly retarded children.' *Journal of Speech and Hearing Research 17*, 510–517.

Christy, P.R. (1975) 'Does use of tangible rewards with individual children affect peer observers?' *Journal of Applied Behavior Analysis 8*, 187–196.

Clark, H.B. and Sherman, J.A. (1975) 'Teaching generative use of sentence answers to three forms of questions.' *Journal of Applied Behavior Analysis 8*, 321–330.

Coleman, S.L. and Stedman, J.M. (1974) 'Use of peer model in language training in an echolalic child.' *Journal of Behavior Therapy and Experimental Psychiatry 5*, 275–279.

Craighead, W.E., O'Leary, K.D. and Allen, J.S. (1973) 'Teaching and generalization of instruction following in an "autistic" child.' *Journal of Behavior Therapy and Experimental Psychiatry 4*, 171–176.

Eyberg, S.M. and Johnson, S.M. (1974) 'Multiple assessment of behavior modification with families: effects of contingency contracting and order of treated problems.' *Journal of Consulting and Clinical Psychology 42*, 594–606.

Favell, J.E., Favell, J.E. and McGimsey, J.F. (1978) 'Relative effectiveness and efficiency of group vs. individual training of severely retarded persons.' *American Journal of Mental Deficiency 83*, 104–109.

Fink, W.T. and Sandall, S.R. (1978) 'One-to-one vs. group academic instruction with handicapped and non-handicapped preschool children.' *Mental Retardation 16*, 236–240.

Flanagan, S., Adams, H.E. and Forehand, R. (1979) 'A comparison of four instructional techniques for teaching parents to use time-out.' *Behavior Therapy 10*, 94–102.

Foxx, R.M. and Azrin, N.H. (1973) 'The elimination of autistic self-stimulatory behavior by overcorrection.' *Journal of Applied Behavior Analysis 6*, 1–14.

Garcia, E.E. (1974) 'The training and generalization of a conversational speech form in nonverbal retardates.' *Journal of Applied Behavior Analysis 7*, 137–151.

Garcia, E.E. (1976) 'The development and generalization of delayed imitation.' *Journal of Applied Behavior Analysis 9*, 499.

Garcia, E.E., Baer, D.M. and Firestone, I. (1971) 'The development of generalized imitation within topographically determined boundaries.' *Journal of Applied Behavior Analysis 4*, 101–113.

Garcia, E.E., Guess, D. and Byrnes, J. (1973) 'Development of syntax in a retarded girl using procedures of imitation, reinforcement, and modeling.' *Journal of Applied Behavior Analysis 6*, 299–311.

Goetz, E.M. and Baer, D.M. (1973) 'Social control of form diversity and the emergence of new forms in children's block building.' *Journal of Applied Behavior Analysis 6*, 209–217.

Greenwood, C.R., Walker, H.M., Todd, N.M. and Hopps, H. (1979) 'Selecting a cost-effective screening device for the assessment of preschool social withdrawal.' *Journal of Applied Behavior Analysis 12*, 639–652.

Guess, D. and Baer, D.M. (1973) 'An analysis of individual differences in generalization between receptive and productive language in retarded children.' *Journal of Applied Behavior Analysis 6*, 311–331.

Hall, R.V., Axelrod, S., Tyler, L., Grief, E., Jones, F.C. and Robertson, R. (1972) 'Modification of behavior problems in the home with a parent as observer and experimenter.' *Journal of Applied Behavior Analysis 5*, 53–64.

Halle, J.W., Marshall, A.M. and Spradlin, J.E. (1979) 'Time delay: a technique to increase language use and facilitate generalization in retarded children.' *Journal of Applied Behavior Analysis 12*, 431–439.

Handleman, J.S. (1979) 'Generalization by autistic-type children of verbal responses across settings.' *Journal of Applied Behavior Analysis 12*, 273–282.

Hardiman, S.A., Goetz, E.M., Reuter, K.E. and LeBlanc, J.M. (1975) 'Primes, contingent attention, and training: effects on a child's motor behavior.' *Journal of Applied Behavior Analysis 8*, 399–410.

Harris, S.L. (1975) 'Teaching language to nonverbal children – with emphasis on problems of generalization.' *Psychological Bulletin 82*, 565–580.

Hart, B. and Risley, T.R. (1975) 'Incidental teaching of language in the preschool.' *Journal of Applied Behavior Analysis 8*, 411–420.

Karoly, P. and Dirks, M.J. (1977) 'Developing self-control in pre-school children through correspondence training.' *Behavior Therapy 8*, 398–405.

Kelley, M.L., Embry, L.H. and Baer, D.M. (1979) 'Skills for child management and family support: training parents for maintenance.' *Behavior Modification 3*, 373–396.

Kirby, F.D. and Toler, H.C. (1970) 'Modification of preschool isolate behavior: a case study.' *Journal of Applied Behavior Analysis 3*, 309–314.

Koegel, R.L. and Covert, A. (1972) 'The relationship of self-stimulation to learning in autistic children.' *Journal of Applied Behavior Analysis 5*, 381–388.

Koegel, R.L. and Egel, A.L. (1979) 'Motivating autistic children.' *Journal of Abnormal Psychology 88*, 418–426.

Koegel, R.L. and Rincover, A. (1974) 'Treatment of psychotic children in a classroom environment: I. Learning in a large group.' *Journal of Applied Behavior Analysis 7*, 45–59.

Koegel, R.L. and Rincover, A. (1976) 'Some detrimental effects of using extra stimuli to guide learning in normal and autistic children.' *Journal of Abnormal Child Psychology 4*, 59–71.

Koegel, R.L. and Rincover, A. (1977) 'Research on the difference between generalization and maintenance in extra-therapy responding.' *Journal of Applied Behavior Analysis 10*, 1–12.

Koegel, R.L. and Schreibman, L. (1977) 'Teaching autistic children to respond to simultaneous multiple cues.' *Journal of Experimental Child Psychology 24*, 299–311.

Koegel, R.L. and Wilhelm, H. (1973) 'Selective responding to the components of multiple visual cues by autistic children.' *Journal of Experimental Child Psychology 15*, 442–453.

Koegel, R.L., Firestone, P.B., Kramme, K.W. and Dunlap, G. (1974) 'Increasing spontaneous play by suppressing self-stimulation in autistic children.' *Journal of Applied Behavior Analysis 7*, 521–528.

Koegel, R.L., Glahn, T.J. and Nieminen, G.S. (1978) 'Generalization of parent-training results.' *Journal of Applied Behavior Analysis 11*, 95–109.

Koegel, R.L., Russo, D.C. and Rincover, A. (1977) 'Assessing and training teachers in the generalized use of behavior modification with autistic children.' *Journal of Applied Behavior Analysis 10*, 197–205.

Lovaas, O.I. and Schreibman, L. (1971) 'Stimulus overselectivity of autistic children in a two-stimulus situation.' *Behaviour Research and Therapy 9*, 305–310.

Lovaas, O.I., Litrownik, A. and Mann, R. (1971) 'Response latencies to auditory stimuli in autistic children engaged in self-stimulatory behavior.' *Behavior Research and Therapy 9*, 39–49.

Lovaas, O.I., Schreibman, L., Koegel, R.L. and Rehm, R. (1971) 'Selective responding by autistic children to multiple sensory input.' *Journal of Abnormal Psychology 77*, 211–222.

Lutzker, J.R. and Sherman, J.A. (1974) 'Producing generative sentence usage by imitation and reinforcement procedures.' *Journal of Applied Behavior Analysis 7, 3*, 447–460.

Martin, J.A. (1971) 'The control of imitative and non-imitative behavior in severely-retarded children through "generalized instruction-following".' *Journal of Experimental Child Psychology 11*, 390–400.

McLean, L.P. and McLean, J.E. (1974) 'A language training program for nonverbal autistic children.' *Journal of Speech and Hearing Disorders 39*, 186–193.

Miller, S.J. and Sloane, H.N. (1976) 'The generalization effects of parent training across stimulus settings.' *Journal of Applied Behavior Analysis 9*, 355–370.

Mithaug, D.E. and Wolfe, M.S. (1976) 'Employing task arrangements and verbal contingencies to promote verbalizations between retarded children.' *Journal of Applied Behavior Analysis 9*, 301–314.

Nedelman, D. and Sulzbacher, S.I. (1972) 'Dicky at 13 years of age: a long-term success following early application of operant conditioning procedures.' In G. Semb (ed) *Behavior Analysis and Education – 1972*. Lawrence, KS: University of Kansas Department of Human Development.

Nelson, R., Gibson, F. and Cutting, D.S. (1973) 'Video taped modeling: the development of three appropriate social responses in a mildly retarded child.' *Mental Retardation 11*, 24–28.

Nordquist, V.M. and Wahler, R.G. (1973) 'Naturalistic treatment of an autistic child.' *Journal of Applied Behavior Analysis 6*, 79–87.

O'Dell, S.L., Blackwell, L.J., Larcen, S.W. and Hogan, J.L. (1977) 'Competency based training for severely behaviorally handicapped children and their parents.' *Journal of Autism and Childhood Schizophrenia 7*, 231–242.

Pinkston, E.M., Reese, N.M., LeBlanc, J.M. and Baer, D.M. (1973) 'Independent control of a preschool child's aggression and peer interaction by contingent teacher attention.' *Journal of Applied Behavior Analysis 6*, 115–124.

Rekers, G.A. and Lovaas, O.I. (1974) 'Behavioral treatment of deviant sex-role behaviors in a male child.' *Journal of Applied Behavior Analysis 7*, 173–190.

Repp, A.C. and Deitz, S.M. (1974) 'Reducing aggressive and self-injurious behavior of institutionalized retarded children through reinforcement of other behaviors.' *Journal of Applied Behavior Analysis 7*, 313–326.

Reynolds, B.S., Newsome, C.D. and Lovaas, O.I. (1974) 'Auditory overselectivity in autistic children.' *Journal of Abnormal Child Psychology 2*, 253–263.

Rincover, A. and Koegel, R.L. (1974) 'Classroom treatment of autistic children II: individualized instruction in a group.' *Journal of Abnormal Child Psychology 5*, 113–126.

Rincover, A. and Koegel, R.L. (1975) 'Setting generality and stimulus control in autistic children.' *Journal of Applied Behavior Analysis 8*, 235–246.

Rincover, A., Newsome, C.D., Lovaas, O.I. and Koegel, R.L. (1977) 'Some motivational properties of sensory reinforcement in psychotic children.' *Journal of Experimental Child Psychology 24*, 312–323.

Risley, T.R. and Baer, D.M. (1973) 'Operant behavior modification: the deliberate development of behavior.' In B. Caldwell and H. Ricciuti (eds) *Review of Child Development Research, Vol. III: Child Development and Social Policy*. Chicago: University of Chicago Press.

Risley, T.R. and Reynolds, N.J. (1970) 'Emphasis as a prompt for verbal imitation.' *Journal of Applied Behavior Analysis 3*, 185–190.

Rogers-Warren, A. and Baer, D.M. (1976) 'Correspondence between saying and doing: teaching children to share and praise.' *Journal of Applied Behavior Analysis 9*, 335–354.

Russo, D.C. and Koegel, R.L. (1977) 'A method for integrating an autistic child into a normal public school classroom.' *Journal of Applied Behavior Analysis 10*, 579–590.

Russo, D.C., Koegel, R.L. and Lovaas, O.I. (1978) 'A comparison of human vs. automated instruction of autistic children.' *Journal of Abnormal Child Psychology 6*, 189–201.

Sailor, W. (1971) 'Reinforcement and generalization of productive plural allomorphs in two retarded children.' *Journal of Applied Behavior Analysis 4*, 305–310.

Sailor, W. and Taman, T. (1972) 'Stimulus factors in the training of prepositional usage in three autistic children.' *Journal of Applied Behavior Analysis 5*, 183–190.

Sajwaj, T., Twardosz, S. and Burke, M. (1972) 'Side effects of extinction procedures in a remedial preschool.' *Journal of Applied Behavior Analysis 5*, 163–175.

Saunders, R. and Sailor, W. (1979) 'A comparison of three strategies of reinforcement on two-choice learning problems with severely retarded children.' *AAESPH Review 4*, 323–333.

Schreibman, L. (1975) 'Effects of within-stimulus and extra-stimulus prompting on discrimination learning in autistic children.' *Journal of Applied Behavior Analysis 8*, 91–112.

Schreibman, L. and Lovaas, O.I. (1973) 'Overselective response to social stimuli by autistic children.' *Journal of Abnormal Child Psychology 1*, 152–168.

Schroeder, G.L. and Baer, D.M. (1972) 'Effects of concurrent and serial training on generalized vocal imitation in retarded children.' *Developmental Psychology 6*, 293–301.

Schumaker, J. and Sherman, J.A. (1970) 'Training generative verb usage by imitation and reinforcement procedures.' *Journal of Applied Behavior Analysis 3*, 273–287.

Solomon, R.W. and Wahler, R.G. (1973) 'Peer reinforcement control of classroom problem behavior.' *Journal of Applied Behavior Analysis 6*, 49–56.

Stevens-Long, J. and Rasmussen, M. (1974) 'The acquisition of simple and compound sentence structure in an autistic child.' *Journal of Applied Behavior Analysis 7*, 473–479.

Stokes, T.F., Baer, D.M. and Jackson, R.L. (1974) 'Programming the generalization of a greeting response in four retarded children.' *Journal of Applied Behavior Analysis 7*, 599–610.

Stokes, T.F., Fowler, S.A. and Baer, D.M. (1978) 'Training preschool children to recruit natural communities of reinforcement.' *Journal of Applied Behavior Analysis 11*, 285–294.

Strain, P.S. and Timm, M.A. (1974) 'An experimental analysis of social interaction between a behaviorally disordered preschool child and her classroom peers.' *Journal of Applied Behavior Analysis 7*, 583–590.

Strain, P.S., Shores, R.E. and Kerr, M.M. (1976) 'An experimental analysis of "spillover" effects on the social interaction of behaviorally handicapped preschool children.' *Journal of Applied Behavior Analysis 9*, 31–40.

Strain, P.S., Shores, R.E. and Timm, M.A. (1977) 'Effects of peer social initiations on the behavior of withdrawn preschool children.' *Journal of Applied Behavior Analysis 10*, 289–298.

Striefel, S., Wetherby, B. and Karlan, G. (1976) 'Establishing generalized verb-noun instruction-following skills in retarded children.' *Journal of Experimental Child Psychology 22*, 247–260.

Sulzbacher, S.I. and Costello, J.M. (1970) 'A behavior strategy for language training of a child with autistic behaviors.' *Journal of Speech and Hearing Disorders 35*, 256–276.

Timm, M.A., Strain, P.S. and Eller, P.H. (1979) 'Effects of systematic, response-dependent fading and thinning procedures on the maintenance of child–child interaction.' *Journal of Applied Behavior Analysis 12*, 308.

Touchette, P.E. (1971) 'Transfer of stimulus control: measuring the moment of transfer.' *Journal of the Experimental Analysis of Behavior 15*, 347–354.

Twardosz, S. and Sajwaj, T. (1972) 'Multiple effects of a procedure to increase sitting in a hyperactive, retarded boy.' *Journal of Applied Behavior Analysis 5*, 73–78.

Varni, J.W., Lovaas, O.I., Koegel, R.L. and Everett, N.L. (1979) 'An analysis of observational learning in autistic and normal children.' *Journal of Abnormal Child Psychology 7*, 31–43.

Walker, H.M. and Buckley, N.K. (1972) 'Programming generalization and maintenance of treatment effects across time and across settings.' *Journal of Applied Behavior Analysis 5*, 209–224.

Warren, S.F., Rogers-Warren, A. and Baer, D.M. (1976) 'The role of offer rates in controlling sharing by young children.' *Journal of Applied Behavior Analysis 9*, 491–497.

Wells, K.C., Forehand, R., Hickey, K. and Green, K.D. (1977) 'Effects of a procedure derived from the overcorrection principle on manipulated and nonmanipulated behaviors.' *Journal of Applied Behavior Analysis 10*, 679–688.

Wheeler, A.J. and Sulzer, B. (1970) 'Operant training and generalization of a verbal response form in a speech-deficient child.' *Journal of Applied Behavior Analysis 3*, 139–147.

Whitman, T.L., Zakaras, M. and Chardos, S. (1971) 'Effects of reinforcement and guidance procedures on instruction-following behavior in retarded children.' *Journal of Applied Behavior Analysis 4*, 283–291.

In the 1980s

Ballard, K. and Crooks, T. (1984) 'Videotape modeling for preschool children with low levels of social interaction and low peer involvement in play.' *Journal of Abnormal Child Psychology 12*, 95–109.

Baum, C.G. and Forehand, R. (1981) 'Long term follow-up assessment of parent training by use of multiple outcome measures.' *Behavior Therapy 12*, 643–652.

Bergsgaard, M.O. and Larsson, E.V. (1984) 'Increasing social interaction between an isolate first-grader and cross-cultural peers.' *Psychology in the Schools 21*, 244–251.

Billingsly, F.F. and Neel, R.S. (1985) 'Competing behaviors and their effects on skill generalization and maintenance.' *Analysis and Intervention in Developmental Disabilities 5*, 357–372.

Blew, P.A., Schwartz, I.S. and Luce, S.C. (1985) 'Teaching functional community skills to autistic children using nonhandicapped peer tutors.' *Journal of Applied Behavior Analysis 18*, 337–342.

Brown, F., Holvoet, J., Guess, D. and Mulligan, M. (1980) 'Individualized curriculum sequencing model (III): small group instruction.' *Journal of the Association for the Severely Handicapped 5*, 352–367.

Carr, E.G. and Durand, V.M. (1985) 'Reducing behavior problems through functional communication training.' *Journal of Applied Behavior Analysis 18*, 111–126.

Carr, E.G., Newsome, C.D. and Binkoff, J.A. (1980) 'Escape as a factor in the aggressive behavior of two retarded children.' *Journal of Applied Behavior Analysis 13*, 101–117.

Charlop, M.H. (1983) 'The effects of echolalia on acquisition and generalization of receptive labeling in autistic children.' *Journal of Applied Behavior Analysis 16*, 111–127.

Charlop, M.H. and Milstein, J.P. (1989) 'Teaching autistic children conversational speech using video modeling.' *Journal of Applied Behavior Analysis 22*, 275–286.

Charlop, M.H. and Walsh, M.E. (1986) 'Increasing autistic children's spontaneous verbalizations of affection: an assessment of time delay and peer modeling procedures.' *Journal of Applied Behavior Analysis 19*, 307–314.

Charlop, M.H., Schreibman, L. and Thibodeau, M.G. (1985) 'Increasing spontaneous verbal responding in autistic children using a time delay procedure.' *Journal of Applied Behavior Analysis 18*, 155–166.

Charlop, M.H., Schreibman, L. and Tryon, A.S. (1983) 'Learning through observation: the effects of peer modeling on acquisition and generalization in autistic children.' *Journal of Abnormal Child Psychology 11*, 355–366.

Clarke, S., Remington, R. and Light, R. (1988) 'The role of referential speech in sign learning by mentally retarded children: a comparison of total communication and sign-alone training.' *Journal of Applied Behavior Analysis 21*, 419–426.

Curl, R.M., Rowbury, T.G. and Baer, D.M. (1985) 'The facilitation of children's social interaction by a picture-cue training program.' *Child and Family Behavior Therapy 7*, 11–39.

Deacon, J.R. and Konarski, E.A. (1987) 'Correspondence training: an example of rule-governed behavior?' *Journal of Applied Behavior Analysis 20*, 391–400.

Deich, R.F. and Hodges, P.M. (1982) 'Teaching nonvocal communication to nonverbal retarded children.' *Behavior Modification 6*, 200–228.

Duker, P.C. and Morsink, H. (1984) 'Acquisition and cross-setting generalization of manual signs with severely retarded individuals.' *Journal of Applied Behavior Analysis 17*, 93–103.

Dunlap, G. (1984) 'The influence of task variation and maintenance tasks on the learning and affect of autistic children.' *Journal of Experimental Child Psychology 37*, 41–46.

Dunlap, G. and Johnson, J. (1985) 'Increasing the independent responding of autistic children with unpredictable supervision.' *Journal of Applied Behavior Analysis 18*, 227–236.

Dunlap, G. and Koegel, R.L. (1980) 'Motivating autistic children through stimulus variation.' *Journal of Applied Behavior Analysis 13*, 619–627.

Dunlap, G., Dyer, K. and Koegel, R.L. (1983) 'Autistic self-stimulation and intertrial interval duration.' *American Journal of Mental Deficiency 88*, 194–202.

Dunlap, G., Koegel, R.L. and Burke, J.C. (1981) 'Educational implications of stimulus overselectivity in autistic children.' *Exceptional Education Quarterly 2*, 3, 37–49.

Dunlap, G., Koegel, R.L., Johnson, J. and O'Neill, R.E. (1986) 'Maintaining performance of autistic clients in community settings with delayed contingencies.' *Journal of Applied Behavior Analysis 20*, 185–192.

Dunlap, G., Koegel, R.L. and Kern, L. (1984) 'Continuity of treatment: toilet training in multiple community settings.' *Journal of the Association for Persons with Severe Handicaps 9*, 134–142.

Durand, V.M. and Carr, E.G. (1987) 'Social influences on "self-stimulatory" behavior: analysis and treatment application.' *Journal of Applied Behavior Analysis 20*, 119–132.

Durand, V.M. and Crimmins, D.B. (1987) 'Assessment and treatment of psychotic speech in an autistic child.' *Journal of Autism and Developmental Disorders 17*, 17–28.

Dyer, K.I. (1987) 'The competition of autistic stereotyped behavior with usual and specially assessed reinforcers.' *Research in Developmental Disabilities 8*, 607–626.

Dyer, K., Christian, W.P. and Luce, S.C. (1982) 'The role of response delay in improving the discrimination performance of autistic children.' *Journal of Applied Behavior Analysis 15*, 231–240.

Dyer, K., Schwartz, I.S. and Luce, S.C. (1984) 'A supervision program for increasing functional activities for severely handicapped students in a residential setting.' *Journal of Applied Behavior Analysis 17*, 249–260.

Eason, L.J., White, M.J. and Newsom, C. (1982) 'Generalized reduction of self-stimulatory behavior: an effect of teaching appropriate play to autistic children.' *Analysis and Intervention in Developmental Disabilities 2*, 157–169.

Edelson, S.M., Taubman, M.T. and Lovaas, O.I. (1982) 'Some social contexts of self-destructive behavior.' *Journal of Abnormal Child Psychology 11*, 299–311.

Egel, A.L. (1981) 'Reinforcer variation: implications for motivating developmentally disabled children.' *Journal of Applied Behavior Analysis 14*, 345–350.

Egel, A.L., Richman, G.S. and Koegel, R.L. (1981) 'Normal peer models and autistic children's learning.' *Journal of Applied Behavior Analysis 14*, 3–12.

Epstein, L.J., Taubman, M.T. and Lovaas, O.I. (1985) 'Changes in self-stimulatory behaviors with treatment.' *Journal of Abnormal Child Psychology 13*, 281–294.

Fink, W.T. and Sandall, S.R. (1980) 'A comparison of one-to-one and small group instructional strategies with developmentally disabled preschoolers.' *Mental Retardation 18*, 34–35.

Foxx, R.M. and Livesay, J. (1984) 'Maintenance of response suppression following overcorrection: a 10-year retrospective examination of eight cases.' *Analysis and Intervention in Developmental Disabilities 4*, 65–80.

Gaylord-Ross, R.J., Haring, T.G., Breen, C. and Pitts-Conway, V. (1984) 'The training and generalization of social interaction skills with autistic youth.' *Journal of Applied Behavior Analysis 17*, 229–248.

Goldstein, H. (1983) 'Recombinative generalization: relationships between environmental conditions and the linguistic repertoires of language learners.' *Analysis and Intervention in Developmental Disabilities 3*, 279–293.

Goldstein, H. and Mousetis, L. (1989) 'Generalized language learning by children with severe mental retardation: effects of peers' expressive modeling.' *Journal of Applied Behavior Analysis 22*, 245–259.

Goldstein, H. and Wickstrom, S. (1986) 'Peer intervention effects on communicative interaction among handicapped and nonhandicapped preschoolers.' *Journal of Applied Behavior Analysis 19*, 209–214.

Goldstein, H., Angelo, D. and Mousetis, L. (1987) 'Acquisition and extension of syntactic repertoires by severely mentally retarded youth.' *Research in Developmental Disabilities 8*, 549–574.

Hall, M.C., Grinstead, J., Collier, H. and Hall, R.V. (1980) 'Responsive parenting: a preventative program which incorporates parents training parents.' *Education and Treatment of Children 3*, 239–259.

Halle, J.W. (1987) 'Teaching language in the natural environment: an analysis of spontaneity.' *Journal of the Association for Persons with Severe Handicaps 12*, 28–37.

Halle, J.W., Baer, D.M. and Spradlin, J.E. (1981) 'Teacher's generalized use of delay as a stimulus control procedure to increase language use in handicapped children.' *Journal of Applied Behavior Analysis 14*, 389–409.

Haring, T.G. (1985) 'Teaching between-class generalization of toy play behavior to handicapped children.' *Journal of Applied Behavior Analysis 18*, 127–140.

Haring, T.G. and Lovinger, L. (1989) 'Promoting social interaction through teaching generalized play initiation responses to preschool children with autism.' *Journal of the Association for Persons with Severe Handicaps 14*, 58–67.

Haring, T.G., Roger, B., Lee, M., Breen, C. and Gaylord-Ross, R. (1986) 'Teaching social language to moderately handicapped students.' *Journal of Applied Behavior Analysis 19*, 159–171.

Harris, S.L. (1984) 'Intervention planning for the family of the autistic child: a multilevel assessment of the family system.' *Journal of Marital and Family Therapy 10*, 157–166.

Hunt, P., Alwell, M. and Goetz, L. (1988) 'Acquisition of conversational skills and the reduction of inappropriate social interaction behaviors.' *Journal of the Association for Persons with Severe Handicaps 13*, 20–27.

Hurlbut, B., Iwata, B. and Green, J. (1982) 'Nonvocal language acquisition in adolescents with severe physical disabilities: Blissymbol versus iconic stimulus formats.' *Journal of Applied Behavior Analysis 15*, 241–258.

Iwata, B.A., Dorsey, M.F., Slifer, K.J., Bauman, K.E. and Richman, G.S. (1982) 'Toward a functional analysis of self-injury.' *Analysis and Intervention in Developmental Disabilities 2*, 3–20.

Jordan, J., Singh, N.N. and Repp, A.C. (1989) 'An evaluation of gentle teaching and visual screening in the reduction of stereotypy.' *Journal of Applied Behavior Analysis 22*, 9–22.

Karlan, G.R., Brenn-White, B., Lentz, A., Hodur, P., Egger, D. and Frankoff, D. (1982) 'Establishing generalized productive verb-noun phrase usage in a manual language system with moderately handicapped children.' *Journal of Speech and Hearing Disorders 47*, 31–42.

Kern, L., Koegel, R.L. and Dunlap, G. (1984) 'The influence of vigorous versus mild exercise on autistic stereotyped behaviors.' *Journal of Autism and Developmental Disorders 14*, 1, 57–67.

Koegel, R.L. and Williams, J. (1980) 'Direct vs. indirect response-reinforcer relationships in teaching autistic children.' *Journal of Abnormal Child Psychology 4*, 536–547.

Koegel, R.L., Dunlap, G. and Dyer, K. (1980) 'Intertrial interval duration and learning in autistic children.' *Journal of Applied Behavior Analysis 13*, 91–99.

Koegel, R.L., Dunlap, G., Richman, G.S. and Dyer, K. (1981) 'The use of specific orienting cues for teaching discrimination tasks.' *Analysis and Intervention in Developmental Disabilities 1*, 187–198.

Koegel, R.L., Dyer, K. and Bell, L.K. (1986) 'The influence of child-preferred activities on autistic children's social behavior.' *Journal of Applied Behavior Analysis 20*, 243–252.

Koegel, R.L., O'Dell, M.C. and Koegel, L.K. (1987) 'A natural language paradigm for teaching autistic children by reinforcing attempts.' *Journal of Autism and Developmental Disorders 17*, 187–199.

Koegel, R.L., Schreibman, L., Britten, K.R., Burke, J.C. and O'Neill, R.E. (1982) 'A comparison of parent training to direct child treatment.' In R.L. Koegel, A. Rincover and A.L. Egel (eds) *Educating and Understanding Autistic Children.* San Diego, CA: College-Hill Press.

Koegel, R.L., Schreibman, L., Johnson, J., O'Neill, R.E. and Dunlap, G. (1984) 'Collateral effects of parent training on families with autistic children.' In R.F. Dangel and R.A. Polster (eds) *Parent Training: Foundations of Research and Practice.* New York: Guilford.

Kohler, F.W. and Fowler, S.A. (1985) 'Training prosocial behaviors to young children: an analysis of reciprocity with untrained peers.' *Journal of Applied Behavior Analysis 18*, 187–200.

Krantz, P.J., Zalenski, S., Hall, L.J., Fenske, E.C. and McClannahan, L.E. (1981) 'Teaching complex language to autistic children.' *Analysis and Intervention in Developmental Disabilities 1*, 259–297.

Lamarre, J. and Holland, J.G. (1985) 'The functional independence of mands and tacts.' *Journal of the Experimental Analysis of Behavior 43*, 5–19.

Larsson, D.G. and Larsson, E.V. (1983) 'Manipulating peer presence to program the generalization of verbal compliance from one-to-one to group instruction.' *Education and Treatment of Children 6*, 109–122.

Laski, K.E., Charlop, M.H. and Schreibman, L. (1988) 'Training parents to use the Natural Language Paradigm to increase their autistic children's speech.' *Journal of Applied Behavior Analysis 21*, 391–400.

Litt, M.D. and Schreibman, L. (1981) 'Stimulus-specific reinforcement in the acquisition of receptive labels by autistic children.' *Analysis and Intervention in Developmental Disabilities 1*, 171–186.

Lovaas, O.I. and Taubman, M.T. (1981) 'Language training and some mechanisms of social and internal control.' *Journal of Analysis and Intervention in Developmental Disabilities 4*, 363–372.

Lovaas, O.I., Newsom, C. and Hickman, C. (1987) 'Self-stimulatory behavior and perceptual reinforcement.' *Journal of Applied Behavior Analysis 20*, 45–68.

Mace, F.C., Hock, M.L., Lalli, J.S., West, B.J., Belfiore, P., Pinter, E. and Brown, D.K. (1988) 'Behavioral momentum in the treatment of noncompliance.' *Journal of Applied Behavior Analysis 21*, 123–142.

Mason, S.A., McGee, G.G., Farmer-Dougan, V. and Risley, T.R. (1989) 'A practical strategy for ongoing reinforcer assessment.' *Journal of Applied Behavior Analysis 22*, 171–179.

Matthews, B.A., Shimoff, E. and Catania, A.C. (1987) 'Saying and doing: a contingency-space analysis.' *Journal of Applied Behavior Analysis 20*, 69–74.

McClannahan, L.E., Krantz, P.J. and McGhee, G.G. (1982) 'Parents as therapists for autistic children: a model for effective parent training.' *Analysis and Intervention in Developmental Disabilities 2*, 223–252.

McEvoy, M., Nordquist, V., Twardosz, S., Heckaman, K.A., Wehby, J. and Denny, K. (1988) 'Promoting autistic children's peer interaction in an integrated early childhood setting using affection activities.' *Journal of Applied Behavior Analysis 18*, 3–16.

McGee, G.G., Krantz, P.J., Mason, D. and McClannahan, L.E. (1983) 'A modified incidental-teaching procedure for autistic youth: acquisition and generalization of receptive object labels.' *Journal of Applied Behavior Analysis 16*, 329–338.

McGee, G.G., Krantz, P.J. and McClannahan, L.E. (1985) 'The facilitative effects of incidental teaching on preposition use by autistic children.' *Journal of Applied Behavior Analysis 18*, 17–32.

McMahon, R.J., Forehand, R.L. and Griest, D.L. (1981) 'Effects of knowledge of social learning principles on enhancing treatment outcome generalization in a parent training program.' *Journal of Consulting and Clinical Psychology 49*, 526–532.

McMorrow, M.J., Foxx, R.M., Faw, G.D. and Bittle, R.G. (1986) 'Cues-pause-point language training: teaching echolalics functional use of their verbal labeling repertoires.' *Journal of Applied Behavior Analysis 20*, 11–22.

Murphy, H.A., Hutchinson, J.M. and Bailey, J.S. (1983) 'Behavioral school psychology goes outdoors: the effect of organized games on playground aggression.' *Journal of Applied Behavior Analysis 16*, 29–36.

Neef, N.A., Shafer, M.S., Egel, A.L., Cataldo, M.F. and Parrish, J.M. (1983) 'The class specific effect of compliance training with "do" and "don't" requests: analogue analysis and classroom application.' *Journal of Applied Behavior Analysis 16*, 81–100.

Neef, N.A., Walters, J. and Egel, A.L. (1984) 'Establishing generative yes/no responses in developmentally disabled children.' *Journal of Applied Behavior Analysis 17*, 453–460.

Odom, S.L. and Strain, P.S. (1986) 'A comparison of peer-initiation and teacher-antecedent interventions for promoting reciprocal social interaction of autistic preschoolers.' *Journal of Applied Behavior Analysis 19*, 59–72.

Odom, S.L., Hoyson, M., Jamieson, B. and Strain, P.S. (1985) 'Increasing handicapped preschoolers' peer social interactions: cross-setting and component analysis.' *Journal of Applied Behavior Analysis 18*, 3–16.

Pace, G.M., Ivancic, M.T., Edwards, G.L., Iwata, B.A. and Page, T.J. (1985) 'Assessment of stimulus preference and reinforcer value with profoundly retarded individuals.' *Journal of Applied Behavior Analysis 18*, 249–255.

Rincover, A. and Newsome, C.D. (1985) 'The relative motivational properties of sensory and edible reinforcers in teaching autistic children.' *Journal of Applied Behavior Analysis 18*, 237–248.

Russo, D.C., Cataldo, M.F. and Cushing, P.J. (1981) 'Compliance training and behavioral covariation in the treatment of multiple behavior problems.' *Journal of Applied Behavior Analysis 14*, 209–222.

Sasso, G.M. and Rude, H.A. (1987) 'Unprogrammed effects of training high-status peers to interact with severely handicapped children.' *Journal of Applied Behavior Analysis 20*, 35–44.

Sasso, G.M., Simpson, R.L. and Novak, C.G. (1985) 'Procedures for facilitating integration of autistic children in public school settings.' *Analysis and Intervention with Developmental Disabilities 5*, 233–246.

Schafer, M.S., Egel, A.L. and Neef, N.A. (1984) 'Training mildly handicapped peers to facilitate changes in the social interaction skills of autistic children.' *Journal of Applied Behavior Analysis 17*, 461–476.

Schreibman, L., O'Neill, R.E. and Koegel, R.L. (1983) 'Behavioral training for siblings of autistic children.' *Journal of Applied Behavior Analysis 16*, 129–138.

Strain, P.S. (1983) 'Generalization of autistic children's social behavior change: effects of developmentally integrated and segregated settings.' *Analysis and Intervention in Developmental Disabilities 3*, 23–34.

Strain, P.S., Hoyson, M.H. and Jamieson, B.J. (1985) 'Normally developing preschoolers as intervention agents for autistic-like children: effects on class deportment and social interactions.' *Journal of the Division for Early Childhood 9*, 105–115.

Strain, P.S., Steele, P., Ellis, T. and Timm, M.A. (1982) 'Long-term effects of oppositional child treatment with mothers as therapists and therapist trainers.' *Journal of Applied Behavior Analysis 15*, 163–169.

Tryon, A.S. and Keane, S.P. (1986) 'Promoting imitative play through generalized observational learning in autistic-like children.' *Journal of Abnormal Child Psychology 14*, 537–549.

Waters, J.M. and Siegel, L.V. (1982) 'Parent recording of speech production of developmentally delayed toddlers.' *Education and Treatment of Children 5*, 109–120.

Williams, J.A., Koegel, R.L. and Egel, A.L. (1981) 'Response-reinforcer relationships and improved learning in autistic children.' *Journal of Applied Behavior Analysis 14*, 53–60.

In the 1990s

Barbetta, P.M., Heron, T.E. and Heward, W.L. (1993) 'Effects of active student response during error correction on the acquisition, maintenance, and generalization of sight words by students with developmental disabilities.' *Journal of Applied Behavior Analysis 26*, 111–120.

Barbetta, P.M., Heward, W.L. and Bradley, D.M. (1993) 'Relative effects of whole-word and phonetic-prompt error correction on the acquisition and maintenance of sight words by students with developmental disabilities.' *Journal of Applied Behavior Analysis 26*, 99–111.

Bay-Hinitz, A.K., Peterson, R.F. and Quilitch, H.R. (1994) 'Cooperative games: a way to modify aggressive and cooperative behaviors in young children.' *Journal of Applied Behavior Analysis 27*, 435–446.

Belchic, J.K. and Harris, S.L. (1994) 'The use of multiple peer exemplars to enhance the generalization of play skills to the siblings of children with autism.' *Child and Family Behavior Therapy 16*, 1–25.

Biederman, G.B., Stepaniuk, S., Davey, V.A., Raven, K. and Ahn, D. (1999) 'Observational learning in children with Down syndrome and developmental delays: the effect of presentation speed in videotaped modelling.' *Downs Syndrome Research and Practice 6*, 12–18.

Bondy, A.S. and Frost, L.A. (1994) 'The Picture Exchange Communication System.' *Focus on Autistic Behavior* (August) 9, 3, 1–19.

Bowman, L.G., Piazza, C.C., Fisher, W.W., Hagopian, L.P. and Kogan, J.S. (1997) 'Assessment of preference for varied versus constant reinforcers.' *Journal of Applied Behavior Analysis 30*, 451–458.

Buch, G.A. (1995) *Teaching Parents and Paraprofessionals How to Provide Behavioral Intensive Early Intervention for Children with Autism and Pervasive Developmental Disorder (Disability)*. Buch, Gregory Allan, PhD. University of California, Los Angeles, 1995. 67 pp. Advisor: Lovaas, O. Ivar.

Camarata, S. (1993) 'The application of naturalistic conversation training to speech production in children with speech disabilities.' *Journal of Applied Behavior Analysis 26*, 173–182.

Celiberti, D.A. and Harris, S.L. (1993) 'Behavioral intervention for siblings of children with autism: a focus on skills to enhance play.' *Behavior Therapy 24*, 4, 573–599.

Charlop, M.H. and Trasowech, J.E. (1991) 'Increasing autistic children's daily spontaneous speech.' *Journal of Applied Behavior Analysis 24*, 747–762.

Charlop, M.H., Kurtz, P.F. and Casey, F.G. (1990) 'Using aberrant behaviors as reinforcers for autistic children.' *Journal of Applied Behavior Analysis 23*, 163–182.

Charlop, M.H., Kurtz, P.F. and Milstein, J.P. (1992) 'Too much reinforcement, too little behavior: assessing task interspersal procedures in conjunction with different reinforcement schedules with autistic children.' *Journal of Applied Behavior Analysis 25*, 795–808.

Charlop-Christy, M.H. and Haymes, L.K. (1998) 'Using objects of obsession as token reinforcers for children with autism.' *Journal of Autism and Developmental Disorders 28*, 189–198.

Connell, M.C., Carta, J.J. and Baer, D.M. (1993) 'Programming generalization of in-class transition skills: teaching preschoolers with developmental delays to self-assess and recruit contingent teacher praise.' *Journal of Applied Behavior Analysis 26*, 345–352.

Cowdery, G.E., Iwata, B.A. and Pace, G.M. (1990) 'Effects and side effects of DRO as treatment for self-injurious behavior.' *Journal of Applied Behavior Analysis 23*, 497–506.

Davis, C.A., Brady, M.P., Hamilton, R., McEvoy, M.A. and Williams, R.E. (1994) 'Effects of high-probability requests on the social interactions of young children with severe disabilities.' *Journal of Applied Behavior Analysis 27*, 619–638.

Drasgow, E., Halle, J.W. and Ostrosky, M.M. (1998) 'Effects of differential reinforcement on the generalization of a replacement mand in three children with severe language delays.' *Journal of Applied Behavior Analysis 31*, 357–374.

Dugan, E., Kamps, D., Leonard, B., Watkins, N., Rheinberger, A. and Stackhaus, J. (1995) 'Effects of cooperative learning groups during social studies for students with autism and fourth-grade peers.' *Journal of Applied Behavior Analysis 28*, 175–188.

Duker, P.C. and van Lent, C. (1991) 'Inducing variability in communicative gestures used by severely retarded individuals.' *Journal of Applied Behavior Analysis 24*, 379–386.

Durand, V.M. and Carr, E.G. (1991) 'Functional communication training to reduce challenging behavior: maintenance and application in new settings.' *Journal of Applied Behavior Analysis 24*, 251–264.

Durand, V.M. and Carr, E.G. (1992) 'An analysis of maintenance following functional communication training.' *Journal of Applied Behavior Analysis 25*, 777–794.

Dyer, K., Dunlap, G. and Winterling, V. (1990) 'Effects of choice making on the serious problem behaviors of students with severe handicaps.' *Journal of Applied Behavior Analysis 23*, 515–524.

Eikeseth, S. and Smith, T. (1992) 'The development of functional and equivalence classes in high-functioning autistic children: the role of naming.' *Journal of the Experimental Analysis of Behavior 58*, 123–133.

Fisher, W.W., Kuhn, D.E. and Thompson, R.H. (1998) 'Establishing discriminative control of responding using functional and alternative reinforcers during functional communication training.' *Journal of Applied Behavior Analysis 31*, 543–560.

Fisher, W.W., Ninness, H.A.C., Piazza, C.C. and Owen-DeSchryver, J.S. (1996) 'On the reinforcing effects of the content of verbal attention.' *Journal of Applied Behavior Analysis 29*, 235–238.

Frea, W.D. and Hepburn, S.L. (1999) 'Teaching parents of children with autism to perform functional assessments to plan interventions for extremely disruptive behaviors.' *Journal of Positive Behavior Interventions 1*, 2, 112–116, 122.

Gena, A., Krantz, P., McClannahan, L.E. and Poulson, C.L. (1996) 'Training and generalization of affective behavior displayed by youth with autism.' *Journal of Applied Behavior Analysis 29*, 291–304.

Goldstein, H., Kaczmarek, L., Pennington, R. and Shafer, K. (1992) 'Peer-mediated intervention: Attending to, commenting on, and acknowledging the behavior of preschoolers with autism.' *Journal of Applied Behavior Analysis 25*, 289–305.

Harris, S.L., Handleman, J.S., Kristoff, B., Bass, L. and Gordon, R. (1990) 'Changes in language development among autistic and peer children in segregated and integrated preschool settings.' *Journal of Autism and Developmental Disorders 20*, 23–31.

Harris, T.A., Peterson, S.L., Filliben, T.L., Glassberg, M. and Favell, J.E. (1998) 'Evaluating a more cost-efficient alternative to providing in-home feedback to parents: the use of spousal feedback.' *Journal of Applied Behavior Analysis 31*, 131–134.

Houlihan, D., Jacobson, L. and Brandon, P.K. (1994) 'Replication of a high-probability request sequence with varied interprompt times in a preschool setting.' *Journal of Applied Behavior Analysis* 27, 737–738.

Ingenmey, R. and Van Houten, R. (1991) 'Using time delay to promote spontaneous speech in an autistic child.' *Journal of Applied Behavior Analysis* 24, 591–596.

Iwata, B.A., Pace, G.M., Cowdery, G.E., Kalsher, M.J. and Cataldo, M.F. (1990) 'Experimental analysis and extinction of self-injurious escape behavior.' *Journal of Applied Behavior Analysis* 23, 11–27.

Kamps, D.M., Barbetta, P.M., Leonard, B.R. and Delquadri, J. (1994) 'Classwide peer tutoring: an integration strategy to improve reading skills and promote peer interactions among students with autism and general education peers.' *Journal of Applied Behavior Analysis* 27, 49–62.

Kamps, D.M., Leonard, B.R., Vernon, S., Dugan, E.P., Delquadri, J.C., Gershon, B., Wade, L. and Folk, L. (1992) 'Teaching social skills to students with autism to increase peer interactions in an integrated first-grade classroom.' *Journal of Applied Behavior Analysis* 25, 281–288.

Koegel, R.L. and Frea, W.D. (1993) 'Treatment of social behavior in autism through the modification of pivotal social skills.' *Journal of Applied Behavior Analysis* 26, 369–378.

Koegel, R.L. and Koegel, L.K. (1990) 'Extended reductions in stereotypic behavior of students with autism through a self-management treatment package.' *Journal of Applied Behavior Analysis* 23, 119–127.

Koegel, R.L., Bimbela, A. and Schreibman, L. (1996) 'Collateral effects of parent training on family interactions.' *Journal of Autism and Developmental Disorders* 26, 347–359.

Koegel, L.K., Koegel, R.L., Hurley, C. and Frea, W.D. (1992) 'Improving social skills and disruptive behavior in children with autism through self-management.' *Journal of Applied Behavior Analysis* 25, 341–353.

Koegel, R.L., Camarata, S., Koegel, L.K., Ben-Tall, A. and Smith, A.E. (1998) 'Increasing speech intelligibility in children with autism.' *Journal of Autism and Developmental Disorders* 28, 241–251.

Koegel, R.L., Koegel, L.K. and Surratt, A. (1992) 'Language intervention and disruptive behavior in preschool children with autism.' *Journal of Autism and Developmental Disorders* 22, 141–153.

Krantz, P.J. and McClannahan, L.E. (1993) 'Teaching children with autism to initiate to peers: effects of a script-fading procedure.' *Journal of Applied Behavior Analysis* 26, 121–132.

Krantz, P.J. and McClannahan, L.E. (1998) 'Social interaction skills for children with autism: a script-fading procedure for beginning readers.' *Journal of Applied Behavior Analysis* 31, 191–202.

Krantz, P.J., MacDuff, M.T. and McClannahan, L.E. (1993) 'Programming participation in family activities for children with autism: parents' use of photographic activity schedules.' *Journal of Applied Behavior Analysis* 26, 137–138.

Lalli, J.S., Mace, F.C., Wohn, T. and Livezy, K. (1995) 'Identification and modification of a response-class hierarchy.' *Journal of Applied Behavior Analysis* 28, 551–559.

Leung, J. and Wu, K. (1997) 'Teaching receptive naming of Chinese characters by incorporating echolalia to children with autism.' *Journal of Applied Behavior Analysis* 30, 59–67.

MacDuff, G.S., Krantz, P.J. and McClannahan, L.E. (1993) 'Teaching children with autism to use photographic activity schedules: maintenance and generalization of complex response chains.' *Journal of Applied Behavior Analysis* 26, 89–97.

Mace, A.B., Shapiro, E.S. and Mace, F.C. (1998) 'Effects of warning stimuli for reinforcer withdrawal and task onset on self-injury.' *Journal of Applied Behavior Analysis* 31, 679–682.

Matson, J.L., Sevin, J.A., Box, M.L., Francis, K.L. and Sevin, B.M. (1993) 'An evaluation of two methods for increasing self-initiated verbalizations in autistic children.' *Journal of Applied Behavior Analysis* 26, 389–398.

McClannahan, L.E., McGee, G.G., MacDuff, G.S. and Krantz, P.J. (1990) 'Assessing and improving child care: a personal appearance index for children with autism.' *Journal of Applied Behavior Analysis 23*, 469–482.

McGee, G.G., Almeida, M.C., Sulzer-Azaroff, B. and Feldman, R.S. (1992) 'Promoting reciprocal interactions via peer incidental teaching.' *Journal of Applied Behavior Analysis 25*, 117–126.

McGee, G., Morrier, M. and Daly, T. (1999) 'An incidental teaching approach to early intervention for toddlers with autism.' *Journal of the Association for Persons with Severe Handicaps 24*, 133–146.

Mineo, B.A. and Goldstein, H. (1990) 'Generalized learning of receptive and expressive action-object responses by language-delayed preschoolers.' *Journal of Speech and Hearing Disorders 55*, 665–678.

Morrison, K. and Rosales-Ruiz, J. (1997) 'The effect of object preferences on task performance and stereotypy of a child with autism.' *Research in Developmental Disabilities 18*, 127–137.

Partington, J.W., Sundberg, M.L., Newhouse, L. and Spengler, S.M. (1994) 'Overcoming an autistic child's failure to acquire a tact repertoire.' *Journal of Applied Behavior Analysis 27*, 733–734.

Piazza, C.C. and Fisher, W. (1991) 'A faded bedtime with response cost protocol for treatment of multiple sleep problems in children.' *Journal of Applied Behavior Analysis 24*, 129–140.

Pierce, K.L. and Schreibman, L. (1994) 'Teaching daily living skills to children with autism in unsupervised settings through pictorial self-management.' *Journal of Applied Behavior Analysis 27*, 471–481.

Pierce, K. and Schreibman, L. (1995) 'Increasing complex social behaviors in children with autism: effects of peer-implemented pivotal response training.' *Journal of Applied Behavior Analysis 28*, 285–296.

Pierce, K. and Schreibman, L. (1997) 'Multiple peer use of pivotal response training to increase social behaviors of classmates with autism: results from trained and untrained peers.' *Journal of Applied Behavior Analysis 30*, 157–160.

Repp, A.C., Karsh, K.G. and Lenz, M.W. (1990) 'Discrimination training for persons with developmental disabilities: a comparison of the task demonstration model and the standard prompting hierarchy.' *Journal of Applied Behavior Analysis 23*, 43–52.

Rodgers, T.A. and Iwata, B.A. (1991) 'An analysis of error-correction procedures during discrimination training.' *Journal of Applied Behavior Analysis 24*, 775–782.

Sainato, D.M., Goldstein, H. and Strain, P.S. (1992) 'Effects of self-evaluation on preschool children's use of social interaction strategies with their classmates with autism.' *Journal of Applied Behavior Analysis 25*, 127–141.

Saunders, K.J. and Spradlin, J.E. (1990) 'Conditional discrimination in mentally retarded adults: the development of generalized skills.' *Journal of the Experimental Analysis of Behavior 54*, 3, 239–250.

Schepis, M.M., Reid, D.H., Behrmann, M.M. and Sutton, K.A. (1998) 'Increasing communicative interactions of young children with autism using a voice output communication aid and naturalistic teaching.' *Journal of Applied Behavior Analysis 31*, 561–578.

Stahmer, A.C. and Schreibman, L. (1992) 'Teaching children with autism: appropriate play in unsupervised environments using a self-management treatment package.' *Journal of Applied Behavior Analysis 25*, 2, 447–459.

Stromer, R., Mackay, H.A. and Remington, B. (1996) 'Naming, the formation of stimulus classes, and applied behavior analysis.' *Journal of Applied Behavior Analysis 29*, 409–431.

Taylor, B.A. and Harris, S.L. (1995) 'Teaching children with autism to seek information: acquisition of novel information and generalization of responding.' *Journal of Applied Behavior Analysis 28*, 3–14.

Taylor, B.A. and Levin, L. (1998) 'Teaching a student with autism to make verbal initiations: effects of a tactile prompt.' *Journal of Applied Behavior Analysis 31*, 651–654.

Taylor, B.A., Levin, L. and Jasper, S. (1999) 'Increasing play-related statements in children with autism toward their siblings: effects of video modeling.' *Journal of Developmental and Physical Disabilities 11*, 253–264.

Thompson, R.H., Fisher, W.W., Piazza, C.C. and Kuhn, D.E. (1998) 'The evaluation and treatment of aggression maintained by attention and automatic reinforcement.' *Journal of Applied Behavior Analysis 31*, 103–116.

Thorp, D.M., Stahmer, A.C. and Schreibman, L. (1995) 'Effects of sociodramatic play training on children with autism.' *Journal of Autism and Developmental Disorders 25*, 3, 265–282.

Vollmer, T.R., Borrero, J.C., Lalli, J.S. and Daniel, D. (1999) 'Evaluating self-control and impulsivity in children with severe behavior disorders.' *Journal of Applied Behavior Analysis 32*, 451–466.

Werle, M.A., Murphy, T.B. and Budd, K.S. (1993) 'Treating chronic food refusal in young children: home-based parent training.' *Journal of Applied Behavior Analysis 26*, 421–434.

Werts, M.G., Caldwell, N.K. and Wolery, M. (1996) 'Peer modeling of response chains: observational learning by students with disabilities.' *Journal of Applied Behavior Analysis 29*, 53–66.

Yamamoto, J. and Miya, T. (1999) 'Acquisition and transfer of sentence construction in autistic students: analysis by computer-based teaching.' *Research in Developmental Disabilities 20*, 355–377.

Young, J.M., Krantz, P.J., McClannahan, L.E. and Poulson, C.L. (1994) 'Generalized imitation and response-class formation in children with autism.' *Journal of Applied Behavior Analysis 27*, 685–697.

Zanolli, K. and Daggett, J. (1998) 'The effects of reinforcement rate on the spontaneous social initiations of socially withdrawn preschoolers.' *Journal of Applied Behavior Analysis 31*, 117–125.

Zanolli, K., Daggett, J. and Adams, T. (1996) 'Teaching preschool age autistic children to make spontaneous initiations to peers using priming.' *Journal of Applied Behavior Analysis 26*, 407–422.

In the 2000s

Allen, K.D. and Warzak, W.J. (2000) 'The problem of parental nonadherence in clinical behavior analysis: effective treatment is not enough.' *Journal of Applied Behavior Analysis 33*, 373–391.

Bernard-Opitz, V., Sriram, N. and Nakhoda-Sapuan, S. (2001) 'Enhancing social problem solving in children with autism and normal children through computer-assisted instruction.' *Journal of Autism and Developmental Disorders 31*, 377–384.

Buggey, T., Toombs, K., Gardener, P. and Cervetti, M. (2000) 'Training responding behaviors in students with autism: using videotaped self-modeling.' *Journal of Positive Behavior Interventions 1*, 205–214.

Carr, J.E., Nicolson, A.C. and Higbee, T.S. (2000) 'Evaluation of a brief multiple-stimulus preference assessment in a naturalistic context.' *Journal of Applied Behavior Analysis 33*, 353–357.

Charlop-Christy, M.H., Le, L. and Freeman, K.A. (2000) 'A comparison of video modeling with in vivo modeling for teaching children with autism.' *Journal of Autism and Developmental Disorders 30*, 537–552.

D'Ateno, P., Mangiapanello, K. and Taylor, B. (2003) 'Using video modeling to teach complex play sequences to a preschooler with autism.' *Journal of Positive Behavioral Interventions 5*, 5–11.

Eikeseth, S. and Jahr, E. (2001) 'The UCLA reading and writing program: an evaluation of the beginning stages.' *Research in Developmental Disabilities 22*, 289–307.

Eikeseth, S. and Nesset, R. (2003) 'Behavioral treatment of children with phonological disorder: the efficacy of vocal imitation and sufficient-response-exemplar training.' *Journal of Applied Behavior Analysis 36*, 325–337.

Geckeler, A.S., Libby, M.E., Graff, R.B. and Ahearn, W.H. (2000) 'Effects of reinforcer choice measured in single-operant and concurrent-schedule procedures.' *Journal of Applied Behavior Analysis 33*, 347–351.

Gottschalk, J.M., Libby, M.E. and Graff, R.B. (2000) 'The effects of establishing operations on preference assessment outcomes.' *Journal of Applied Behavior Analysis 33*, 85–88.

Hastings, R.P. and Symes, M.D. (2002) 'Early intensive behavioral intervention for children with autism: parental therapeutic self-efficacy.' *Research in Developmental Disabilities 23*, 332–341.

Jahr, E., Eldevik, S. and Eikeseth, S. (2000) 'Teaching children with autism to initiate and sustain cooperative play.' *Research in Developmental Disabilities 21*, 151–169.

Lerman, D.C., Swiezy, N., Perkins-Parks, S. and Roane, H.S. (2000) 'Skill acquisition in parents of children with developmental disabilities: interaction between skill type and instructional format.' *Research in Developmental Disabilities 21*, 183–196.

Marcus, B.A., Swanson, V. and Vollmer, T.R. (2001) 'Effects of parent training on parent and child behavior using procedures based on functional analyses.' *Behavioral Interventions 16*, 87–104.

Moore, M. and Calvert, S. (2000) 'Brief report: vocabulary acquisition for children with autism: teacher or computer instruction.' *Journal of Autism and Developmental Disorders 30*, 359–362.

Nikopoulos, C.K. and Keenan, M. (2003) 'Promoting social initiation in children with autism using video modeling.' *Behavioral Interventions 18*, 87–108.

Perez-Gonzalez, L.A. and Williams, G. (2002) 'Multicomponent procedure to teach conditional discriminations to children with autism.' *American Journal of Mental Retardation 107*, 293–301.

Sherer, M., Pierce, K.L., Paredes, S., Kisacky, K.L., Ingersoll, B. and Schreibman, L. (2001) 'Enhancing conversation skills in children with autism via video technology. Which is better, "self" or "other" as a model?' *Behavior Modification 25*, 140–158.

Shipley-Benamou, R., Lutzker, J.R. and Taubman, M. (2002) 'Teaching daily living skills to children with autism through instructional video modeling.' *Journal of Positive Behavioral Interventions 4*, 165–175.

Smith, T., Lovaas, N.W. and Lovaas, O.I. (2002) 'Behaviors of children with high-functioning autism when paired with typically developing versus delayed peers: a preliminary study.' *Behavioral Interventions 17*, 129–143.

Stahmer, A. and Gist, B. (2001) 'The effects of an accelerated parent education program on technique mastery and child outcome.' *Journal of Positive Behavior Interventions 3*, 75–82.

Wert, B.Y. and Neisworth, J.T. (2003) 'Effects of video self-modeling on spontaneous requesting in children with autism.' *Journal of Positive Behavioral Interventions 5*, 30–34.

Whalen, C. and Schreibman, L. (2003) 'Joint attention training for children with autism using behavior modification procedures.' *Journal of Child Psychology and Psychiatry 44*, 456–468.

Contributors

Aisling Ardiff is behavioural supervisor at Saplings School for children with autism in Rathfarnham, Dublin. Her areas of particular interest are precision teaching and direct instruction. She is studying for a Master's degree in behaviour analysis from the University of Bangor, Wales. Aisling is a parent of a child with autism.

Helen Byrne and **Dr Tony Byrne** are parents of five children; two of their boys are diagnosed with ASD. They have been involved in ABA parent training for many years and Tony is the Chair of the PEAT group.

Dr Mecca Chiesa is a Certified Behaviour Analyst presently at the Tizard Centre, University of Kent. She has been working and researching ABA with children on the autism spectrum for many years. She was joint recipient of the 2002 International Development Grant of the Society for the Advancement of Behavior Analysis to help fund the development of the first postgraduate programme in applied behaviour analysis in England to satisfy the education coursework requirements of the Behavior Analyst Certification Board. She has published widely on philosophical and experimental issues in the science of behaviour and is the author of the classic text, *Radical Behaviorism: The Philosophy and the Science* (1994, Boston: Author's Cooperative).

Mary Clark trained as a nurse and undertook graduate study in oncology nursing in London. She then qualified as a midwife after teaching nursing full time. She is the mother of two children, one of whom has high functioning Asperger's, now aged 15. She is on the committee of Autism New Zealand, Inc. (Waikato) and has recently returned to full-time study at the University of Waikato, New Zealand, working towards a BSocSci in psychology.

Marc de Salvo is a parent of three children, one of whom is on the autistic spectrum. He has lobbied for ABA services since 1999 and has played a pivotal role in establishing ABA as a viable nationwide option in Ireland. He co-founded Saplings Model of Education, a school for 30 children with autism in Kildare, Ireland, and has played an active role in the Irish Autism Alliance. He also was a key influence in arranging Ireland's first course in applied behaviour analysis open to parents and professionals alike.

Dr Karola Dillenburger is a Chartered Clinical Psychologist (BPS), qualified social worker, and mother of four young children. She is Senior Lecturer and Director of Research for Children and Families at the School of Sociology, Social Policy and Social Work at Queen's University of Belfast. Her main research interests include applied behaviour analysis in the areas of parent training, bereavement, child sex abuse, and autism. She has published widely in national and international journals and is author of *Violent Bereavement: Widows in Northern*

Ireland (1992, Aldershot: Avebury), co-author of *The Abuse of Women Within Child Care Work* (1995, Buckingham: Open University Press) and co-editor of *Advances in Behaviour Analysis* (1997, Dublin: University College Dublin Press) and *Parents' Education as Autism Therapists: Applied Behaviour Analysis in Context* (2000, London: Jessica Kingsley Publishers).

Erika Ford is the Managing Supervisor for the New Zealand branch of the Center for Autism and Related Disorders (CARD). After receiving her training in the United States, she returned to Auckland to open the New Zealand satellite office in 2002. Since then Erika has been instrumental in the development and promotion of the application of ABA principles to the wider Auckland community. She has over nine years' experience working with children on the spectrum.

Dr Stephen Gallagher is Director of Training for PEAT. He has been involved in the design of home programmes for early intensive behavioural intervention with children with autism for many years. His research interests include applied behaviour analysis, parent training, autism and gerontology. He has published peer-reviewed papers in international academic and applied journals. He obtained his PhD in applied behaviour analysis at the University of Ulster.

Professor Gina Green is Director of Professional Training and Research at the Institute for Effective Education in San Diego, CA, and adjunct faculty member in the Department of Behavior Analysis, University of North Texas. She co-edited the books *Behavioral Intervention for Young Children with Autism* and *Making a Difference: Behavioral Intervention for Autism*. She serves or has served on the editorial boards of several professional journals in developmental disabilities and behaviour analysis. Professor Green also serves on the Board of Trustees and the Autism Advisory Group of the Cambridge Center for Behavioral Studies, the Board of Directors of the Behavior Analyst Certification Board, and the advisory boards of several autism programmes and organizations. She is a Board Certified Behavior Analyst, former president of the Association for Behavior Analysis, and a Fellow of the American Psychological Association and the Council for Scientific Medicine and Mental Health. *Psychology Today* named her 'Mental Health Professional of the Year' in 2000. She was awarded an Honorary Doctorate from Queen's University, Belfast.

Mary Henderson is a parent of a nine-year-old child, diagnosed with moderate functioning autism. Her child has had ABA therapy since he was two years old. Mary has experienced AAPTC (Precision Teaching Centre) in Auckland, a school that showed that children advanced with intensive intervention. She is the co-founder of Bright Sparks Sports and Recreation for ASD children and established a charitable trust for Bright Sparks to enable individual families to raise money for their child for therapies and activities. She is a business owner and partner of an international business, travelling and presenting internationally. She is currently chairperson of Autism NZ Auckland branch.

Jonny (17) is the eldest of a family of five and has two brothers diagnosed with autism and lives in Northern Ireland. He has experienced intensive ABA home-based treatments for both brothers for many years. He presently is studying for his A-levels.

Dr Mickey Keenan is a Senior Lecturer and Distinguished Community Fellow at the School of Psychology of the University of Ulster at Coleraine, Northen Ireland. He is Founder of PEAT and received the Award for Promoting Equality of Opportunity from the British Psychological Society and the Personal Achievement Award from the New York State Association for Behaviour Analysis for his work of bringing ABA to children with ASD in Ireland. He is the father of four young children. His research interests include imitation learning, the analysis of social behaviours, schedules of reinforcement, equivalence responding, community psychology, autism, hypnosis, teaching behaviour analysis, and child sex abuse. He supervises a large group of doctoral students in a variety of research areas. He has published widely in national and international journals and is co-editor of *Advances in Behaviour Analysis* (1997, Dublin: University College Dublin Press) and *Parents' Education as Autism Therapists: Applied Behaviour Analysis in Context* (2000, London: Jessica Kingsley Publishers).

Dr Ken P. Kerr is an Acting Principal Psychologist for Western Care Association, John Moore Road, Castlebar, Co. Mayo, Ireland. Prior to this appointment he has been director of Saplings School in Kildare and director of training of PEAT. He has been involved with training parents and supervising home-based treatment programmes for many years. His main research interests include precision teaching, early intervention for children with autism, and positive behaviour support. He has published widely in national and international journals and is co-editor of *Parents' Education as Autism Therapists: Applied Behaviour Analysis in Context* (2000, London: Jessica Kingsley Publishers).

Claire Lacey is the Behaviour Support Specialist for the Children's Autism Service with Western Care Association, John Moore Road, Castlebar, Co. Mayo. She has published in national and international journals on assessment and treatment of behavioural difficulties of individuals with disabilities. She has previously taught on undergraduate and postgraduate courses in behaviour analysis, psychology, and developmental disabilities in Ireland. Her main interests include applied behaviour analysis, assessment and treatment of behavioural difficulties, early intervention for children with autism, and supporting the inclusion of children with autism.

Dr Eric V. Larsson, Board Certified Behavior Analyst, is Executive Director, Clinical Services, in The Lovaas Institute for Early Intervention, Midwest of USA. For further information see www.lovaas.com.

He can be contacted at:

Eric V. Larsson
Executive Director
LIFE-Midwest: The Lovaas Institute for Early Intervention
2925 Dean Parkways, Suite 300
Minneapolis, MN 55416
USA
elarsson@lovaas.com

Lynne McKerr is the mother of five children, the youngest of whom has Asperger's syndrome and ADHD. The family have been following an ABA programme with Cillian since he was just over three years old in 1995 when Mickey Keenan introduced them to ABA. Lynne became a founder member of PEAT and has been involved in the pre-school group STARS in Kilrea, Co. Derry, which was founded in 2001 by parents and teachers in response to a dismal lack of ABA provision in the local area.

Meghan (11) is the only sister in a family of five and has two brothers diagnosed with autism and lives in Northern Ireland. She has experienced intensive ABA home-based treatments for both brothers for many years.

Eric Messick is a Board Certified Behavior Analyst and holds a Master's in educational psychology from West Virginia University. He is currently Programme Director for Autism New Zealand, Inc. (Waikato), team leader of Youth Horizons Intensive Clinical Service Waikato/Bay of Plenty, Associate to the Behaviour Analysis Programme at the University of Waikato, and doctoral candidate at the university.

Judith Petry is currently a full-time mother of three children, aged two, four and eight. Her middle child Gordon was diagnosed with autism at the age of two and a half. Gordon commenced the CARD ABA home programme six weeks later and Judith has managed the day-to-day running of this for two years. Gordon is now at the high-functioning end of the spectrum, thanks to ABA. Judith has a Bachelor of Management Studies (Marketing) from the University of Waikato.

Dr Phil Smyth BSc is currently Director of Education for Saplings Model of Education in Kildare. Prior to this appointment she was a consultant with Behaviour Intervention Services (Ireland) and has participated in training courses nationally and internationally. She has published in the area of precision teaching and other interests include early intervention for children with autism, verbal behaviour, and functional assessment of challenging behaviour. She received her D.Phil in behaviour analysis from the University of Ulster.

Shelley Wise is a mother of three, her middle child being an eight-year-old son diagnosed at the age of three and a half with severe autism. Her initial involvement with ABA began when her son was three and a half when overseas specialists were brought into the family home to write and supervise an ABA programme for her son. Shelley managed the daily implementation of this programme for two years until he started school. Since then her involvement has extended to working as a senior ABA therapist for two families in her local area, teacher aiding a severely autistic child in a mainstream school using ABA techniques. She is past chairperson and a current committee member for Autism New Zealand, Inc. (Waikato), having sat on the committee for the past three years, and is currently working as their service coordinator.

Subject Index

Author Index